D1414330

ENGR 162

Prepared For

Robert Mulder

University of Virginia
Engineering Academic Programs

Course: Introduction to Engineering
Course Number: ENGR 162
Term: Fall 2002

Prentice Hall
Upper Saddle River, NJ 07458

Vice President and Editorial Director, ECS: **Marcia J. Horton**
Executive Editor: **Eric Svendsen**
Associate Editor: **Dee Bernhard**
Vice President and Director of Production and Manufacturing, ESM:
  David W. Riccardi
Executive Managing Editor: **Vince O'Brien**
Managing Editor: **David A. George**
Director of Creative Services: **Paul Belfanti**
Creative Director: **Carole Anson**
Art Director: **Jayne Conte**
Art Editor: **Adam Velthaus, Gregory L. Dulles**
Manufacturing Manager: **Trudy Pisciotti**
Manufacturing Buyer: **Lisa McDowell**
Marketing Manager: **Holly Stark**

© 2003 by Prentice-Hall, Inc.
Upper Saddle River, New Jersey 07458

Printed in the United States of America

10 9 8 7 6 5 4 3 2 1

013029635X

Prentice-Hall International (UK) Limited, *London*
Prentice-Hall of Australia Pty. Limited, *Sydney*
Prentice-Hall Canada, Inc., *Toronto*
Prentice-Hall Hispanoamericana, S.A., *Mexico City*
Prentice-Hall of India Private Limited, *New Delhi*
Prentice-Hall of Japan, Inc., *Tokyo*
Prentice-Hall (Singapore), Pte., Ltd., *Singapore*
Editora Prentice-Hall do Brazil, Ltda., *Rio de Janeiro*

About ESource

ESource—The Prentice Hall Engineering Source gives professors the power to harness the full potential of their text and their first-year engineering course. More than just a collection of books, ESource is a unique publishing system revolving around the ESource website—www.prenhall.com/esource. ESource enables you to put your stamp on your book just as you do your course. It lets you:

Control You choose exactly what chapter or sections are in your book and in what order they appear. Of course, you can choose the entire book if you'd like and stay with the authors' original order.

Optimize Get the most from your book and your course. ESource lets you produce the optimal text for your students needs.

Customize You can add your own material anywhere in your text's presentation, and your final product will arrive at your bookstore as a professionally formatted text. Of course, all titles in this series are available as stand-alone texts, or as bundles of two or more books sold at a discount. Contact your PH sales rep for discount information.

ESource ACCESS

Professors who choose to bundle two or more texts from the ESource series for their class, or use an ESource custom book will be providing their students with complete access to the library of ESource content. All bundles and custom books will come with a student password that gives web ESource ACCESS to all information on the site. This passcode is free and is valid for one year after initial log-on. We've designed ESource ACCESS to provide students a flexible, searchable, on-line resource. Professors may also choose to deliver custom ESource content via the web only using ESource ACCESS passcodes. Contact your PH sales rep for more information.

ESource Content

All the content in ESource was written by educators specifically for freshman/first-year students. Authors tried to strike a balanced level of presentation, an approach that was neither formulaic nor trivial, and one that did not focus too heavily on advanced topics that most introductory students do not encounter until later classes. Because many professors do not have extensive time to cover these topics in the classroom, authors prepared each text with the idea that many students would use it for self-instruction and independent study. Students should be able to use this content to learn the software tool or subject on their own.

While authors had the freedom to write texts in a style appropriate to their particular subject, all followed certain guidelines created to promote a consistency that makes students comfortable. Namely, every chapter opens with a clear set of **Objectives**, includes **Practice Boxes** throughout the chapter, and ends with a number of **Problems**, and a list of **Key Terms**. **Applications Boxes** are spread throughout the book with the intent of giving students a real-world perspective of engineering. **Success Boxes** provide the student with advice about college study skills, and help students avoid the common pitfalls of first-year students. In addition, this series contains an entire book titled **Engineering Success** by Peter Schiavone of the University of Alberta intended to expose students quickly to what it takes to be an engineering student.

Creating Your Book

Using ESource is simple. You preview the content either on-line or through examination copies of the books you can request on-line, from your PH sales rep, or by calling 1-800-526-0485. Create an on-line outline of the content you want, in the order you want, using ESource's simple interface. Either type or cut and paste your own material and insert it into the text flow. You can preview the overall organization of the text you've created at anytime (please note, since this preview is immediate, it comes unformatted.), then press another button and receive an order number for your own custom book. If you are not ready to order, do nothing—ESource will save your work. You can come back at any time and change, re-arrange, or add more material to your creation. Once you're finished and you have an ISBN, give it to your bookstore and your book will arrive on their shelves four to six weeks after they order. Your custom desk copies with their instructor supplements will arrive at your address at the same time.

To learn more about this new system for creating the perfect textbook, go to www.prenhall.com/esource. You can either go through the on-line walkthrough of how to create a book, or experiment yourself.

Supplements

Adopters of ESource receive an instructor's CD that contains professor and student code from the books in the series, as well as other instruction aides provided by authors. The website also holds approximately **350 PowerPoint transparencies** created by Jack Leifer of University of Kentucky–Paducah available to download. Professors can either follow these transparencies as pre-prepared lectures or use them as the basis for their own custom presentations.

Titles in the ESource Series

Design Concepts for Engineers, 2/e
0-13-093430-5
Mark Horenstein

Engineering Success, 2/e
0-13-041827-7
Peter Schiavone

Engineering Design and Problem Solving, 2E
ISBN 0-13-093399-6
Steven K. Howell

Exploring Engineering
ISBN 0-13-093442-9
Joe King

Engineering Ethics
0-13-784224-4
Charles B. Fleddermann

Engineering Design—A Day in the Life of Four Engineers
0-13-085089-6
Mark N. Horenstein

Introduction to Engineering Analysis
0-13-016733-9
Kirk D. Hagen

Introduction to Engineering Experimentation
0-13-032835-9
Ronald W. Larsen, John T. Sears, and Royce Wilkinson

Introduction to Mechanical Engineering
0-13-019640-1
Robert Rizza

Introduction to Electrical and Computer Engineering
0-13-033363-8
Charles B. Fleddermann and Martin Bradshaw

Introduction to MATLAB 6
0-13-032845-6
Delores Etter and David C. Kuncicky, with Douglas W. Hull

Introduction to MATLAB
0-13-013149-0
Delores Etter with David C. Kuncicky

Introduction to Mathcad 2000
0-13-020007-7
Ronald W. Larsen

Introduction to Mathcad
0-13-937493-0
Ronald W. Larsen

Introduction to Maple
0-13-095133-1
David I. Schwartz

Mathematics Review
0-13-011501-0
Peter Schiavone

Power Programming with VBA/Excel
0-13-047377-4
Steven C. Chapra

Introduction to Excel 2002
0-13-008175-2
David C. Kuncicky

Introduction to Excel, 2/e
0-13-016881-5
David C. Kuncicky

Engineering with Excel
ISBN 0-13-017696-6
Ronald W. Larsen

Introduction to Word 2002
0-13-008170-1
David C. Kuncicky

Introduction to Word
0-13-254764-3
David C. Kuncicky

Introduction to PowerPoint 2002
0-13-008179-5
Jack Leifer

Introduction to PowerPoint
0-13-040214-1
Jack Leifer

Graphics Concepts
0-13-030687-8
Richard M. Lueptow

Graphics Concepts with SolidWorks
0-13-014155-0
Richard M. Lueptow and Michael Minbiole

Graphics Concepts with Pro/ENGINEER
0-13-014154-2
Richard M. Lueptow, Jim Steger, and
Michael T. Snyder

Introduction to AutoCAD 2000
0-13-016732-0
Mark Dix and Paul Riley

Introduction to AutoCAD, R. 14
0-13-011001-9
Mark Dix and Paul Riley

Introduction to UNIX
0-13-095135-8
David I. Schwartz

Introduction to the Internet, 3/e
0-13-031355-6
Scott D. James

Introduction to Visual Basic 6.0
0-13-026813-5
David I. Schneider

Introduction to C
0-13-011854-0
Delores Etter

Introduction to C++
0-13-011855-9
Delores Etter

Introduction to FORTRAN 90
0-13-013146-6
Larry Nyhoff and Sanford Leestma

Introduction to Java
0-13-919416-9
Stephen J. Chapman

About the Authors

No project could ever come to pass without a group of authors who have the vision and the courage to turn a stack of blank paper into a book. The authors in this series, who worked diligently to produce their books, provide the building blocks of the series.

Martin D. Bradshaw was born in Pittsburg, KS in 1936, grew up in Kansas and the surrounding states of Arkansas and Missouri, graduating from Newton High School, Newton, KS in 1954. He received the B.S.E.E. and M.S.E.E. degrees from the University of Wichita in 1958 and 1961, respectively. A Ford Foundation fellowship at Carnegie Institute of Technology followed from 1961 to 1963 and he received the Ph.D. degree in electrical engineering in 1964. He spent his entire academic career with the Department of Electrical and Computer Engineering at the University of New Mexico (1961-1963 and 1991-1996). He served as the Assistant Dean for Special Programs with the UNM College of Engineering from 1974 to 1976 and as the Associate Chairman for the EECE Department from 1993 to 1996. During the period 1987-1991 he was a consultant with his own company, EE Problem Solvers. During 1978 he spent a sabbatical year with the State Electricity Commission of Victoria, Melbourne, Australia. From 1979 to 1981 he served an IPA assignment as a Project Officer at the U.S. Air Force Weapons Laboratory, Kirkland AFB, Albuquerque, NM. He has won numerous local, regional, and national teaching awards, including the George Westinghouse Award from the ASEE in 1973. He was awarded the IEEE Centennial Medal in 2000.

Acknowledgments: Dr. Bradshaw would like to acknowledge his late mother, who gave him a great love of reading and learning, and his father, who taught him to persist until the job is finished. The encouragement of his wife, Jo, and his six children is a never-ending inspiration.

Stephen J. Chapman received a B.S. degree in Electrical Engineering from Louisiana State University (1975), the M.S.E. degree in Electrical Engineering from the University of Central Florida (1979), and pursued further graduate studies at Rice University.

Mr. Chapman is currently Manager of Technical Systems for British Aerospace Australia, in Melbourne, Australia. In this position, he provides technical direction and design authority for the work of younger engineers within the company. He also continues to teach at local universities on a part-time basis.

Mr. Chapman is a Senior Member of the Institute of Electrical and Electronics Engineers (and several of its component societies). He is also a member of the Association for Computing Machinery and the Institution of Engineers (Australia).

Steven C. Chapra presently holds the Louis Berger Chair for Computing and Engineering in the Civil and Environmental Engineering Department at Tufts University. Dr. Chapra received engineering degrees from Manhattan College and the University of Michigan. Before joining the faculty at Tufts, he taught at Texas A&M University, the University of Colorado, and Imperial College, London. His research interests focus on surface water-quality modeling and advanced computer applications in environmental engineering. He has published over 50 refereed journal articles, 20 software packages and 6 books. He has received a number of awards including the 1987 ASEE Merriam/Wiley Distinguished Author Award, the 1993 Rudolph Hering Medal, and teaching awards from Texas A&M, the University of Colorado, and the Association of Environmental Engineering and Science Professors.

Acknowledgments: To the Berger Family for their many contributions to engineering education. I would also like to thank David Clough for his friendship and insights, John Walkenbach for his wonderful books, and my colleague Lee Minardi and my students Kenny William,

Robert Viesca and Jennifer Edelmann for their suggestions.

Mark Dix began working with AutoCAD in 1985 as a programmer for CAD Support Associates, Inc. He helped design a system for creating estimates and bills of material directly from AutoCAD drawing databases for use in the automated conveyor industry. This system became the basis for systems still widely in use today. In 1986 he began collaborating with Paul Riley to create AutoCAD training materials, combining Riley's background in industrial design and training with Dix's background in writing, curriculum development, and programming. Mr. Dix received the M.S. degree in education from the University of Massachusetts. He is currently the Director of Dearborn Academy High School in Arlington, Massachusetts.

Delores M. Etter is a Professor of Electrical and Computer Engineering at the University of Colorado. Dr. Etter was a faculty member at the University of New Mexico and also a Visiting Professor at Stanford University. Dr. Etter was responsible for the Freshman Engineering Program at the University of New Mexico and is active in the Integrated Teaching Laboratory at the University of Colorado. She was elected a Fellow of the Institute of Electrical and Electronics Engineers for her contributions to education and for her technical leadership in digital signal processing.

Charles B. Fleddermann is a professor in the Department of Electrical and Computer Engineering at the University of New Mexico in Albuquerque, New Mexico. All of his degrees are in electrical engineering: his Bachelor's degree from the University of Notre Dame, and the Master's and Ph.D. from the University of Illinois at Urbana-Champaign. Prof. Fleddermann developed an engineering ethics course for his department in response to the ABET requirement to incorporate ethics topics into the undergraduate engineering curriculum. *Engineering Ethics* was written as a vehicle for presenting ethical theory, analysis, and problem solving to engineering undergraduates in a concise and readily accessible way.

Acknowledgments: I would like to thank Profs. Charles Harris and Michael Rabins of Texas A & M University whose NSF sponsored workshops on engineering ethics got me started thinking in this field. Special thanks to my wife Liz, who proofread the manuscript for this book, provided many useful suggestions, and who helped me learn how to teach "soft" topics to engineers.

Kirk D. Hagen is a professor at Weber State University in Ogden, Utah. He has taught introductory-level engineering courses and upper-division thermal science courses at WSU since 1993. He received his B.S. degree in physics from Weber State College and his M.S. degree in mechanical engineering from Utah State University, after which he worked as a thermal designer/analyst in the aerospace and electronics industries. After several years of engineering practice, he resumed his formal education, earning his Ph.D. in mechanical engineering at the University of Utah. Hagen is the author of an undergraduate heat transfer text.

Mark N. Horenstein is a Professor in the Department of Electrical and Computer Engineering at Boston University. He has degrees in Electrical Engineering from M.I.T. and U.C. Berkeley and has been involved in teaching engineering design for the greater part of his academic career. He devised and developed the senior design project class taken by all electrical and computer engineering students at Boston University. In this class, the students work for a virtual engineering company developing products and systems for real-world engineering and social-service clients.

Acknowledgments: I would like to thank Prof. James Bethune, the architect of the Peak Performance event at Boston University, for his permission to highlight the competition in my text. Several of the ideas relating to brainstorming and teamwork were derived from a workshop on engineering design offered by Prof. Charles Lovas of Southern Methodist University. The principles of estimation were derived in part from a freshman engineering problem posed by Prof. Thomas Kincaid of Boston University.

Steven Howell is the Chairman and a Professor of Mechanical Engineering at Lawrence Technological University. Prior to joining LTU in 2001, Dr. Howell led a knowledge-based engineering project for Visteon Automotive Systems and taught computer-aided design  classes for Ford Motor Company engineers. Dr. Howell also has a total of 15 years experience as an engineering faculty member at Northern Arizona University, the University of the Pacific, and the University of Zimbabwe. While at Northern Arizona University, he helped develop and implement an award-winning interdisciplinary series of design courses simulating a corporate engineering-design environment.

Douglas W. Hull is a graduate student in the Department of Mechanical Engineering at Carnegie Mellon University in Pittsburgh, Pennsylvania. He is the author of *Mastering Mechanics 1 Using Matlab 5*, and contributed to *Mechanics of Materials* by Bedford and Liechti. His  research in the Sensor Based Planning lab involves motion planning for hyper-redundant manipulators, also known as serpentine robots.

Scott D. James is a staff lecturer at Kettering University (formerly GMI Engineering & Management Institute) in Flint, Michigan. He is currently pursuing a Ph.D. in Systems Engineering with an emphasis on software engineering and computer-integrated manufac-  turing. He chose teaching as a profession after several years in the computer industry. "I thought that it was really important to know what it was like outside of academia. I wanted to provide students with classes that were up to date and provide the information that is really used and needed."

Acknowledgments: Scott would like to acknowledge his family for the time to work on the text and his students and peers at Kettering who offered helpful critiques of the materials that eventually became the book.

Joe King received the B.S. and M.S. degrees from the University of California at Davis. He is a Professor of Computer Engineering at the University of the Pacific, Stockton, CA, where he teaches courses in digital design, computer design, artificial intelligence, and com-  puter networking. Since joining the UOP faculty, Professor King has spent yearlong sabbaticals teaching in Zimbabwe, Singapore, and Finland. A licensed engineer in the state of California, King's industrial experience includes major design projects with Lawrence Livermore National Laboratory, as well as independent consulting projects. Prof. King has had a number of books published with titles including MATLAB, MathCAD, Exploring Engineering, and Engineering and Society.

David C. Kuncicky is a native Floridian. He earned his Baccalaureate in psychology, Master's in computer science, and Ph.D. in computer science from Florida State University. He has served as a faculty member in the Department of Electrical Engineering at the FAMU–

FSU College of Engineering and the Department of Computer Science at Florida State University. He has taught computer science and computer engineering courses for over 15 years. He has published research in the areas of intelligent hybrid systems and neural networks. He is currently the Director of Engineering at Bioreason, Inc. in Sante Fe, New Mexico.

Acknowledgments: Thanks to Steffie and Helen for putting up with my late nights and long weekends at the computer. Finally, thanks to Susan Bassett for having faith in my abilities, and for providing continued tutelage and support.

Ron Larsen is a Professor of Chemical Engineering at Montana State University, and received his Ph.D. from the Pennsylvania State University. He was initially attracted to engineering by the challenges the profession offers, but also appreciates that engineering is a serving profession. Some of the greatest challenges he has faced while teaching have involved non-traditional teaching methods, including evening courses for practicing engineers and teaching through an interpreter at the Mongolian National University. These experiences have provided tremendous opportunities to learn new ways to communicate technical material. Dr. Larsen views modern software as one of the new tools that will radically alter the way engineers work, and his book *Introduction to Math-CAD* was written to help young engineers prepare to meet the challenges of an ever-changing workplace.

Acknowledgments: To my students at Montana State University who have endured the rough drafts and typos, and who still allow me to experiment with their classes—my sincere thanks.

Sanford Leestma is a Professor of Mathematics and Computer Science at Calvin College, and received his Ph.D. from New Mexico State University. He has been the long-time co-author of successful textbooks on Fortran, Pascal, and data structures in Pascal. His current research interest are in the areas of algorithms and numerical computation.

Jack Leifer is an Assistant Professor in the Department of Mechanical Engineering at the University of Kentucky Extended Campus Program in Paducah, and was previously with the Department of Mathematical Sciences and Engineering at the University of South Carolina–Aiken. He received his Ph.D. in Mechanical Engineering from the University of Texas at Austin in December 1995. His current research interests include the modeling of sensors for manufacturing, and the use of Artificial Neural Networks to predict corrosion.

Acknowledgments: I'd like to thank my colleagues at USC–Aiken, especially Professors Mike May and Laurene Fausett, for their encouragement and feedback; and my parents, Felice and Morton Leifer, for being there and providing support (as always) as I completed this book.

Richard M. Lueptow is the Charles Deering McCormick Professor of Teaching Excellence and Associate Professor of Mechanical Engineering at Northwestern University. He is a native of Wisconsin and received his doctorate from the Massachusetts Institute of Technology in 1986. He teaches design, fluid mechanics, an spectral analysis techniques. Rich has an active research program on rotating filtration, Taylor Couette flow, granular flow, fire suppression, and acoustics. He has five patents and over 40 refereed journal and proceedings papers along with many other articles, abstracts, and presentations.

Acknowledgments: Thanks to my talented and hard-working co-authors as well as the many colleagues and students who took the tutorial for a "test drive." Special thanks to Mike Minbiole for his major contributions to Graphics Concepts with SolidWorks. Thanks also to Northwestern University for the time to work on a book. Most of all, thanks to my loving wife, Maiya, and my children, Hannah and Kyle, for supporting me in this endeavor. (Photo courtesy of Evanston Photographic Studios, Inc.)

Larry Nyhoff is a Professor of Mathematics and Computer Science at Calvin College. After doing bachelor's work at Calvin, and Master's work at Michigan, he received a Ph.D. from Michigan State and also did graduate work in computer science at Western Michigan. Dr. Nyhoff has taught at Calvin for the past 34 years—mathematics at first and computer science for the past several years.

Acknowledgments: We thank our families—Shar, Jeff, Dawn, Rebecca, Megan, Sara, Greg, Julie, Joshua, Derek, Tom, Joan; Marge, Michelle, Sandy, Lory, Michael—for being patient and understanding. We thank God for allowing us to write this text.

Paul Riley is an author, instructor, and designer specializing in graphics and design for multimedia. He is a founding partner of CAD Support Associates, a contract service and professional training organization for computer-aided design. His 15 years of business experience and  20 years of teaching experience are supported by degrees in education and computer science. Paul has taught AutoCAD at the University of Massachusetts at Lowell and is presently teaching AutoCAD at Mt. Ida College in Newton, Massachusetts. He has developed a program, Computer-aided Design for Professionals that is highly regarded by corporate clients and has been an ongoing success since 1982.

Robert Rizza is an Assistant Professor of Mechanical Engineering at North Dakota State University, where he teaches courses in mechanics and computer-aided design. A native of Chicago, he received the Ph.D. degree from the Illinois Institute of Technology. He is  also the author of *Getting Started with Pro/ENGINEER*. Dr. Rizza has worked on a diverse range of engineering projects including projects from the railroad, bioengineering, and aerospace industries. His current research interests include the fracture of composite materials,

repair of cracked aircraft components, and loosening of prostheses.

Peter Schiavone is a professor and student advisor in the Department of Mechanical Engineering at the University of Alberta, Canada. He received his Ph.D. from the University of Strathclyde, U.K. in 1988. He has authored several books in the area of student academic  success as well as numerous papers in international scientific research journals. Dr. Schiavone has worked in private industry in several different areas of engineering including aerospace and systems engineering. He founded the first Mathematics Resource Center at the University of Alberta, a unit designed specifically to teach new students the necessary *survival skills* in mathematics and the physical sciences required for success in first-year engineering. This led to the Students' Union Gold Key Award for outstanding contributions to the university. Dr. Schiavone lectures regularly to freshman engineering students and to new engineering professors on engineering success, in particular about maximizing students' academic performance.

Acknowledgements: Thanks to Richard Felder for being such an inspiration; to my wife Linda for sharing my dreams and believing in me; and to Francesca and Antonio for putting up with Dad when working on the text.

David I. Schneider holds an A.B. degree from Oberlin College and a Ph.D. degree in Mathematics from MIT. He has taught for 34 years, primarily at the University of Maryland. Dr. Schneider has authored 28 books, with one-half of them computer programming books. He has developed three customized  software packages that are supplied as supplements to over 55 mathematics textbooks. His involvement with computers dates back to 1962, when he programmed a special purpose computer at MIT's Lincoln Laboratory to correct errors in a communications system.

David I. Schwartz is an Assistant Professor in the Computer Science Department at Cornell University and earned his B.S., M.S., and Ph.D. degrees in Civil Engineering from State University of New York at Buffalo. Throughout his graduate studies, Schwartz combined principles of computer science to applications of civil engineering. He became interested in helping students learn how to apply software tools for solving a variety of engineering problems. He teaches his students to learn incrementally and practice frequently to gain the maturity to tackle other subjects. In his spare time, Schwartz plays drums in a variety of bands.

Acknowledgments: I dedicate my books to my family, friends, and students who all helped in so many ways. Many thanks go to the schools of Civil Engineering and Engineering & Applied Science at State University of New York at Buffalo where I originally developed and tested my UNIX and Maple books. I greatly appreciate the opportunity to explore my goals and all the help from everyone at the Computer Science Department at Cornell.

John T. Sears received the Ph.D. degree from Princeton University. Currently, he is a Professor and the head of the Department of Chemical Engineering at Montana State University. After leaving Princeton he worked in research at Brookhaven National Laboratory and Esso Research and Engineering, until he took a position at West Virginia University. He came to MSU in 1982, where he has served as the Director of the College of Engineering Minority Program and Interim Director for BioFilm Engineering. Prof. Sears has written a book on air pollution and economic development, and over 45 articles in engineering and engineering education.

Michael T. Snyder is President of Internet startup Appointments123.com. He is a native of Chicago, and he received his Bachelor of Science degree in Mechanical Engineering from the University of Notre Dame. Mike also graduated with honors from Northwestern University's Kellogg Graduate School of Management in 1999 with his Masters of Management degree. Before Appointments123.com, Mike was a mechanical engineer in new product development for Motorola Cellular and Acco Office Products. He has received four patents for his mechanical design work. "Pro/ENGINEER was an invaluable design tool for me, and I am glad to help students learn the basics of Pro/ENGINEER."

Acknowledgments: Thanks to Rich Lueptow and Jim Steger for inviting me to be a part of this great project. Of course, thanks to my wife Gretchen for her support in my various projects.

Jim Steger is currently Chief Technical Officer and cofounder of an Internet applications company. He graduated with a Bachelor of Science degree in Mechanical Engineering from Northwestern University. His prior work included mechanical engineering assignments at Motorola and Acco Brands. At Motorola, Jim worked on part design for two-way radios and was one of the lead mechanical engineers on a cellular phone product line. At Acco Brands, Jim was the sole engineer on numerous office product designs. His Worx stapler has won design awards in the United States and in Europe. Jim has been a Pro/ENGINEER user for over six years.

Acknowledgments: Many thanks to my co-authors, especially Rich Lueptow for his leadership on this project. I would also like to thank my family for their continuous support.

Royce Wilkinson received his under-graduate degree in chemistry from Rose-Hulman Institute of Technology in 1991 and the Ph.D. degree in chemistry from Montana State University in 1998 with research in natural product isolation from fungi. He currently resides in Bozeman, MT and is involved in HIV drug research. His research interests center on biological molecules and their interactions in the search for pharmaceutical advances.

Reviewers

ESource benefited from a wealth of reviewers who on the series from its initial idea stage to its completion. Reviewers read manuscripts and contributed insightful comments that helped the authors write great books. We would like to thank everyone who helped us with this project.

Concept Document

Naeem Abdurrahman *University of Texas, Austin*
Grant Baker *University of Alaska, Anchorage*
Betty Barr *University of Houston*
William Beckwith *Clemson University*
Ramzi Bualuan *University of Notre Dame*
Dale Calkins *University of Washington*
Arthur Clausing *University of Illinois
   at Urbana–Champaign*
John Glover *University of Houston*
A.S. Hodel *Auburn University*
Denise Jackson *University of Tennessee, Knoxville*
Kathleen Kitto *Western Washington University*
Terry Kohutek *Texas A&M University*
Larry Richards *University of Virginia*
Avi Singhal *Arizona State University*
Joseph Wujek *University of California, Berkeley*
Mandochehr Zoghi *University of Dayton*

Books

Stephen Allan *Utah State University*
Naeem Abdurrahman *University of Texas, Austin*
Anil Bajaj *Purdue University*
Grant Baker *University of Alaska–Anchorage*
Betty Burr *University of Houston*
William Beckwith *Clemson University*
Haym Benaroya *Rutgers University*
Tom Bledsaw *ITT Technical Institute*
Tom Bryson *University of Missouri, Rolla*
Ramzi Bualuan *University of Notre Dame*
Dan Budny *Purdue University*
Dale Calkins *University of Washington*
Arthur Clausing *University of Illinois*
James Devine *University of South Florida*
Patrick Fitzhorn *Colorado State University*
Dale Elifrits *University of Missouri, Rolla*

Frank Gerlitz *Washtenaw College*
John Glover *University of Houston*
John Graham *University of North Carolina–Charlotte*
Malcom Heimer *Florida International University*
A.S. Hodel *Auburn University*
Vern Johnson *University of Arizona*
Kathleen Kitto *Western Washington University*
Robert Montgomery *Purdue University*
Mark Nagurka *Marquette University*
Romarathnam Narasimhan *University of Miami*
Larry Richards *University of Virginia*
Marc H. Richman *Brown University*
Avi Singhal *Arizona State University*
Tim Sykes *Houston Community College*
Thomas Hill *SUNY at Buffalo*
Michael S. Wells *Tennessee Tech University*
Joseph Wujek *University of California, Berkeley*
Edward Young *University of South Carolina*
Mandochehr Zoghi *University of Dayton*
John Biddle *California State Polytechnic University*
Fred Boadu *Duke University*
Harish Cherukuri *University of North Carolina–Charlotte*
Barry Crittendon *Virginia Polytechnic and State University*
Ron Eaglin *University of Central Florida*
Susan Freeman *Northeastern University*
Frank Gerlitz *Washtenaw Community College*
Otto Gygax *Oregon State University*
Donald Herling *Oregon State University*
James N. Jensen *SUNY at Buffalo*
Autar Kaw *University of South Florida*
Kenneth Klika *University of Akron*
Terry L. Kohutek *Texas A&M University*
Melvin J. Maron *University of Louisville*
Soronadi Nnaji *Florida A&M University*
Michael Peshkin *Northwestern University*
Randy Shih *Oregon Institute of Technology*
Neil R. Thompson *University of Waterloo*
Garry Young *Oklahoma State University*

Patrick Fitzhorn *Colorado State University*
Dale Elifrits *University of Missouri, Rolla*
Frank Gerlitz *Washtenaw College*
John Glover *University of Houston*

CONTENTS

1

Mathcad: The Engineer's Scratch Pad

SECTIONS

- 1.1   Introduction to Mathcad
- 1.2   Mathcad as a Design Tool
- 1.3   Mathcad as a Mathematical Problem Solver
- 1.4   Mathcad as a Unit Converter
- 1.5   Mathcad for Presenting Results
- 1.6   Mathcad's Place in an Engineer's Tool Kit
- 1.7   Objectives of the Text
- 1.8   Conventions Used in the Text
- Key Terms

OBJECTIVES

- begin to understand how Mathcad solves problems;
- be able to describe the unique features that make Mathcad a valuable tool for engineers and scientists, especially Mathcad's value as a design tool
- be able to describe the unique features that make Mathcad a valuable tool for engineers and scientists, especially Mathcad's value as a mathematical problem solver
- be able to describe the unique features that make Mathcad a valuable tool for engineers and scientists, especially Mathcad's value as a unit converter
- be able to describe the unique features that make Mathcad a valuable tool for engineers and scientists, especially Mathcad's value as a good way to present your results
- know what to expect from the text, the objectives, and a typical chapter layout; and
- become familiar with some conventions that will be used in the text.

1.1   INTRODUCTION TO MATHCAD

Mathcad[1] is an equation-solving software package that has proven to have a wide range of applicability to engineering problems. Mathcad's ability to display equations the same way you would write them on paper makes a Mathcad worksheet easy to read. For example, if you wanted to calculate the mass of water in a storage tank, you might solve the problem on paper like this:

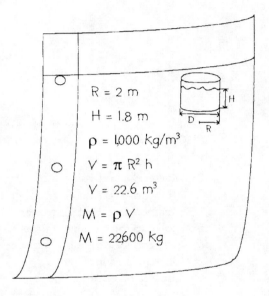

The same calculation in Mathcad might look like this:

```
R  := 2·m
H  := 1.8·m
```

$$\rho := 1000 \bullet \frac{kg}{m^3}$$

```
V  := π·R²·H
V  = 22.6·m³
M  := ρ·V
M  = 2.26·10⁴·kg
```

One of the nicest features of Mathcad is its ability to solve problems much the same way people do, rather than making your solution process fit the program's way of doing things. For example, you could also solve this problem in a spreadsheet by entering the constants and the equations for volume and mass into various cells:

[1] Mathcad is a registered trademark of Mathsoft, Inc. of Cambridge, Massachusetts.

	A	B	C
1	R:	2	
2	H:	1.8	
3	Rho:	1000	
4			
5	V:	22.6	
6	M:	22619	
7			

In the C programming language, the problem might be solved with the following program:

```
#include stdio.h
#include math.h

main()
{
    float R, H, Rho, V, M;

    R = 2;
    H = 1.8;
    V = 3.1416 * pow (R, 2) * H;
    M = Rho * V;
    printf('V = %f \n M = % f', V, M);
}
```

While spreadsheets and programming languages can produce the solution, Mathcad's presentation is much more like the way people solve equations on paper. This makes Mathcad easier for you to use. It also makes it easier for others to read and understand your results.

PROFESSIONAL SUCCESS

Work to develop communication skills as well as technical skills.

An engineer's job is to find a solution to someones problem. Finding the solution requires good technical skills, but the solution must *always* be communicated to other people. An engineer's communication skills are just as important as her or his technical skills.

Because Mathcad's worksheets are easy to read, they can help you communicate your results to others. You can improve the readability of your worksheets by

- performing your calculations in an orderly way (plan your work),
- adding comments to your worksheet, and
- using units on your variables.

The last two items will be discussed in more detail in the next chapter.

Mathcad's user interface is an important feature, but Mathcad has other features that make it excel as a *design* tool, a mathematical problem solver, a unit converter, and a communicator of results.

1.2   MATHCAD AS A DESIGN TOOL

A Mathcad *worksheet* is a collection of variable definitions, equations, text regions, and graphs displayed on the screen in pretty much the same fashion you would write them on paper. A big difference between a Mathcad worksheet and your paper scratch pad is *automatic recalculation*: If you make a change to any of the definitions or equations in your worksheet, the rest of the worksheet is automatically updated. This makes it easy to do the "what if" calculations that are so common in engineering. For example, what if the water level rises to 2.8 m? Would the mass in the tank exceed the tank's maximum design value of 40,000 kg?

To answer these questions, simply edit the definition of H in the Mathcad worksheet. The rest of the equations are automatically updated, and the new result is displayed:

$$R := 2 \cdot m$$
$$H := 2.8 \cdot m$$

$$\rho := 1000 \cdot \frac{kg}{m^3}$$

$$V := \pi \cdot R^2 \cdot H$$
$$V := 35.2 \cdot m^3$$
$$M := \rho \cdot V$$
$$M = 3.52 \cdot 10^4 \cdot kg$$

From this calculation, we see that even at a height of 2.8 m, the mass in the tank is still within the design specifications.

The ability to develop a worksheet for a particular case and then vary one or more parameters to observe their impact on the calculated results makes a Mathcad worksheet a valuable tool for evaluating multiple designs.

Mathcad has another feature, called a QuickPlot, that is very useful for visualizing functions, and this can also speed the design process. With a QuickPlot, you simply create a graph, put the function on the *y*-axis, and place a dummy variable on the *x*-axis. Mathcad evaluates the function for a range of values and displays the graph.

For example, if you want to see what the hyperbolic sine function looks like, use a QuickPlot, such as the following:

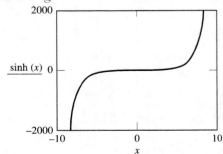

QuikPlots are discussed in more detail in later chapters—we will use them a lot.

1.3   MATHCAD AS A MATHEMATICAL PROBLEM SOLVER

Mathcad has the ability to solve problems numerically (computing a value) or symbolically (working with the variables directly). It has a large collection of built-in functions for trigonometric calculations, statistical calculations, data analysis (e.g., regression), and matrix operations. Mathcad can calculate derivatives and evaluate integrals, and it can handle many differential equations. It can work with imaginary numbers and handle Laplace transforms. Iterative solutions are tedious by hand, but very straightforward in Mathcad. In sum, while it is possible to come up with problems that are beyond Mathcad's capabilities, Mathcad can handle the bulk of an engineer's day-to-day calculations—and do them very well.

Some of these features, like Laplace transforms and functions for solving differential equations, are beyond the scope of this text, but many of Mathcad's commonly used features and functions will be presented and used.

1.4   MATHCAD AS A UNIT CONVERTER

Mathcad allows you to build units into most equations. (There are a couple of restrictions, which will be discussed in the next chapter.) Allowing Mathcad to handle the chore of getting all the values converted to a consistent set of units can be a major time-saver. For example, if the storage tank's radius had been measured in feet and the depth in inches, then

$$R = 6.56 \text{ ft (equivalent to 2 m)}$$
$$H = 70.87 \text{ in (equivalent to 1.8 m)}$$

We could convert the feet and inches to meters ourselves, or let Mathcad do it as shown here:

```
R := 6.56·ft
H := 70.87·in

ρ := 1000•kg/m³

V := π·R2·H
V := 22.609·m³
M := ρ·V
M = 22609·kg
```

(*Note:* The mass is slightly lower here than in the first example because of rounding of the R and H values.)

For complicated problems, and when your input values have many different units, Mathcad's ability to handle the *unit conversions* is a very nice feature.

1.5   MATHCAD FOR PRESENTING RESULTS

Engineering and science are both fields in which a person's computed results have little meaning unless they are given to someone else. A circuit design has to be passed along to a manufacturer, for example. Getting the results in a useful form can often take as long as computing the results. This is an area where Mathcad can help speed up the process.

Practicing engineers use spreadsheets for many routine calculations, but spreadsheets can be frustrating because they display only the calculated results while hiding the equations. If someone gives you a spreadsheet printout, it probably shows only numbers, and you have to take the person's word for the equations or ask for a copy of the spreadsheet file. If you dig into the spreadsheet to see the equations, they are still somewhat cryptic because they typically use cell references (e.g., B12) rather than variable names.

Computer program listings make it clear how the results were calculated, and recognizable variable names can be used, but long equations on a single line can still be difficult to decipher. Mathcad's ability to show the equations and the results the way people are used to reading them makes a Mathcad worksheet a good way to give your results to someone else. If there is a question about a result, the solution method is obvious. Mathcad's ability to print equations in the order we would write them, but with typeset quality, is a bonus.

Still, there are times when you need to get your results into a more formal report. Mathcad helps out in that area too. Equations and results (e.g., values, matrices, graphs) on a Mathcad worksheet can be inserted (via copy and paste operations) into other software programs, such as word processors. You don't have to retype the equations in the word processor, which can be a major time-saver. This compatibility with other software also means you can get a matrix from Mathcad into a spreadsheet or create a Mathcad matrix from a column of values in a spreadsheet. These features will be described in much more detail later.

1.6   MATHCAD'S PLACE IN AN ENGINEER'S TOOL KIT

Spreadsheets, programming languages, and mathematical problem solvers all have their place, and the tools you will use routinely will depend on where your career takes you, or perhaps vice versa. There is no single "right" tool for most problems, but Mathcad seems a logical choice when the requirements of the problem align with Mathcad's strengths, which include

- equations that are displayed in a highly readable form,
- the ability to work with units,
- a symbolic math capability,
- an iterative solution capability, and
- an extensive function library.

Deciding on which software product to use requires an understanding of the various products. For example,

- Spreadsheets can solve equations requiring iteration, but the process is much easier to follow in Mathcad.
- Mathcad can handle lists of numbers (e.g., analyses of experimental data sets), but columns of numbers fit well into the strengths of a spreadsheet.
- Spreadsheets cannot handle symbolic mathematics, so Mathcad (or Maple, or Mathematica)[2] must be used for that type of work.

This text demonstrates some of Mathcad's capabilities; hopefully, it will help you learn where the package fits in your tool kit.

---

[2] Maple is product of Waterloo Maple, Inc., 57 Erb Street, W. Waterloo, Ontario, Canada. Mathematica is produced by Wolfram Research, Inc., Champaign, Illinois.

1.7   OBJECTIVES OF THE TEXT

The first objective of the text is to teach you how to use Mathcad to solve engineering problems. The second objective is to show the wide range of career areas open to engineers and to demonstrate how Mathcad fits into all these areas. Finally, the third objective is to address a few of the challenges and opportunities that the next generation of engineers will face. With these objectives in mind, a typical chapter includes the following features:

- an introduction to one of the expanding fields of engineering;
- information on Mathcad, initially using simple examples for clarity;
- "Practice!" boxes—an opportunity for you to try Mathcad's features for yourself, using quick and easy problems;
- application boxes, showing how Mathcad can be used to solve real problems.

At the end of each chapter are several homework problems, some related to the challenges and opportunities mentioned. The following themes appear throughout the text:

- *global warming*, an issue the next generation of engineers will have to address;
- *biomedical engineering*, an opportunity for future engineers;
- *optics*, an old field that is expanding rapidly into new areas;
- *risk analysis*, a necessary and challenging part of many engineering activities;
- *total recycle*, Can we eliminate waste products entirely? It's being tried.
- *composite materials*, engineered materials that require the skills of a variety of engineering disciplines and that have the potential to change the way we do a lot of things.

1.8   CONVENTIONS USED IN THE TEXT

Stdev(v)	Function names and variable names in text are shown in a different font.
[Ctrl-6]	Keystrokes are shown in brackets. This example indicates that the control key and 6 key should be pressed simultaneously.
File / Save As	Menu selections are listed with the main menu item and submenu items separated by " / ".
$A := \pi \cdot r^2$	Mathcad examples are shown in the Times New Roman font and are indented.
Keyword	Keywords are shown in italics the first time they are used.

KEY TERMS

automatic recalculation	unit conversions	worksheet
design		

2

Mathcad Fundamentals

OBJECTIVES

* begin to understand how to work with Mathcad, including knowing how the Mathcad workspace is laid out
* begin to understand how to work with Mathcad, including knowing how to control the order in which Mathcad evaluates equations;
* begin to understand how to work with Mathcad, including knowing how to enter an equation,
* begin to understand how to work with Mathcad, including knowing know how Mathcad handles unit conversionsconversions; and
* begin to understand how to work with Mathcad, including knowing how to display a result, and
* begin to understand how to work with Mathcad, including knowing know how to enter and format text in a Mathcad worksheet.

9

GLOBAL WARMING

The *greenhouse effect* is an atmospheric phenomenon in which a buildup of greenhouse gases (carbon dioxide, methane, etc.) increases the amount of infrared radiation from the earth that is reflected back to the earth. If the concentration of greenhouse gases in the atmosphere increases, the surface temperature will rise, and *global warming* will result.

Our world's problem with global warming is hotly debat-ed, but there are a few points that are generally agreed upon:

1. The concentration of greenhouse gases (principally CO_2) in our atmosphere is increasing.
2. The average surface temperature of our planet is slowly increasing.
3. The greenhouse effect could cause global warming.

It is the likelihood and significance of the potential problem that are being questioned. In the worst-case scenario, the polar ice packs melt, flooding coastal cities around the world, changing climates, and turning America's grain belt (for example) into a desert. In the best-case scenarios, atmospheric CO_2 concentrations level off as the earth's ecosystem responds to the changing atmospheric conditions, and the problem goes away. The science is likely to be debated for many years to come. Even then, we may decide that we simply cannot know for certain what will happen. But even if we cannot know, that does not imply that we should not act—uncertainty does not justify inaction if there is a real possibility of catastrophe. This has led the leaders of the world's industrialized nations to commit to reducing their nations' emissions of CO_2. Because of this commitment, global warming has become a very real problem for engineers and one that may well be a significant part of your career.

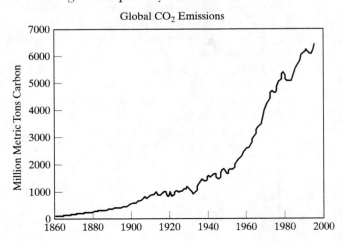

Historical Perspective

Energy has been a major contributor to economic growth ever since the Industrial Revolution, and much of that energy has come from fossil fuels. One result has been increased emissions of greenhouse gases into the atmosphere. Because there are many greenhouse gases, the total emissions are often reported in terms of carbon only.

The accompanying graph looks a lot like an exponential growth curve with a few perturbations. For example, 1918 to 1945 was a period of reduced growth in CO_2 emissions that coincides with World Wars I and II and the Great Depression. There's a bump around 1980 that coincides with a worldwide recession. Finally, there's a flat spot in the early 1990s that is being attributed to emission reductions in eastern Europe following the collapse of the Soviet Union.

There is good evidence that hard times coincide with reduced CO_2 emissions. Accordingly, many people are concerned that attempting to reduce CO_2 emissions may bring about hard times. Finding ways to reduce emissions while maintaining economic growth will require some very creative solutions. But finding creative solutions is what engineering is all about.

2.1 THE MATHCAD WORKPLACE

When you start Mathcad, you should see the following on your screen :

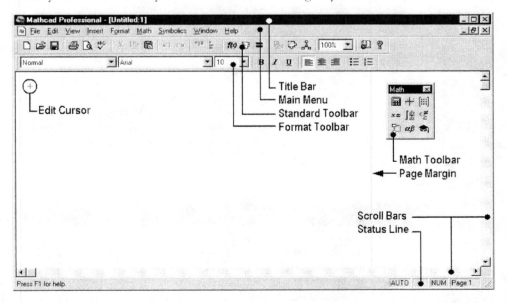

(The exact appearance of the screen depends upon the version of Mathcad you are using and the options that have been selected. Some of these options will be described in this chapter. The screen examples in this text are from Mathcad 2000.)

Several of the features near the top of the screen should be pretty familiar to Windows users. The Title Bar and Menu Bar are common to most Windows applications. Many of the most common menu commands are also available as buttons on the Toolbar. The Format Toolbar is very similar to that used by most word processors, but in Mathcad it displays the font type and size only when you are actually editing text or equations. The bold, italic, and underline buttons on the Format Toolbar apply to text only, not equations.

When you enter an equation or some text, it is initially formatted using a predefined *style*. There are separate styles defined for constants, variables, and text. You can change the formatting of any text or equations that you have selected by using the Format Toolbar, or you can change the formatting of all constants, variables, or text by redefining their respective styles. You access the styles by using the Format menu.

The *Math* Toolbar, shown just under the Format Bar toward the top of the screen (but it can be moved to other locations), is unique to Mathcad and provides access to a variety of useful mathematical symbols and functions. Clicking on any of the buttons on the Math Toolbar causes another toolbar to be displayed. For example, clicking the Matrix Toolbar button displays the Matrix Toolbar—a collection of functions that are useful for performing matrix operations. The Mathcad Toolbars available from the Math Toolbar include the following:

- Calculator Toolbar.
- Evaluation and Boolean Toolbar.
- Graph Toolbar.
- Vector and Matrix Toolbar.
- Calculus Toolbar.
- Programming Toolbar.
- Greek Symbol Toolbar.
- Symbolic Keyword Toolbar.

The majority of the workspace is a blank, white space called the *worksheet*. This is the area available for you to enter your equations, text, graphs, etc. The worksheet scrolls if you need more space.

There is a small crosshair cursor displayed on the worksheet. This is the *edit cursor*, and it indicates where the next equation or text region will be displayed. Clicking the mouse anywhere on the worksheet moves the edit cursor to the mouse pointer's location. If the edit cursor is located between two equations, you can add lines between the equations by pressing [Enter] or delete lines between the equations by pressing [Delete].

PROFESSIONAL SUCCESS

Practice, Practice, Practice!

This does not mean that you should perform the same tasks over and over again (you're not trying to improve your manual dexterity), but you can take conceptual information in a textbook and make it your own by putting it into practice.

The fastest way to learn Mathcad is to use it. Try working through the examples in this text on a computer. There are "Practice!" boxes throughout the text that have been designed to help you learn what Mathcad can do—to help you put this new knowledge into practice.

2.2   DETERMINING THE ORDER OF SOLVING EQUATIONS IN MATHCAD

It is usually very important to solve a set of equations in a particular order. In Mathcad, you use the placement of equations on the worksheet to control the order of their solution. Mathcad evaluates equations from left to right and top to bottom. When two equations are side by side on the worksheet, the equation on the left will be evaluated first, followed by the equation on the right. When there are no more equations to evaluate on a line, Mathcad moves down the worksheet and continues evaluating equations from left to right.

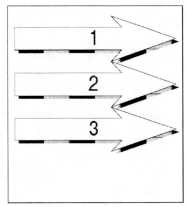

Some equations take a lot more space on the screen than others, so how do you determine which equation will be evaluated first? Mathcad assigns each equation an *anchor point* on the screen. The anchor point is located to the left of the first character in the equation, at the character baseline. You can ask Mathcad to display the anchor points by selecting Regions from the View Menu (View/Regions). When View/Regions is on, the background of the worksheet is dimmed, and the equation regions appear as bright boxes. The anchor point is indicated by a black dot.

anchor point

In the preceding figure, the equation on the left would be evaluated first, since the anchor points are the same distance from the top of the worksheet, but the anchor point on the s is to the left of the anchor point on the P. For simple variable definitions, like those of s and P shown here, the anchor point is always located at the bottom-left corner of the variable name.

2.3   FOUR DIFFERENT KINDS OF EQUAL SIGNS!

In high school algebra, you learned that the equal sign indicates that the left and right sides of an equation are equal. Then, in a programming course, you may have seen a statement such as

```
COUNT = COUNT + 1
```

This statement is never an algebraic equality, but it is a valid programming statement because the equal sign, in a programming context, means *assignment*, not algebraic equality. That is, the result of the calculation on the right side is assigned to the variable on the left. Mathcad allows both types of usage (algebraic equality and assignment) within a single worksheet, but different types of equal signs are used to keep things straight.

In Mathcad, four different symbols are available to represent equality or assignment (more if you count the "symbolic evaluation" and the programming "temporary assignment" symbols). Fortunately, some are used less often than others.

2.3.1 Assignment (:=)

The most commonly used *assignment operator* is :=, which is entered by using the colon key [:]. It is often called the "define as equal to" operator. This type of equal sign was used to assign values to variables s and P in the previous figure.

2.3.2 Display the Value of a Variable or Result of a Calculation (=)

Once a variable has been assigned a value (either directly or by means of a calculation), you can display the value by using the plain equal sign [=]. Displaying a value is the only usage of the plain equal sign in Mathcad; it is never used for assignment or algebraic equality. To display the value of the calculated variable s, you first define the equation used to compute s and then display the result using the equal sign. For example, we might have

```
s := 4·π
s = 12.566
```

You can also display a calculated result without assigning it to a variable. This displays the result of the calculation, but you cannot use that result in further calculations without assigning it to a variable. An example is

```
4·π = 12.566
```

2.3.3 Symbolic Equality (=)

A *symbolic equality* is used to indicate that the combination of variables on the left side of an equation is equal to the combination of variables on the right side of an equation—the high school algebra meaning of the equal sign. Symbolic equality is shown as a heavy boldface equal sign in Mathcad and is entered by pressing [Ctrl - =]. (Hold down the control key while pressing the equal key.) An example of a formula that uses this operation is

```
P·V = n·R·T
```

Symbolic equality is used to show a relationship between variables. There is no assignment of a value to any variable when symbolic equality is used. This type of equal sign is used for symbolic math and for solving equations by means of iterative methods.

2.3.4 Global Assignment (≡)

There is one way to override the left-to-right, top-to-bottom evaluation order in Mathcad: use a *global assignment* operator. Mathcad actually evaluates a worksheet in two passes. In the first pass, all global assignment statements are evaluated (from left to right and top to bottom). Then, in the second pass, all other equations are evaluated. Defining a variable with the use of a global assignment equal sign has the same effect as putting the equation at the top of the worksheet, since both cause the statement to be evaluated first.

Global assignments are not used a lot, but it is fairly common to use them for unit definitions. For example, Mathcad already knows what a year (yr) is, but you could define a new unit, decade, in terms of years as

    Decade ≡ 10·yr

(*Note:* You could also define the decade by using the regular assignment operator, := . It is common, but not required, to use global assignment for units.)

PRACTICE!

What will Mathcad display as the value of x in each of the examples that follow? (Try each in a separate worksheet.)

a. Use of "define as equal to" ...
    $y := 3$
    $x := y$
    $x =$

b. Use of a symbolic equality ...
    $y = 3$
    $x := y$
    $x =$

c. With units ...
    $y := 3 \cdot cm$
    $x := y$
    $x =$

d. Use of a "global define as equal to" ...
    $x := y$
    $x =$
    $y \equiv 3$

2.4   ENTERING AN EQUATION

To enter an equation, you simply position the edit cursor (crosshair) where you want the equation to go, and start typing. Mathcad creates an *equation region* and displays the equation as you enter it. (Whenever Mathcad is waiting for you to type in the workspace, it waits in *equation edit mode* so that you can easily enter a new equation.) To enter the defining equation for the variable s, you would type [s] [:] [4] [°] [Ctrl-Shift-p][Enter].[1] To see the result of this calculation, move the cursor to the right or down (or both), and type [s] [=]. Mathcad will display the result after the equal sign:

    s := 4·π
    s = 12.566

---

[1] The keyboard shortcut for pi is [Ctrl-Shift-p] in recent versions of Mathcad, but prior to version 8 the shortcut was [Ctrl-p].

2.4.1 Predefined Variables

Pi is such a commonly used value, that it comes as a *predefined variable* in Mathcad. You can get the π symbol either from the Greek Symbols Toolbar or by pressing [Ctrl-Shift-p], the shortcut used in the previous paragraph. Pi comes predefined in Mathcad with a value of 3.14159265. ... You can redefine pi (or any other predefined variable) simply by building it into a new definition:

```
π  := 7
s  := 4·π
s  = 28
```

However, redefining a commonly used constant is not a good idea in most situations. Four common predefined values in Mathcad are π, e, g, and %. These are entered by using [Ctrl-Shift-p], [e], [g], and [%], respectively.

2.4.2 Exponents

Use the *caret* [^] or [Shift-6] to enter an exponent in an equation. The right-hand side of the equation for the area of a circle would be entered as [Ctrl-Shift-p] [°] [r] [^] [2], which gives

```
Area := π·r²
```

Note that once Mathcad has moved the cursor up so that you can enter the exponent, it *stays* in the exponent. That is, if you were to enter a plus sign after the 2 in the preceding equation, you would be adding to the 2 (the exponent), not to the r^2. If you need to add something to the r^2, you must first select a portion of the equation and then enter the plus sign.

(*Note*: Mathcad uses standard mathematical *operator precedence rules*: exponentiation before multiplication and division, and multiplication and division before addition and subtraction. Parentheses can be used to ensure that an equation is evaluated in the desired order.)

2.4.3 Entering Nondecimal Values

To enter a hexadecimal value when defining a variable, simply add the letter h after the value. Hexadecimal values can contain the digits 0 through 9 and the letters a through f. No decimal points are allowed. Similarly, octal values can be used in variable definitions simply by adding the letter o after the value. Only digits 0 through 7 may be used. Mathcad allows binary values (consisting of zeroes and ones only) to be entered by adding a letter b at the end of the value. The following examples are representative:

A := 12	A = 12	decimal
B := 12o	B = 10	octal
C := 12h	C = 18	hexadecimal
D := 1011b	D = 11	binary

To see a result expressed as an octal, a hexadecimal, or a binary value, double-click the value and change the *radix* of the displayed result on the Format Result dialog.[2]

---

[2] In version 7 of Matchad, it is called the Format Number dialog.

```
E := 201                              E = 201
                                      E = 311o
                                      E = 0c9h
                                      E = 11001001b
```

2.4.4 Selecting Part of an Equation

If you want to compute the surface area of a cylinder, you need to add the areas of the circles on each end ($2\pi r^2$) and the area of the side of the cylinder ($2\pi rL$). After entering the exponent on the first term, you need to add another piece to the equation. If you don't select the r^2 before entering the plus sign, you will end up adding to the exponent as follows:

$$A_{cyl} := 2 \cdot \pi \cdot r^{2+2 \cdot \pi \cdot r}$$

This is obviously not what we want. To get what we want, right after entering the 2 in the r^2, you need to press the [Space] key once to select the r^2. (Mathcad will indicate the selected portion of the equation with an underline. There is also a vertical line, called the *insert bar*, that shows where the next typed character will go.) After you enter the exponent, the worksheet should look like this:

$$A_{cyl} := 2 \bullet \pi \bullet r^{2|}$$

After you enter the exponent and press [Space], the worksheet should look like this:

$$A_{cyl} := 2 \bullet \pi \bullet \underline{r^2}|$$

The underline beneath the r_2 indicates that the next operation will be applied to the entire selected region, which is what we want—we want to add $2\pi rL$ to the selected region. The final result is:

$$A_{cyl} := 2 \cdot \pi \cdot r^2 + 2 \cdot \pi \cdot r \cdot L$$

(*Note:* You might think you should select the entire term, $2 \cdot \pi \cdot r^2$, instead of just the r^2. That would work, too. You would just press [Space] two more times to select the π and the 2. To reduce the number of keystrokes required to enter an equation, Mathcad keeps multiplied variables together when you add to the collection. This is just a convenience; it is handy, but does take some getting used to.)

PRACTICE!

What does Mathcad display when you enter the following key sequences?

a. [P][°][V][Ctrl =][n] [°] [R] [°] [T]
b. [P][:][n] [°] [R] [°] [T][/][V]
c. [P][:][n] [°] [R] [°] [T][Space][Space] [/][V]
d. [r][:][k][1][°][C][A][^][2][-][k][2][°][C][B]
e. [r][:][k][1][°][C][A][^][2][Space][-][k][2][°][C][B]

2.4.5 Text Subscripts and Index Subscripts

The "cyl" in the variable name A_{cyl} presented earlier is slightly lower than the A—this is an example of a *text subscript*. Mathcad will allow the use of a text subscript as part of a variable name, which can be useful when one is naming related variables. For example, the areas of a circle, sphere, and cylinder might be indicated as A_{circle}, A_{sphere}, and A_{cyl}, respectively. The variable name A_{cyl} was entered as [A] [.] [c] [y] [l], where the period was used to indicate that a text subscript follows.

The *index subscript*, which may look similar to the text subscript, is used for an entirely different purpose. Index subscripts indicate a particular element of an array (a vector or matrix). The first element of an array is called element zero in Mathcad. For example, if you have a three-element array called Z, containing the values 2, 5, and 7—that is

$$Z := \begin{bmatrix} 2 \\ 5 \\ 7 \end{bmatrix}$$

then the value of element zero of array Z is 2. The zero element can be accessed individually using an index subscript, as in

$$Z_0 = 2$$

While it looks similar to a text subscript, an index subscript is entered differently and has a different meaning than a text subscript. The preceding index subscript was entered as [Z] [[ ] [0], where [[ ] means the left-square-bracket key.

PRACTICE!

What does Mathcad display when you enter the following key sequences?

a. [r][.][A][:][k][.][0][°][C][.][A][^][2]—this expression has a *text* subscript on k

b. [r][.][A][:][k][[ ][0][°][C][.][A][^][2]—this expression has an *index* subscript on k

c. [r][.][A][:][k][[ ][0][space][°][C][.][A][^][2]

2.4.6 Changing a Value or a Variable Name

If you click in the middle of a value or a variable name, a vertical insert bar (cursor) will be displayed. The insert bar indicates where any edits will take place. You can use the left- and right-arrow keys to move the bar. The delete key will remove the character to the right of the insert bar, while the backspace key will remove the character to the left.

Not all characters that are entered are displayed by Mathcad, but they can still be deleted. For example, the [.] used to enter a text subscript is not shown on the screen, but if you position the insert bar at the beginning of the subscript text and press [Backspace], the [.] will be removed, and the subscript will become regular text.

For example, if the ideal-gas constant (0.08206 liter atm/mole K) had been entered incorrectl y as 0.08506, you would click next to the 5, as in the following figure:

$$R_{gas} := 0.085|06$$

Then press [Backspace] to remove the 5, and press [2] to enter the correct value. The final result would look like this:

$$R_{gas} := 0.08206$$

2.4.7 Changing an Operator

When you need to change an operator, such as a symbolic equality (**=**) to an assignment operator (**:=**), you click just to the right of the operator itself. This puts insert bars around the character just to the right of the operator. Press [Insert] to move the vertical bar to the left side of the character (just to the right of the operator):

$$s\ =\ \lfloor 4 \cdot \pi$$

Then press [Backspace] to delete the operator. An open placeholder appears, indicating where the new operator will be placed:

$$s\ \square\ \lfloor 4 \cdot \pi$$

Enter the new assignment operator by pressing the colon key [:]:

$$s\ :=\ \lfloor 4 \cdot \pi$$

2.4.8 Inserting a Minus Sign

Special care must be taken when you need to insert a minus sign, because the same key is used to indicate both negation and subtraction. Here is how Mathcad decides which symbol to insert when you press the [-] key:

If the insert bar is to the left of a character (to the right of the open placeholder), as in

$$A\ :=\ 12 \cdot x^2\ \square\ \lfloor 5 \cdot y^2$$

then the sign of the character to the right of the placeholder is changed (indicating negation):

$$A\ :=\ 12 \cdot x^2\ \square -5 \cdot y^2$$

If the insert bar is to the right of a character (to the left of the open placeholder), as in

$$A\ :=\ 12 \cdot x^2 \rfloor \square 5 \cdot y^2$$

then the open placeholder is filled by a subtraction operator:

$$A\ :=\ 12 \cdot x^2 - 5 \cdot y^2$$

2.4.9 Highlighting a Region

To make your results stand out, Mathcad allows you to show them in a highlighted region. The highlighting can consist of a border around the result or a colored background.

To highlight a result, right-click on it, and select Properties from the pop-up menu:

$$M := 10 \cdot kg \qquad a := 9.8 \cdot \frac{m}{s^2}$$

$$F := M \cdot a \qquad F = 98 \cdot N$$

- Cut
- Copy
- Paste
- Properties...
- Disable Evaluation
- Bring to Front
- Send to Back

On the Properties dialog, select Highlight Region and Choose Color, or check the Show Border box:

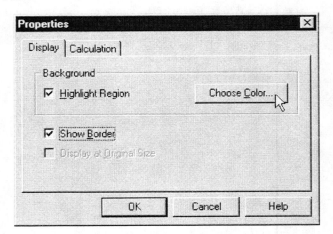

2.4.10 Changing the Way Operators are Displayed

Mathcad uses specific symbols for operators, such as the := to indicate assignment. While these symbols help you read to a Mathcad worksheet, they can confuse people who are not used to working with the software. You can change the way operators are displayed using the Math Options dialog. Several of the common operators used in Mathcad have alternative display symbols (e.g., ·, ·, and × for multiplication:); the assignment operator, :=, will be used as an example.

To bring up the Math Options dialog, use Math/Options from the Mathcad menu:

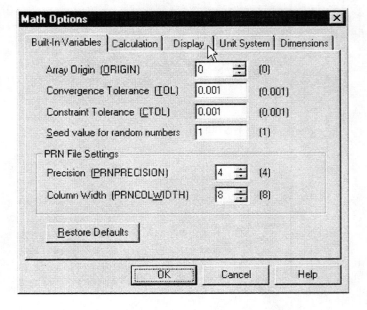

Click on the Display tab to change the way operators are displayed:

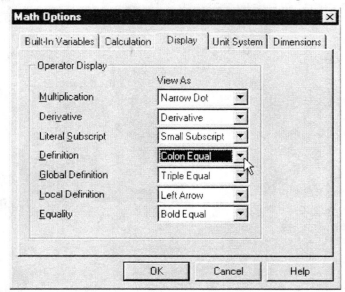

To change the way assignment (i.e., variable definition) is indicated, click on the drop-down list on the Definition line, and select Equal:

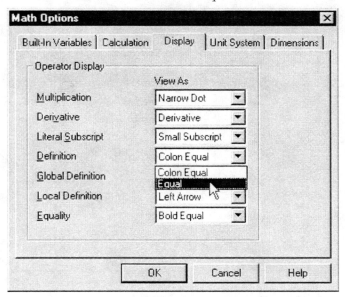

Now, every := your worksheet will be displayed without the colon before the equal sign. The following lists show a few examples of what is displayed before and after changing the assignment operator:

Before changing the assignment operators

R := 3·cm

L := 12·cm

A := 2·π·R^2+2·R·π·L

A = 282.7cm^2

After changing the assignment operator

R = 3·cm

L = 12·cm

A = 2·π·R^2+2·R·π·L

A = 282.7cm^2

2.5   WORKING WITH UNITS

Mathcad supports units. Its ability to automatically handle unit conversions is a *very* nice feature for engineering calculations, since the number of required unit conversions can be considerable. Mathcad handles units by storing all values in a base set of units (SI by default, but you can change it):

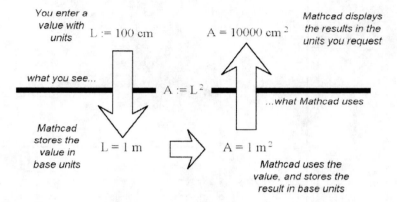

Values are converted from the units you enter to the base set before the value is stored. Then, when a value is displayed, the conversions required to give the requested units are automatically performed. Mathcad's unit handling works very well for most situations, but it does have some limitations, which will be discussed shortly.

Mathcad supports the following *systems of units*:

- SI—default units (meter, kilogram, second, etc.);
- MKS—meter, kilogram, second;
- CGS—centimeter, gram, second;
- US—foot, pound, second;
- none—disables all built-in units, but user-defined units still work.

Within each system, certain *dimensions* are supported. But not all dimensions are supported in all systems. The following table shows the dimensions the various systems support in Mathcad:

DIMENSION	SYSTEM				
	SI	MKS	CGS	US	None
Mass	✓	✓	✓	✓	✓
Length	✓	✓	✓	✓	✓
Time	✓	✓	✓	✓	✓
Current	✓	no	no	no	no
Charge	no	✓	✓	✓	✓
Temperature	✓	✓	✓	✓	✓
Luminosity	✓	no	no	no	no
Substance	✓	no	no	no	no

If you plan to work with current (typical units, amps), luminosity (typical units, candelas) or substance (typical units, moles), then you want to use the default SI units. If these units are not important to you, you have more system options available. You set the system of units to be used as base units from the menu bar: Math/Options .../Unit System.

The following are some common unit abbreviations, by category:

mass	kg, gm, lb
length	m, cm, ft
time	sec, hr
current	amp
charge	coul
temperature	K, R
substance	mole
volume	liter, gal, galUK (Imperial gallon)
force	N, dyne, lbf
pressure	Pa, atm, torr, in_Hg, psi
energy and work	joule, erg, cal, BTU
power	watt, kW, hp

Cautions on Unit Names

g—predefined as gravitational acceleration, not grams;

gm—unit name for grams;

R—unit name for °R (degrees Rankine), not the gas constant;

mole—gram mole, defined in the SI system only.

You can overwrite the symbols used as predefined unit names by declaring them as variables in a worksheet. For example, if you included the statement

$$m := 1 \cdot kg$$

in a worksheet, the symbol 'm' would become a variable and no longer represent meters. Redefining unit names is usually not a good idea.

These units are only a small subset of the predefined units in Mathcad. A list of available units may be obtained by pressing [Ctrl-u]. You can select units from the list or simply type the unit name (using Mathcad's abbreviation).

For example, you could find the area of a circle with a radius of 7 cm by using the following equations:

```
r := 7·cm
Area := π·r²
```

In the first line, the 7 is multiplied by the unit name, 'cm'; then the area is computed on the second line. The result is displayed as

$$\underline{Area} = 0.015 \bullet m^2$$

The box around this equation and the vertical bar at the right side of `Area` indicate that we haven't completed editing the equation; that is, we haven't pressed [Enter] yet. As soon as you press [=], Mathcad shows the value currently assigned to the variable `Area` in the base units (SI, by default). A *placeholder* is also shown to the right of the units (only while the equation is being edited), so that you can request that the value be displayed in different units. If you want the result displayed in cm², click on the placeholder and then enter [c] [m] [^] [2] [Enter]. The result is displayed in the requested units:

```
Area = 153.938·cm²
```

You can put any defined (predefined, or defined part of the worksheet) unit in the placeholder. If the units you enter have the wrong dimensions, Mathcad will make that apparent by showing you the "leftover" dimensions in base units. For example, if you had placed 'atm' (atmospheres) in the placeholder, the dimensions would be quite wrong, and the displayed result would make this apparent:

```
Area = 1.519·10⁻⁷·kg⁻¹·m³·s² * atm
```

2.5.1 Defining a New Unit

New units are defined in terms of predefined units. For example, a commonly used unit of viscosity is the centipoise, or cP. The poise is predefined in Mathcad, but the centipoise is not. The new unit can be defined like this:

$$cP := \frac{poise}{100}$$

Once the new unit has been defined, it can be used throughout the rest of the worksheet. Here, the viscosity of honey is defined as 10,000 cP, and then the value is displayed by using another common unit for viscosity, Pascal·seconds:

```
visc_honey := 10000·cP
visc_honey = 10 * Pa·s
```

PRACTICE!

Try these obvious unit conversions:

    a.   100 cm → m

    b.   2.54 cm → in

    c.   454 gm → lb

Now try these less obvious conversions:

    a.   1 hp → KW

    b.   1 liter·atm → joule

    c.   1 joule → watt (This is an invalid conversion. How does Mathcad respond?)

First, make sure your method [or design/computer code/Mathcad worksheet] works correctly on a test case with a known answer. Then try your method [design/computer code/Mathcad worksheet] on a new problem.

In the last "Practice"! box, you were asked to try Mathcad on some obvious cases before trying some less obvious ones. Testing against a known result is a standard procedure in engineering. If you get the right answer in the test case, you have increased confidence (though not total confidence) that your method is working. If you get the wrong answer, it is a lot easier to find out what went wrong using the test problem than it is to try to fix the method and solve the real problem simultaneously.

You'll see this technique used throughout the text.

2.5.2 Editing the Units on a Value or Result

Once you have entered units, simply edit the unit name to change them. Click on the unit name, delete characters as needed, and then type in the desired units.

2.5.3 Limitations to Mathcad's Units Capabilities

- Mathcad's unit conversions must be multiplicative—no additive constants can be used in unit conversions. This means that Mathcad can convert kelvins to °R (degrees Rankine), but cannot convert °C to kelvins (add 273) or °C to °F (add 32). Similarly, Mathcad can handle absolute pressure conversions, but cannot automatically convert gauge pressures to absolute (add the barometric pressure).

- Some of Mathcad's built-in functions do not support, or do not fully support, units. For example, the linear regression function `linfit( )` does not accept values with units. The iterative solver (`given-find` solve block) does allow units, but if you are solving for two or more variables simultaneously, the variables must have the same units.

- Mathcad's built-in graphics always display the values in the base (stored) units.

- Only the SI system of units fully supports moles. In the other systems, Mathcad allows you to use the term "mole" as a unit, but does not consider it a dimension and does not display it when presenting units. This means that *you should use the SI system if you plan to work with moles.*

- The mole defined in Mathcad's SI system is the gram-mole. I like to make this obvious by defining a new unit, the gmol:

```
gmol := mole
```

You can define the other commonly used molar units as well:

```
kmol  := 1000·mole
lbmol := 453.593·mole
```

With these definitions, Mathcad can convert between the various types of moles (but only if you are using the SI system of units.)

APPLICATIONS: DETERMINING THE CURRENT IN A CIRCUIT

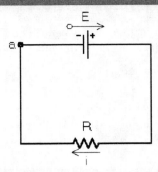

Consider a simple circuit containing a 9-volt battery and a 90-ohm resistor, as shown in the accompanying diagram. What current would flow in the circuit? To solve this problem, you need to know *Ohm's law*,

$$V = iR,$$

and *Kirchhoff's law of voltage*,

> *For a closed (loop) circuit, the algebraic sum of all changes in voltage must be zero.*

Kirchhoff's law is perhaps easier to understand if you consider the following analogy:

> If you are hiking in the hills and you end up back at the same spot you started from (a loop trail), then the sum of the changes in elevation must be zero: You must end up at the same elevation at which you started.

The electrons moving through the circuit from point 'a' may have their electric potential (volts) increased (by the battery) or decreased (by the resistor), but if they end up back where they started from (in a loop circuit), they must end up with the same potential they started with. We can use Kirchhoff's law to write an equation describing the voltage changes through the circuit. Starting at an arbitrary point 'a' and moving through the circuit in the direction of the current flow the voltage is first raised by the battery ($V_B = E$) and then lowered by the resistor (V_R). These are the only two elements in the circuit, so

$$V_B - V_R = 0$$

by Kirchhoff's law. Now, we know that the battery raises the electric potential by 9 volts, and Ohm's law relates the current flowing through the resistor (and the rest of the circuit) to the resistance, 90 ohms. Thus,

$$V_B - iR = 0.$$

The Mathcad equations needed to calculate the current through the circuit look like this:

$$V_B := 9 \cdot \text{volt}$$

$$R := 90 \cdot \text{ohm}$$

$$i := \frac{V_B}{R}$$

$$i = 0.1 \circ \text{amp}$$

2.6   CONTROLLING HOW RESULTS ARE DISPLAYED

The Result Format dialog allows you to control the way individual numbers, matrices, and units are displayed. If you have not selected a result when you change a setting in the Result Format dialog, you will change the way all results on the worksheet will be displayed. However, if you select a value before you open the Result Format dialog, the changes you make in the Result Format dialog will affect only that one result. The Result Format dialog can be opened in two ways:

1. from the menu, using Format / Result, or
2. by double-clicking on a displayed result.

2.6.1 Controlling the Way Numbers Are Displayed

Mathcad tries to present results in a readable form, with only a few decimal places displayed. You may want to change the way results are displayed, in any of following ways:

1. Format: You can use General, Decimal, Scientific, or Engineering Format. (The default is General format, which displays small values without exponents, but switches to scientific notation for larger values.)
2. Number of decimal places displayed (three by default).
3. Whether or not to display trailing zeros. (By default, they are not displayed.)
4. Exponential threshold (for General format only): You can indicate how large values can get before Mathcad switches to scientific notation.

You can bring up the Result Format dialog by double-clicking on a displayed result. As an example, we'll use B = 1 / 700, a very small value with lots of decimal points:

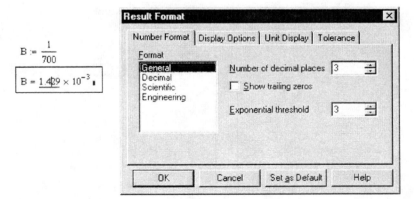

The Mathcad defaults are shown in the Result Format dialog:

*   general format;
*   three decimal places;
*   trailing zeros not shown;
*   exponential threshold of 3 (i.e., 999 displayed as decimal, 1,000 displayed in scientific notation)

If you were to select Decimal format, the result would be displayed in standard notation, but still with only three decimal places:

$$B := \frac{1}{700}$$

$$B = 0.001$$

To see more decimal places, change the number of displayed decimal places from 3 to some larger value, say 7:

$$B := \frac{1}{700}$$

$$B = 0.0014286$$

The following table compares general, scientific, and engineering formats.

DEFINITION X	GENERAL FORMAT	SCIENTIFIC FORMAT	ENGINEERING FORMAT
$x := \begin{pmatrix} 10 \\ 100 \\ 1000 \\ 10000 \\ 100000 \\ 1000000 \end{pmatrix}$	$x = \begin{pmatrix} 10.000 \\ 100.000 \\ 1.000 \times 10^3 \\ 1.000 \times 10^4 \\ 1.000 \times 10^5 \\ 1.000 \times 10^6 \end{pmatrix}$	$x = \begin{pmatrix} 1.000 \times 10^1 \\ 1.000 \times 10^2 \\ 1.000 \times 10^3 \\ 1.000 \times 10^4 \\ 1.000 \times 10^5 \\ 1.000 \times 10^6 \end{pmatrix}$	$x = \begin{pmatrix} 10.000 \times 10^0 \\ 100.000 \times 10^0 \\ 1.000 \times 10^3 \\ 10.000 \times 10^3 \\ 100.000 \times 10^3 \\ 1.000 \times 10^6 \end{pmatrix}$

General format displays small values without a power, but switches large values (greater than the exponential threshold) to scientific notation. Scientific format uses scientific notation for values of any size. Engineering format is similar to scientific notation, except that the powers are always multiples of 3 (- 6, - 3, 0, 3, 6, 9, etc.).

2.6.2 Controlling the Way Matrices Are Displayed

By default, Mathcad shows small matrices (arrays) in their entirety, but switches to scrolling tables when the matrices get large. You can change the way a matrix result is displayed by double-clicking on the matrix:

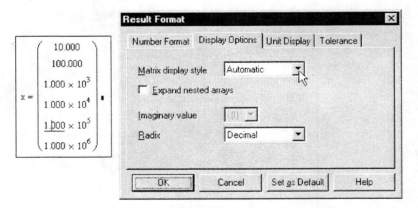

The x matrix used in this example is a pretty small matrix, so the Automatic selection (default) displays the result as a matrix. You can change the display style using the drop-down list and selecting Table:

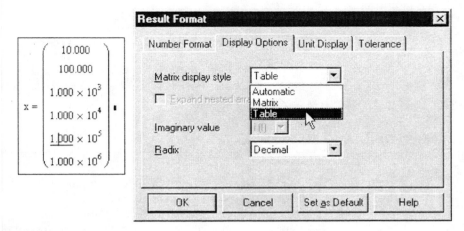

When you click on the OK button, the x matrix is displayed as a scrolling table:

	0
0	10.000
1	100.000
2	$1.000 \cdot 10^3$
3	$1.000 \cdot 10^4$
4	$1.000 \cdot 10^5$
5	$1.000 \cdot 10^6$

$x =$ (to the left of the table)

2.6.3 Controlling the Way Units Are Displayed

By default, Mathcad tries to simplify units whenever possible. Because of this, the units on the result in the following example are newtons rather than $\text{kg} \cdot \text{m} / \text{s}^2$:

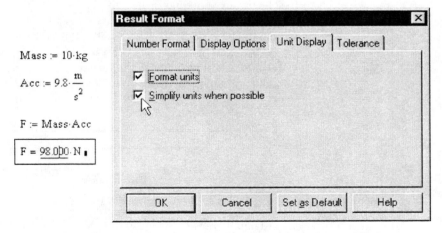

If you do not want Mathcad to simplify the units for a particular result, double-click on that result to bring up the Result Format dialog. Then clear the 'Simplify units when possible' check box. When you leave the dialog box, the result will be displayed without simplifying the units:

$\text{Mass} := 10 \cdot \text{kg}$

$\text{Acc} := 9.8 \cdot \dfrac{\text{m}}{\text{s}^2}$

$$F \; := \; Mass \cdot Acc$$

$$F = 98.000 \cdot \frac{kg \;\; m}{s^2}$$

The "Format units" check box indicates that units should be displayed in "common" form. If the "Format units" check box is cleared, the result would be displayed as

$$F = 98.000 \cdot kg \;\; m \;\; s^{-2}$$

2.7 ENTERING AND EDITING TEXT

Mathcad defaults to equation edit mode, so if you just start typing, Mathcad will try to interpret your entry as an equation. If you type a series of letters and then a space, Mathcad will recognize that you are entering text and will switch to *text edit mode* and create a *text region*. Or you can tell Mathcad you want to enter text by pressing the double-quote key ["].

To create a text region, position the edit cursor (crosshair) in the blank portion of the worksheet where you want the text to be placed, and then press ["] (the double-quote key). A small rectangle with a vertical line (the insert bar) inside appears on the worksheet, indicating that you are creating a text region. The text region will automatically expand as you type, until you reach the page margin (the vertical line at the right side of the screen, shown in the next figure). Then the text will automatically wrap to the next line.

> This text region will expand until reaches the page margin, then the text will automatically wrap...

You can change the size or location of an existing text region by clicking on the text to select the region and display the border. Then, drag the border to move the box, or drag one of the handles to change the size of the box. If you change the width of a text region, the text will wrap as necessary to fit in the new width.

Once you have a block of text in a text region, you can select all or part of the text with the mouse and then use the formatting buttons on the Format Toolbar. These buttons allow you to make the font boldface, add italics, or underline the text. For example, to create a heading for some global-warming calculations, you might type in some text and then select "Global Warming":

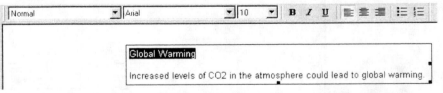

Then increase the font size of the selected text by using the Format Toolbar:

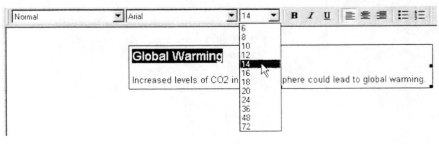

Finally, make the font in the heading boldface by using the Format Toolbar.

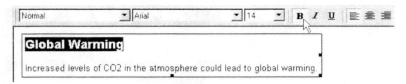

You can also create sub- or superscripts within the text region by selecting the characters to be raised or lowered. Next, using Format/Text ...from the Menu Bar, and select Subscript or Superscript from the Text Format dialog box as follows:

1. Select the text you want to make into a subscript:

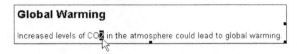

2. Select Text ... from the Format menu:

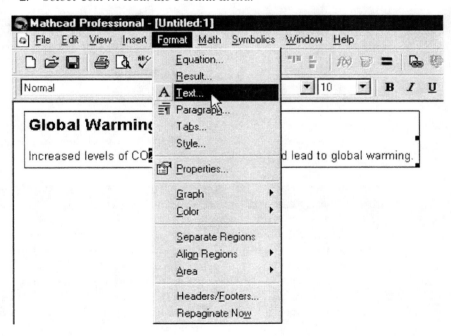

3.   Select Subscript on the Text Format dialog box:

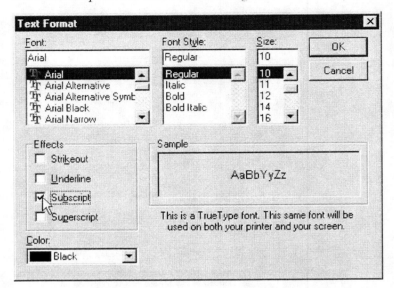

After these changes, the worksheet heading looks like this:

Global Warming

Increased levels of CO_2 in the atmosphere could lead to global warming.

Mathcad gives you a great deal of control over the appearance of your text, and adding headings and notes to your worksheets can make them much easier for others to read and understand.

PROFESSIONAL SUCCESS

Document your results.

Taking the time to document your worksheets by adding headings and comments can have a big payoff later (sometimes years later), when you need to perform a similar calculation and want to refer to your worksheets to see how it was done.

The skills you develop and the knowledge you acquire in your academic and professional careers combine to form the resource base, or expertise, that you bring to a new job or project. But when your resource base gets stale, you can spend a lot of time relearning things you once knew. Plan ahead and make the relearning as easy as possible by making your worksheets easy to understand.

Note: If you want to make a change to all text regions—italicizing all the text so that it is easier to see the difference between your text regions and equations, for example—then change the *style* used to display all text regions. To modify the text style sheet, select Format/Style .../Normal/Modify/Font from the menu bar. This will bring up a dialog box describing the Normal style (used for regular text). If you click on the italic property and close the dialog box, all text created using the Normal style will be in italics. (Format changes to individual text boxes or selected characters override the style sheet. If you select one word in a text box and remove the italics using the Format Bar, that individual change would override the style sheet, and the italics would be removed for that word.)

2.7.1 Sizing and Moving a Text or Equation Region

If you click outside of a region and drag the mouse into the region, Mathcad will show you the size and location of the region by drawing a line around it. For resizable regions, like text regions, Mathcad will also show three small black squares on the edges of the region, called *handles*. Grab a handle with the mouse, and drag it to change the size or shape of a region. (Some regions automatically resize, so they might snap back again when you release the handle.) To move a single selected region, move the mouse over the border until it changes to a hand symbol. While the hand symbol is displayed, drag the border (and the region) to the new location on the worksheet. If multiple regions are selected, dashed lines are drawn around each region. They cannot be resized, but they can be moved together by clicking inside any of the selected regions and dragging all the selected regions to a new location.

2.7.2 Inserting Equations Inside Text Regions

You can move an existing equation into a text region so that the equation is read as part of the text. When equations are moved inside text regions, they are still functioning equations in the Mathcad worksheet and are evaluated just like any other equation.

As an example, consider a force calculation with a paragraph describing Newton's second law:

```
M := 10•kg
```

$$a := 9.8 \cdot \frac{m}{s^2}$$ *The relationship between force, mass, and acceleration was defined by Isaac Newton. The commonly used version of the equation is called Newton's second law.*

```
F := M•a
```
```
F = 98 N
```

The equation for calculating force can be moved inside the paragraph, and it will still calculate the force:

```
M := 10•kg
```

$$a := 9.8 \cdot \frac{m}{s^2}$$ *The relationship between force, mass, and acceleration was defined by Isaac Newton. The commonly used version of the equation,* $F := M \cdot a$, *is called Newton's second law.*

```
F = 98 N
```

2.8   A SIMPLE EDITING SESSION

We will use one of the examples mentioned earlier, namely, determining the surface area of a cylinder, to demonstrate how to solve a simple problem using Mathcad. Even in this simple example, the following Mathcad features will be used:

- text editing and formatting;
- variable definitions (r and L);
- equation definition;
- exponentiation (r^2);

- displaying the result (=);
- working with units.

2.8.1 Statement of the problem

Determine the surface area of a cylinder with a radius of 7 cm and a length of 21 cm.

The solution will be presented with a step-by-step commentary. For this simple example, the complete Mathcad worksheet will be shown as it develops at each step.

**STEP 2.1
USE A TEXT
REGION TO
DESCRIBE THE
PROBLEM**

1. Position the edit cursor (crosshair) near the top of the blank worksheet and click the left mouse button.
2. Press ["] to create a text region.
3. Enter the statement of the problem.
4. Click outside of the text region when you are done entering text.

The result might look something like this (italic text is not the Mathcad default, but adding italics can help differentiate text regions from equations):

Statement of the Problem
Determine the surface area of a cylinder with a radius of 7 cm and a length of 21 cm.

**STEP 2.2
ENTER THE
KNOWN
VALUES OF
RADIUS AND
LENGTH, WITH
APPROPRIATE
UNITS**

1. Position the edit cursor below the text region and near the left side of the worksheet. Click the left mouse button.
2. Define the value of r by typing [r] [:] [7] [°] [c] [m] [Enter].
3. Similarly, position the edit cursor, and enter the value of L (21 cm).

The positions of the r and L equations are arbitrary, but they might look like the following:

Statement of the Problem
Determine the surface area of a cylinder with a radius of 7 cm and a length of 21 cm.

```
r := 7·cm
L := 21·cm
```

STEP 2.3 ENTER THE EQUATION FOR COMPUTING THE SURFACE AREA OF A CYLINDER

1. Position the edit cursor below or to the right of the definitions of r and L.
2. Enter the area variable name, A_{cyl}, by using a text subscript, as [A] [.] [c] [y] [l].
3. Press [:] to indicate that you are defining the A_{cyl} variable.
4. Enter the first term on the right side ($2\pi r^2$) as [2] [°] [Ctrl-Shift-p] [°] [r] [^] [2].[3]
5. Press [Space] to select the r^2 in the $2\pi r^2$ term.
6. Press [+] to add to the selected term.
7. Enter the second term on the right side ($2\pi rL$) as [2] [°] [Ctrl-Shift-p] [°] [r] [°] [L].
8. Press [Enter] to conclude the equation entry.

The result will look like this:

Statement of the Problem

Determine the surface area of a cylinder with a radius of 7 cm and a length of 21 cm.

r := 7·cm
L := 21·cm
A_{cyl} := $2·\pi·r^2+2·\pi·r·L$

STEP 2.4 DISPLAY THE RESULT IN THE DESIRED UNITS

1. Position the edit cursor below or to the right of the A_{cyl} equation.
2. Ask Mathcad to display the result of the calculation by typing [A] [.] [c] [y] [l] [=].
3. Click on the units placeholder (to the right of the displayed base units).
4. Enter the desired units (e.g., cm^2).
5. Press [Enter] to conclude the entry.

The worksheet will look like this:

Statement of the Problem

Determine the surface area of a cylinder with a radius of 7 cm and a length of 21 cm.

r := 7·cm
L := 21·cm
A_{cyl} := $2·\pi·r^2+2·\pi·r·L$
A_{cyl} = $1.232·10^3·cm^2$

PRACTICE!

Calculate the surface area and volume of

a. a cube 1 cm on a side.
b. a sphere with a radius of 7 cm.

Equations for the sphere are $A = 4 \pi r^2$ and $V = (4/3) \pi r^3$.

---

[3] The keyboard shortcut is [Ctrl-Shift-p] in recent versions of Mathcad and [Ctrl-p] in version 7.

APPLICATIONS: GLOBAL WARMING

The Kyoto Accords of 1997 commit the United States and Canada to reducing CO_2 emissions to levels 7% below the 1990 baseline. European countries have committed to lower their emissions to 8% below the baseline. Developing nations such as India and China were asked to voluntarily lower their CO_2 emissions as well. Apart from the issue of whether or not the various governments ratify the accords, there is now a strong worldwide emphasis on trying to reduce CO_2 emissions to delay or prevent global warming.

Carbon dioxide is extremely abundant on our planet, and the vast majority of the gaseous CO_2 produced each year is from natural sources: plant and animal respiration, aerobic decay of vegetation, and releases of CO_2 from the oceans. The planet also has considerable resources for removing CO_2 from the atmosphere, mostly by uptake into the oceans and plant photosynthesis. These natural sources and sinks for CO_2 are approximately in balance. The source of the increasing CO_2 in our atmosphere is human-made, or anthropogenic, CO_2. (See accompanying table.)

TABLE 2-1 The Global CO_2 Imbalance
(units are million metric tons of carbon per year)

SOURCES		SINK
Natural	Anthropogenic	Natural
150,000	7,100	154,000

Source: Intergovernmental Panel on Climate Change, *Climate Change 1995: The Science of Climate Change* (Cambridge, UK: Cambridge University Press, 1996), pp. 17-19, reported in *Emissions of Greenhouse Gases in the United States 1996,* Energy Information Agency, U.S. Department of Energy.

Natural removal processes can handle all of the naturally produced CO_2 and a substantial part of the anthropogenic CO_2. But the excess CO_2 has nowhere to go and is building up in our atmosphere. In order to restore the balance, we must either reduce one or the other of the source terms, increase the sink term, or add another term to the equation (give the CO_2 someplace else to go.) The Kyoto solution focuses on reducing the anthropogenic source term to move towards balance.

The Kyoto Accords have made the 1997 emissions (estimates at the time of the Kyoto meeting) and the 1990 emissions data of primary significance. These data are summarized in following table:

TABLE 2-2 U.S. CO_2

CATEGORY	1990	1997 (PREDICTED)
	Million Metric Tons Carbon	
Residential, Commercial	459.9	528.3
Industrial	453.8	487.6
Transportation	432.1	484.5
Total	1,345.8	1,493.2

Sources: 1990 Data: *Emissions of Greenhouse Gases in the United States, 1996,* Energy Information Agency, U.S. Department of Energy. 1997 Predictions: *Annual Energy Outlook 1998,* U.S. Department of Energy.

The global estimate for CO_2 emissions in 1990 is 6,120 million metric tons of carbon.[1] We can use Mathcad to determine the percentage of global CO_2 emissions that came from the United States in 1990:

$$MMT \equiv 1 \cdot 10^6 \cdot tonne \qquad \textit{define unit: million metric ton}$$

$$CO_{2\ US} := 1345.8 \cdot MMT \qquad \textit{set U.S. emissions in 1990}$$

$$CO_{2\ Global} := 6120 \cdot MMT \qquad \textit{set global emissions in 1990}$$

$$\frac{CO_{2\ US}}{CO_{2\ Global}} = 0.22 \qquad \textit{result expressed as fraction}$$

$$\frac{CO_{2\ US}}{CO_{2\ Global}} = 21.99 \circ \% \qquad \textit{result expressed as percentage}$$

In 1990, the United States emitted almost 22% of the world's anthropogenic (human-generated) CO_2, making it the world's largest emitter of this gas.

The U.S. is supposed to reduce CO_2 emissions to 7% below the 1990 level. We can see what this target means in terms of millions of metric tons of CO_2:

$$CO_{2\ target} := CO_{2\ US} - (0.07 \cdot CO_{2\ US})$$
$$CO_{2\ target} = 1251.6 \cdot MMT$$

And we can calculate the required reduction in CO_2 emissions by using the following equations:

$$CO_{2\ US97} := 1493.2 \cdot MMT$$
$$CO_{2\ reduction} := CO_{2\ US97} - CO_{2\ target}$$
$$CO_{2\ reduction} = 241.6 \cdot MMT$$

This represents a 16.18% reduction in CO_2 emissions from the 1997 levels:

$$\frac{CO_{2\ reduction}}{CO_{2\ US97}} = 16.18 \cdot \%$$

The levels requested by the Kyoto Accords will be hard to achieve—but even if they are achieved, they will not "fix" the problem. They are only a beginning.

[1]Greg Marl and Tom Boden, *Global, Regional, and National Annual Carbon Dioxide Emission from Fossil-Fuel Burning and Cement Production: 1950-1994*, Environmental Sciences Division, Oak Ridge National Laboratory, Oak Ridge, TN.

MATHCAD SUMMARY   *Four Kinds of Equal Signs*

:=	Assigns a value or the result of a calculation to a variable.
=	Displays a value or the result of a calculation.
=	Symbolic equality; shows the relationship between variables.
≡	Global assignment; these are evaluated before the rest of the worksheet.

Predefined Variables

π	3.141592 …	Press [Ctrl-Shift-p] or choose π from the Greek Symbols Toolbar.
e	2.718281 …	
g	9.8 m/s^2	
%	multiplies the displayed value by 100 and displays the percent symbol.	

Entering Equations

+, -	addition and subtraction.	
°, /	multiplication and division.	Press [Shift-8] for the multiplication symbol.
^	exponentiation.	Press [Shift-6] for the caret symbol.
[Space]	enlarges the currently selected region—used after typing in exponents and denominators.	
[Insert]	moves the vertical edit cursor between the front and back of a selected region—used when you need to delete an operator to the left of a selected region.	
[.]	text subscript.	
[[ ]	index subscript—used to indicate a particular element of an array.	

Operator Precedence

^	Exponentiation is performed before multiplication and division.
°, /	Multiplication and division are performed before addition and subtraction.
+, -	Addition and subtraction are performed last.

Text Regions

["]	Creates a text region—if you type in characters that include a space (i.e., two words), Mathcad will automatically create a text region around these characters.

KEY TERMS

anchor point
assignment operator
dimensions
edit cursor
equation region
global assignment

greenhouse effect
index subscript
Kirchhoff's law of voltage
Ohm's law
operator precedence rules
placeholder

predefined variable
style
symbolic equality
text region
text subscript
worksheet

Problems

1. UNIT CONVERSIONS

   a. speed of light in a vacuum — 2.998×10^5 m/sec to miles per hour.

   b. density of water at room temperature — 62.3 lb/ft^3 to kg/m^3.

   c. density of water at 4°C — 1,000 kg/m^3 to lb/gal.

   d. viscosity of water at room temperature (approx.) — 0.01 poise to lb/ft sec. 0.01 poise to kg/m sec.

   e. ideal gas constant — 0.08206 L · atm/mole · K to joules/mole · K.

Note: The "lb" in parts b, c, and d is a pound mass, and "mole" in part e is a gram mole.

2. **VOLUME AND SURFACE AREA OF A SPHERE**

    Calculate the volume and surface area of a sphere with a radius of 3 cm. Use

    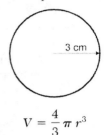

    $$V = \frac{4}{3}\,\pi\,r^3$$

    and

    $$A = 4\,\pi\,r^2.$$

3. **VOLUME AND SURFACE AREA OF A TORUS**

    A doughnut is roughly shaped like a torus. The surface area and volume functions for a torus are

    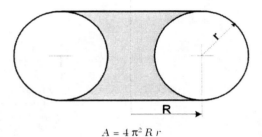

    $$A = 4\,\pi^2\,R\,r$$

    and

    $$V = 2\,\pi^2\,R\,r^2,$$

    respectively. Calculate the surface area and volume of a doughnut with R = 3 cm and r = 1.5 cm.

4. **IDEAL GAS BEHAVIOR, I**

    a. A glass cylinder fitted with a movable piston contains 5 grams of chlorine gas. When the gas is at room temperature (25°C), the piston is 2 cm from the bottom of the container. The pressure on the gas is 1 atm. What is the volume of gas in the glass cylinder (in liters)?

    b. The gas is heated at constant pressure until the piston is 5 cm from the bottom of the container. What is the final temperature of the chlorine (in kelvins)? Assume chlorine behaves as an ideal gas under these conditions. The molecular weight of chlorine is 35.45 grams per mole.

    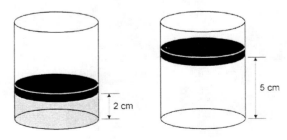

5.   IDEAL GAS BEHAVIOR, II

a.   Chlorine gas is added to a glass cylinder 2.5 cm in radius, fitted with a movable piston. Gas is added until the piston is lifted 5 cm off the bottom of the glass. The pressure on the gas is 1 atm, and the gas and cylinder are at room temperature (25°C). How many moles of chlorine were added to the cylinder?

b.   Pressure is applied to the piston, compressing the gas until the piston is 2 cm from the bottom of the cylinder. When the temperature returns to 25°C, what is the pressure in the cylinder (in atm)?

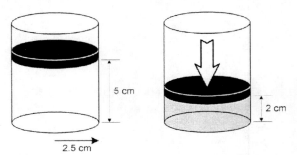

Assume that chlorine behaves as an ideal gas under these conditions. The molecular weight of chlorine is 35.45 grams per mole.

6.   RELATING FORCE AND MASS

This problem is the first in a series that introduces the concepts needed to design a suspension bridge. Fundamental to the design of the bridge is the relation between the mass of the deck and the force on the wires supporting the deck. The relationship between force and mass is called *Newton's law* and in physics courses is usually written as

$$F = ma$$

In engineering courses, we often build in the gravitational constant, g_c, to help keep the units straight:

$$F = m\frac{a}{g_c}.$$

Note that g_c has a value of 1 (no units) in SI and a value of 32.174 ft · lb/lb$_f$ · s^2 in American Engineering units. If the mass is being acted on by gravity, Newton's law can be written as

$$F = m\frac{g}{g_c},$$

where $g = 9.8$ m/s^2 or 32.174 ft/s^2 is the acceleration due to gravity.

Note: While the acceleration due to gravity, g, is predefined in Mathcad, g_c is not. If you want to use g_c, it can easily be defined in your worksheet with the use of the SI value and letting Mathcad take care of the unit conversions. The definition is simply

$$g_c \; := \; 1$$

a. If a 150-kg mass is hung from a hook by a fine wire (of negligible mass), what force (N) is exerted on the hook? See accompanying diagram.

b. If the mass in part a were suspended by two wires, the force on the hook would be unchanged, but the tension in each wire would be halved. If the duty rating on the wire states that the tension in any wire should not exceed 300 N, how many wires should be used to support the mass?

7. **SPRING CONSTANTS**

Springs are so common that we hardly even notice them, but if you are designing a component that needs a spring, you have to know enough about them to specify them correctly. Common springs obey *Hooke's law* (if they are not overstretched), which simply states that the spring extension, x (the amount of stretch), is linearly related to the force exerted on the spring, F.

$$F = k\,x,$$

where k is the linear proportionality constant, called the *spring constant*. Use Mathcad's unit capabilities to determine the spring constants in N/m for the following springs:

a. extended length, 12 cm; applied force, 800 N.
b. extended length, 0.3 m; applied force, 1200 N.
c. extended length, 1.2 cm; applied force, 100 dynes.
d. extended length, 4 inches; applied force, 2000 lb_f.

(*Note:* The preceding equation is actually only a simplified version of Hooke's law that is applicable when the force is in the direction of motion of the spring. Sometimes you will see a minus sign in Hooke's law. It all depends on whether the force being referred to is being applied to the spring or is within the spring, restraining the applied force.)

8. **SPECIFYING A SPRING CONSTANT**

The backrest of a chair is to be spring loaded to allow the chair to recline slightly. The design specifications call for a deflection of no more than 2 inches when a 150-lb person leans 40% of his or her body weight on the backrest. (Assume that there are no lever arms between the backrest and the spring to account for in this problem.)

a. Use Newton's law (described in Problem 6) to determine the force applied to the backrest when a 150-lb person leans 40% of his or her body weight against it.

b. Determine the constant required for the spring.

c. If a 200-lb person puts 70% of his or her body weight on the backrest, what spring extension would be expected? (Assume that the applied force is still within the allowable limits for the spring.)

9. SIMPLE HARMONIC OSCILLATOR

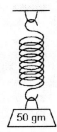

If a 50-gram mass is suspended on a spring and the spring is stretched slightly and released, the system will oscillate. The period, T, and natural frequency, f_n, of this simple harmonic oscillator can be determined using the formulas

$$T = \frac{2\pi}{\sqrt{k/m}}$$

$$f_n = \frac{1}{T},$$

where k is the spring constant and m is the suspended mass. (This equation assumes that the spring has negligible mass.)

a. If the spring constant is 100 N/m, determine the period of oscillation of the spring.

b. What spring constant should be specified to obtain a period of 1 second?

10. DETERMINING THE CURRENT IN A CIRCUIT

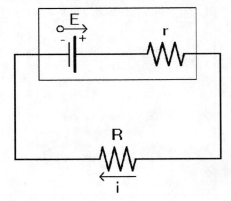

A real battery has an internal resistance, often shown by combining a cell symbol and a resistor symbol, as illustrated in the preceding figure. If a 9-volt battery has an internal resistance, r, of 15 ohms and is in a circuit with a 90-ohm resistor, what current would flow in the circuit?

(*Note:* When resistors are connected in series, the combined resistance is simply the sum of the individual resistance values.)

11. RESISTORS IN PARALLEL

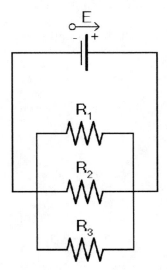

When multiple resistors are connected in parallel (see preceding diagram), the equivalent resistance of the collection of resistors can be computed as

$$\frac{1}{R_{eq}} = \sum_{i=1}^{N} \frac{1}{R_i},$$

where N is the number of resistors connected in parallel:

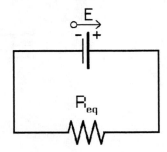

Compute the equivalent resistance, R_{eq}, in the circuit, and determine the current that would flow through the equivalent resistor. The data are as follows:

$$E = 9 \text{ volts};$$

$$R_1 = 20 \text{ ohms};$$

$$R_2 = 30 \text{ ohms};$$

$$R_3 = 40 \text{ ohms}.$$

12. REDUCING CO_2 EMISSIONS

The Kyoto Accords call for the United States to reduce emissions of CO_2 to 7% below 1990 levels. Those reductions will almost certainly have to come from three sectors —residential and commercial, industrial, and transportation—since the emissions from each sector are of the same magnitude. This problem demonstrates how significant a reduction would be required if only one sector were used to accomplish the entire task. If the targeted reduction in CO_2 emissions came entirely from the transportation sector (cars, buses, trains, planes), what percentage reduction in CO_2 emissions would be required to achieve the target? Use the data presented in the global-warming applications box to solve this problem.

13. AVERAGE FLUID VELOCITY

When a fluid is flowing in a pipe, the rate and direction of flow of the fluid —the fluid velocity—is not the same everywhere in the pipe. The fluid near the wall moves more slowly than the fluid near the center of the pipe, and things that cause the flow field to bend, such as obstructions and bends in the piping, cause some parts of the flow to move faster and in different directions than other parts of the flow. For many calculations, the details of the flow pattern are not important, and an *average fluid velocity* can be used in design calculations. The average velocity, V_{avg}, can be determined by measuring the volumetric flow rate, Q, and dividing that by the cross-sectional area of the pipe, A_{flow}:

$$V_{avg} = \frac{Q}{A_{flow}} .$$

a. If 1,000 gallons per minute (gpm) of water are flowing through a 4-inch (inside diameter) pipe, what is the average velocity of the water in the pipe?

b. If the flow passes into a section of 2-inch pipe, what is the average velocity in the smaller pipe?

c. A common rule of thumb for trying to keep pumping costs low is to design for an average fluid velocity of about 3 ft/sec. What pipe diameter is required to obtain this average velocity with a volumetric flow rate of 1,000 gpm?

(*Note:* You may need to take a square root in part c. You can use either an exponent of 0.5 or Mathcad's square-root operator, which is available by pressing [\ ] (backslash).)

14. ORIFICE METER

An *Orifice Meter* is a commonly used flow measuring device. The flow must squeeze through a small opening (the orifice), generating a pressure drop across the orifice plate. The higher the flow rate, the higher is the pressure drop, so if the pressure drop is measured, it can be used to calculate the flow rate through the orifice.

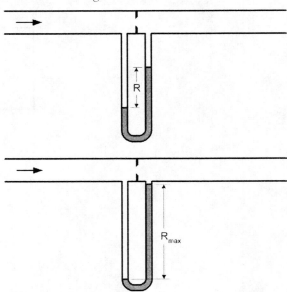

In the past, mercury manometers were often used to measure the pressure drop across the orifice plate. The manometer reading, R, can be related to the pressure drop, δP, by the differential manometer equation

$$\Delta P = \left(\rho_m - \rho \right) \frac{g}{g_c} R ,$$

where ρ_m is the density of the manometer fluid, ρ is the density of the process fluid in the pipe, g is the acceleration due to gravity, g_c is the gravitational constant (used to help manage units in the American Engineering system), and R is the difference in height of the manometer fluid on the two sides of the manometer, which is called the manometer reading.

a.   Given the following data, what is the pressure drop (atm) across the manometer when the manometer reading is R=32 cm?

b. $\rho_m = 13,600$ kg/m^3;

   $\rho = 1,000$ kg/m^3;

   $g = 9.80$ m/sec^2;

   $g_c = 1$ (SI);

c.   If the flow rate gets too high, the mercury in the manometer can be washed out of the device into the pipe downstream of the orifice plate. To avoid this, the orifice must be designed to produce a pressure drop smaller than the maximum permissible δP for the manometer. If $R_{max} = 70$ cm, what is the maximum permissible δP (atm) for the manometer?

15. **DESIGNING AN IRRIGATION SYSTEM**

In arid areas, one cannot rely on periodic rains to water crops, so many farmers depend on irrigation systems. Center-pivot irrigation systems are a type of system that is commonly used. These systems have a 1/4-mile-long water pipe on wheels that rotates (pivots) around the water source. The result is an irrigated circle with a diameter of 1/2 mile, centered on the source. From an airplane, you can easily see where center-pivot systems are in use.

In the past, one large pulsating sprinkler was used for each wheeled section (120 feet) of pipe, and the sprinkler head was placed high to try to get wide coverage. In an attempt to utilize the water better, these systems have been radically reengineered. The large pulse sprinkler heads have been replaced by a series of small water spray nozzles 20 feet apart, and these have been placed much lower, just above crop level, to reduce the impact of wind on the water distribution pattern.

a.   How many acres of cropland would be irrigated using the center-pivot system just described?

b.   An acre-inch of water is the volume of water needed to cover an acre of ground with water to a depth of one inch (assuming no ground infiltration). How many acre-inches of water are required to provide one inch (depth) of water to the field? How many gallons is that?

c.   If the system makes a complete rotation every 40 hours, at what rate (gallons per minute) must water be pumped into the system?

An important feature of these irrigation systems is their ability to distribute water evenly. We'll return to this problem to see what is required to get a uniform water distribution.

3

Mathcad Functions

SECTIONS

OBJECTIVES

- know how to use Mathcad's built-in functions, including trigonometric functions
- know how to use Mathcad's built-in functions, including logarithmic functions
- know how to use Mathcad's built-in functions, including advanced math functions
- know how to use Mathcad's built-in functions, including functions to read and write data files
- know how to write your own functions.

3.1 OPTICS

The use of *optics* can be dated back at least to the time when someone noticed that putting a curved piece of metal behind a lamp could concentrate the light. Or perhaps it goes back to the time when someone noticed that the campfire felt warmer if it was built next to a large rock. In any case, while the use of optics might be nearly as old as humanity itself, optics itself is a field that has seen major changes in the past 20 years. And these changes are affecting society in a variety of ways:

- Fiber-optic communication systems are now widely used and will become even more commonplace in the future.
- Lasers have moved from laboratory bench tops to supermarket checkout scanners and CD players.
- Traffic signs are much more visible at night now that they incorporate microreflective optical beads.

As these optical systems continue to develop, they will require the skills of engineers from many disciplines. Fiber-optic communication systems alone will make use of the following scientists and engineers:

- *Material scientists*, to select and manipulate the properties of glass.
- *Chemical engineers*, to design glass-processing facilities.
- *Mechanical engineers*, to develop equipment designs for fiber production, cladding, wrapping, handling, and installation.
- *Civil engineers*, to design the support structures for transmission lines.
- *Electrical engineers*, to develop data transfer techniques.
- *Computer scientists*, to design systems to encode and decode transmissions.

Optics is a field that has been studied for centuries, but still has room for growth and continues to change the way we live. Any field that uses technology in society is a field in which engineers will be working.

3.2 MATHCAD FUNCTIONS

In a programming language, the term *function* is used to mean a piece of the program dedicated to a particular calculation. A function accepts input from a list of *parameters*, performs calculations, and then *returns* a value or a set of values. Functions are used whenever you want to

- perform the same calculations multiple times using different input values,
- reuse the function in another program without retyping it, or
- make a complex program easier to comprehend.

Mathcad's functions work the same way and serve the same purposes. They receive input from a parameter list, perform a calculation, and return a value or a set of values. Mathcad's functions are useful when you need to perform the same calculation multiple times. You can also cut and paste a function from one worksheet to another.

PROFESSIONAL SUCCESS

When do you use a calculator to solve a problem, and when should you use a computer?
These three questions will help you make this decision:

1. Is the calculation long and involved?
2. Will you need to perform the same calculation numerous times?
3. Do you need to document the results for the future, either to give them to someone else or for you own reference?

A "yes" answer to any of these questions suggests that you consider using a computer. Moreover, a "yes" to the second question suggests that you may want to write a reusable function to solve the problem.

Mathcad provides a wide assortment of built-in functions. While most Mathcad functions *can* accept arrays as input, some Mathcad functions *require* data arrays as input. For example, the mean( ) function needs a column of data values in order to compute the average value of the data set. The functions that take arrays as input will be discussed in later chapters, after we describe how Mathcad handles matrices. In this chapter, we present only functions that can take single-valued (scalar) inputs.

The following are the commonly used scalar functions:

*   elementary mathematical functions and operators;
*   trigonometric functions;
*   advanced mathematical functions;
*   string functions;
*   file-handling functions.

3.3 ELEMENTARY MATHEMATICS FUNCTIONS AND OPERATORS

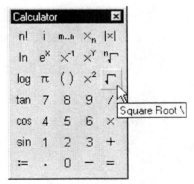

Many of the functions available in programming languages are implemented as *operators* in Mathcad. For example, to take the square root of four in FORTRAN, you would use SQRT(4). SQRT( ) is FORTRAN's square-root function. In Mathcad, the square-root symbol is an operator available on the Calculator Toolbar, and shows up in a

Mathcad worksheet just as you would write it on paper. Here are a couple of examples of Mathcad's square-root function:

$$\sqrt{4} = 2$$

$$\sqrt{\frac{4 - \pi}{2}} = 0.655$$

Notice that the square-root symbol changes size as necessary as you enter your equation.

3.3.1 Common Mathematical Operators

The following table presents some common mathematical operators in Mathcad:

Operator	Mathematical Operation	Source Palette	Alternate Keystroke
Square Root	$\sqrt{}$	Calculator toolbar	[ ] (backslash)
n^{th}Root	$^n\sqrt{}$	Calculator toolbar	[Ctrl-\]
Absolute Value	$|x|$	Calculator toolbar	[|] (vertical bar)
Factorial	$x!$	Calculator toolbar	[!]
Summation	Σx	Calculator toolbar	[Shift-4]
Product	Πx	Calculus toolbar	[Shift-3]
NOT	$\neg A$	Boolean toolbar	[Ctrl-Shift-1]
AND	$A \wedge B$	Boolean toolbar	[Ctrl-Shift-7]
OR	$A \vee B$	Boolean toolbar	[Ctrl-Shift-6]
XOR	$A \oplus B$	Boolean toolbar	[Ctrl-Shift-5]

Many additional mathematical operations are available as built-in functions. Some of these elementary mathematical functions are the logarithm and exponentiation functions and the *round-off* and *truncation* functions.

(*Note:* Mathcad's help files include descriptions of every built-in function, including information about requirements on arguments or parameters. Excerpts from the Mathcad help files are shown in text boxes.)[1]

3.3.2 Logarithm and Exponentiation Functions

The following shows Mathcad's *logarithm* and *exponentiation functions*:

exp(z)	The number e raised to the power z
log(z)	Base-10 log of z
ln(z)	Natural logarithm (base e) of z

Arguments:
- z must be a scalar (real, complex, or imaginary).
- z must be dimensionless.
- For log and ln functions, z cannot be zero.

[1] The Mathcad help file text is reprinted here with permission of Mathsoft, Inc.

But e is also a predefined variable in Mathcad, so the following two calculations are equivalent:

```
exp(3)  =  20.086
e³  =  20.086
```

If you know or can guess a function name and want to see the Help for information on the function in order to find out what arguments are required, type the function name on the worksheet, and while the edit lines are still around the function name, press the [F1] key. If Mathcad recognizes the function name you entered, it will display information on that function. For example, if you type log and press [F1], the information shown in the preceding text box will be displayed.

If you don't know the function name, use the Help menu and search the Mathcad index for your subject. For example, you can access the index list from the Help menu by clicking Help/Mathcad Help/Index. A search box will appear. When you type the word "function", you will receive a lot of information about Mathcad's functions.

PRACTICE!

Try out Mathcad's operators and functions. First try these obvious examples:

    a. $\sqrt{4}$

    b. $\sqrt[3]{8}$

    c. |-7| (This is the absolute-value operator from the Calculator Toolbar.)

    d. 3!

    e. log(100)

Then try these less obvious examples and check the results with a calculator:

    a. 20!

    b. ln(-2)

    c. exp(-0.4)

3.3.3 Using QuickPlots to Visualize Functions

Mathcad has a feature called a *QuickPlot* that produces the graph of a function. For example, to obtain a visual display of the natural logarithm function, you would follow these steps:

1. First, create a graph by either selecting X-Y Graph from the Graph Toolbar or pressing [Shift-2].
2. Enter ln (x) in the *y*-axis placeholder. (The *x* can be any unused variable, but you need to use the same variable in step 3.)
3. Enter *x* in the *x*-axis placeholder.

The result will look like this:

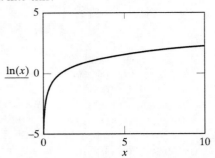

Mathcad shows what the function looks like over an arbitrary range of x values. The default range is -10 to +10, but the natural logarithm is not defined for negative numbers, so Mathcad used only positive numbers for this function. If you want to see the plot over a different range, just click on the x-axis and change the plot limits.

3.3.4 3-d QuickPlots

QuickPlots can also be used to visualize functions of two variables. For example, the function $Z(x, y) = 2 x^2 - 2 y^2$ can be plotted as a contour plot as follows:

1. Define the function in your worksheet.
2. Create the graph by either selecting Surface Graph from the Graph toolbar or pressing [Ctrl-2].
3. Put the variable name, Z, in the placeholder on the surface plot.
4. Double-click on the graph to change display characteristics if desired.

The following is the resulting graph:

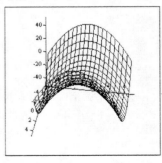

3.4   TRIGONOMETRIC FUNCTIONS

Mathcad's *trigonometric functions* work with angles in radians, but deg is a predefined unit, so you can also display your calculated results in degrees. In addition, there is a predefined unit rad. You probably won't need to use it, since Mathcad assumes radians if the unit is not included, but you can include the rad unit label to make your worksheet easier to read. For example, you might have

```
angle := 2 · π
angle = 6.283
angle = 6.283 + rad
angle = 360 + deg
```

Mathcad's basic trigonometric functions are displayed in the following box:

```
sin(z)          cos(z)

tan(z)          cot(z)

sec(z)          csc(z)
```
Arguments:
- z must be in radians.
- z must be a scalar (real, complex, or imaginary).
- z must be dimensionless.

3.4.1 Standard Trigonometric Functions

Mathcad's trigonometric functions require angles in radians, but as the examples that follow illustrate, you can work with either degrees or radians in Mathcad. To understand how this works, remember how Mathcad handles units: When you enter a value with units, Mathcad converts those units to its base units and stores the value. Then it performs the calculation using the base units and displays the result:

```
sin(30 · deg) = 0.5
cos (π) = -1
```

When sin(30·deg) = was entered in the preceding example, Mathcad converted the units that were entered (degrees) to base units (radians) and stored the value. Then the sine was computed using the stored value in base units, and the result was displayed. In the second example, no units were entered with the π, so Mathcad used the default unit, radians, and computed the result.

(**Remember:** You can work with degrees with Mathcad's trigonometric functions, but you must include the deg unit abbreviation on each angle. When you do so, Mathcad automatically converts the units to radians before performing the calculations.)

PROFESSIONAL SUCCESS

Validate your functions and worksheets as you develop them.

If you are "pretty sure" that the tangent of an angle is equal to the sine of the angle divided by the cosine of the angle, test the tan ( ) function before building it into your worksheet. Learning to devise useful tests is a valuable skill. In this case, you could test the relationship between the functions like this:

$$tan(30·deg) = 0.577$$

$$\frac{sin(30·deg)}{cos(30·deg)} = 0.577$$

It only takes a second to test, and building a number of "pretty sure" items into a worksheet will quickly lead to a result with low confidence.

3.4.2 Inverse Trigonometric Functions

The following box shows Mathcad's inverse trigonometric functions:

```
asin(z)

acos(z)

atan(z)
```

Arguments:
- z must be a scalar.
- z must be dimensionless.

Values returned are angles in radians between 0 and 2π. Values returned are from the principal branch of these functions.

The angles returned by these functions will be in radians. You can display the result in degrees by using the deg unit abbreviation with it. You can also append the rad unit abbreviation; doing so won't change the displayed angle, but it might help someone else understand your results. For example, you might have

```
asin(0.5) = 0.524
asin(0.5) = 30°deg
asin(0.5) = 0.524°rad
```

APPLICATIONS: RESOLVING FORCES

If one person pulls on a rope connected to a hook imbedded in a floor with a force of 400 N and another person pulls on the same hook with a force of 200 N, what is the total force on the hook?

Answer: Can't tell—there's not enough information.

What's missing in the statement is some indication of the direction of the applied forces, as force is a vector. If two people are pulling in the same direction, then the combined force is 600 N. But if they are pulling in different directions, it's a little tougher to determine the net force on the hook. To help find the answer, we often *resolve* the forces into horizontal and vertical components:

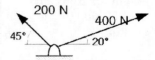

One person pulls to the right on a rope connected to a hook imbedded in a floor with a force of 400 N at an angle of 20° from the horizontal. Another person pulls to the left on the same hook with a force of 200 N at an angle of 45° from the horizontal. What is the net force on the hook?

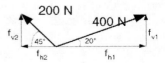

Since both people are pulling upwards, their vertical contributions add. But since one is pulling left and the other right, they are (in part) counteracting each other's efforts. To quantify this distribution of forces, we can calculate the horizontal and vertical components of the force being applied by each person. Mathcad's trigonometric functions are helpful for these calculations.

The 400-N force from person 1 resolves into a vertical component f_{v1} and a horizontal component f_{h1}. The magnitudes of these force components can be calculated as follows:

$$f_{v1} \eth\ 400\ \texttt{sin(20 deg)} \qquad f_{v1} \quad 136.808\ \texttt{N}$$
$$f_{h1} \eth\ 400\ \texttt{N cos(20 deg)} \qquad f_{h1} \quad 375.877\ \texttt{N}$$

Similarly, the 200-N force from person 2 can be resolved into the following component forces:

$$f_{v2} \eth\ 200\ \texttt{sin(45 deg)} \qquad f_{v2} \quad 141.421\ \texttt{N}$$
$$f_{h2} \eth\ 200\ \texttt{N cos(45 deg)} \qquad f_{h2} \quad 141.421\ \texttt{N}$$

Actually, force component f_{h2} would usually be written as $f_{h2} = -141.421$ N, since it is pointed in the $-x$ direction. If all angles had been measured from the same position (usually the three-o'clock angle is called $0°$), the angle on the 200-N force would have been at $135°$ and the signs would have taken care of themselves:

$$f_{h2} \eth\ 200\ \texttt{N cos(135 deg)} \quad f_{h2} \quad \eth 141.421\ \texttt{N}$$

Once the force components have been computed, the net force in the horizontal and vertical directions can be determined. (Force f_{h2} has a negative value in this calculation.) We obtain

$$f_{v\_net} \eth\ f_{v1} \downdownarrows f_{v2} \qquad f_{v\_net} \quad 278.229\ \texttt{N}$$
$$f_{h\_net} \eth\ f_{h1} \downdownarrows f_{h2} \qquad f_{h\_net} \quad 234.456\ \texttt{N}$$

The net horizontal and vertical components can be recombined to find a combined net force on the hook, F_{net}, and angle, θ:

$$F_{net} := \sqrt{f_{h\_net}^2 + f_{v\_net}^2}$$

$$\theta := \operatorname{atan}\left(\frac{f_{v\_net}}{f_{h\_net}}\right)$$

(*Note:* In this text, horizontal and vertical force components are named with lowercase letters, while forces at arbitrary angles are given uppercase names.)

3.4.3 Hyperbolic Trigonometric Functions

Mathcad's hyperbolic trigonometric functions are as follows:

`sinh(z)`	`cosh(z)`
`tanh(z)`	`csch(z)`
`sech(z)`	`coth(z)`

Arguments:
- z must be in radians.
- z must be a scalar.
- z must be dimensionless.

3.4.4 Inverse Hyperbolic Trigonometric Functions

The following box shows the inverse hyperbolic trigonometric functions in Mathcad:

```
asinh(z)
acosh(z)
atanh(z)
```
Arguments:
- z must be a scalar.
- z must be dimensionless.

Values returned are from the principal branch of these functions.

The angles returned by the inverse hyperbolic trigonometric functions will be in radians, but you can put deg in the units placeholder to convert the displayed units.

PRACTICE!

Try out these Mathcad trigonometric functions:

a. $\sin(\pi/4)$
b. $\sin(90{\cdot}\text{deg})$
c. $\cos(180{\cdot}\text{deg})$
d. $\operatorname{asin}(0)$
e. $\operatorname{acos}(2{\cdot}\pi)$

Try QuickPlots of these functions over the indicated ranges:

a. $\sin(x)$ $-\pi \le x \le \pi$
b. $\tan(x)$ $-\pi/2 \le x \le \pi/2$
c. $\sinh(x)$ $-10 \le x \le 10$

3.5 ADVANCED MATHEMATICS FUNCTIONS

3.5.1 Round-off and Truncation Functions

Mathcad provides two functions that determine the nearest integer value. The `floor(x)` function returns the largest integer that is less than or equal to x, while the `ceil(x)` function returns the smallest integer that is greater than or equal to x. To remove the decimal places following a value, use the `floor( )` function. For example, to find the greatest integer less than or equal to π, either of the following will work:

```
floor(3.1416) = 3
floor(π)  = 3
```

The second example used Mathcad's predefined variable for π.

If you want the values after the decimal point (i.e., the mantissa), use the mod ( ) function, which performs *modulo division*, returning the remainder after the division calculation:

---

mod(x,y)   This function returns the remainder on dividing x by y. The result has the same sign as x.

Arguments:

- x and y should both be real scalars.
- y must be nonzero.

Using the example of π again, we have

```
mod(3.1416,3) = 0.1416
mod(π,3) = 0.1416
```

Notice that the mod ( ) function will return the trailing decimal places only when the y argument is the integer less than or equal to x. You can create a user-written function that will always return the trailing decimal places using mod ( ) and floor ( ) together like this:

```
trail(x) := mod(x,floor(x))
trail(3.1416) = 0.1416
trail(π) = 0.1416
```

The new trail ( ) function doesn't work correctly when x is negative, because it tries to divide -3.1416 by -4, which does not yield the trailing digits. An improved version uses Mathcad's absolute-value operator, which is available on the Calculator Toolbar. For example, we might have

```
trail(x) := mod(x, floor(|x|))
trail(3.1416) = 0.1416
trail(-3.1416) = -0.1416
```

The result has the same sign as the x value, which might be useful. If not, another absolute-value operator around the entire right-hand side would force a positive result:

```
trail(x) := | mod(x, floor(|x|)) |
trail(3.1416) = 0.1416
trail(-3.1416) = 0.1416
```

PRACTICE!

You can compute the mantissa by subtracting floor (x) from x, but this approach also has trouble with negative numbers:

```
mantissa(x) := x-floor(x)
mantissa(3.1416) = 0.1416
mantissa(-3.1416) = 0.8584
```

Modify the mantissa ( ) function shown here so that it returns the correct mantissa when x is negative.

3.5.2 The if() Function

Mathcad provides an `if ( )` function for making logical decisions, as well as functions for handling discontinuous systems and generating random numbers.

Rules for the `if ( )` function in Mathcad are as follows:

```
if(cond, Tval, Fval)        This function returns one of two values, depending on the
                            value of a logical condition.
```

Arguments:
- cond is usually an expression involving a logical operator. For example, you can use
  ```
  (i < 2)
  (x < 1) * (x > 0) for an 'and' gate
  (x > 1) + (x < 0) for an 'or' gate
  ```
- Tval is the value returned when cond is true.
- Fval is the value returned when cond is false.

The value that is returned can be a simple scalar value, a computed value, or even a text string. For example, the `if ( )` function can be used to determine whether water would be a liquid or a solid by checking the temperature of the water:

```
state(Temp) := if(Temp > 0,"liquid","solid")
state(25) = "liquid"
state(-3) = "solid"
```

Tval and Fval can be formulas. Thus, we can create an absolute-value function by using `if ( )` and changing the sign on x if $x < 0$:

```
abs(x) := if(x ≥ 0,x,-x)
abs(12) = 12
abs(-6) = 6
```

PRACTICE

Write an expression that returns a value of 1 if the volume in a tank is greater than or equal to 5,000 gallons and a value of 0 otherwise. An expression like this might be used to control a valve through which a liquid flows into the tank, shutting the valve when the tank is full. Test your expression in Mathcad.

3.5.3 Discontinuous Functions

Mathcad supports the following *discontinuous functions*:

```
KRONECKER DELTA
δ(m,n)          This function returns 1 if m=n and returns 0 otherwise.
    Arguments:
    • Both m and n must be integers without units.

HEAVISIDE STEP FUNCTION
φ(x)            This function returns 0 if x is negative and returns 1 otherwise.
    Arguments:
    • x must be a real scalar.
```

3.5.4 Boolean (Logical) Operators

Mathcad provides the following *Boolean (logical) operators* on the Boolean toolbar.

¬A	NOT Operator—returns 1 if A is zero; returns 0 otherwise.
A ∧ B	AND Operator—returns 1 if A and B both have nonzero values; otherwise returns 0.
A ∨ B	OR Operator—returns 1 if A or B is nonzero; otherwise returns 0.
A ⊕ B	XOR (Exclusive OR) Operator—returns 1 if A or B, but not both, is nonzero; otherwise returns 0.

3.5.5 Random-Number-Generating Function

`rnd(x)`	Returns a random number (not an integer) between 0 and *x*.

A set of *random numbers* generated by `rnd(x)` will have a uniform distribution. Mathcad provides a number of other random-number-generating functions that produce sets of numbers with various distributions. For example, the `rnorm(m, μ, σ)` function produces a vector of m values that are normally distributed about the value μ with a standard deviation σ.

3.6   STRING FUNCTIONS

Because text regions can be used anywhere on a worksheet, the need for *string-handling functions* is greatly reduced in Mathcad. Still, Mathcad does provide the typical functions for manipulating text strings:

`concat(S1,S2)`	Concatenates string S2 to the end of string S1. Returns a string.
`strlen(S)`	Determines the number of characters in the string S. Returns an integer.
`substr(S,n,m)`	Extracts a substring of S, starting with the character in position n and having at most m characters. The arguments m and n must be integers.
`search(S,SubS,x)`	Finds the starting position of the substring SubS in S, beginning from position x in S.
`str2num(S)`	Converts a string of numbers S into a constant.
`num2str(x)`	Converts the number x into a string.

The example that follows illustrates the use of the `search( )` function to find the word `Mathcad` in the string called `MyString`. The position of the M in `Mathcad` is returned by the function. Since `Mathcad` says the first character of the string (the `T` in `This`) is in position zero, the M in `Mathcad` is in position 10 (the 11th character of the string). The `Mathcad` code is

```
MyString := "This is a mathcad example."
pos := search(MyString, "mathcad", 0)
pos = 10
pos := search(MyString, "mathcad", 0)
pos = -1
```

The last two lines illustrate that Mathcad differentiates between uppercase and lowercase letters. That is, Mathcad is *case sensitive*. The `search( )` function returns a -1 when the search string is not found.

3.7   FILE-HANDLING FUNCTIONS

Mathcad can read and write data to *ASCII text files*. The following functions are provided to accomplish those tasks:

READ('file')	Reads a single value from a data file.
WRITE('file')	Writes a single value to a data file.
APPEND('file')	Appends a single value to an existing data file.
READPRN('file')	Reads an array of values from a data file.
WRITEPRN('file')	Writes an array of values to a data file.
APPENDPRN('file')	Appends an array of values to an existing data file.

`file` is a text string containing either a file name (which should be in Mathcad's default directory) or a complete path name (preferred). The files created with these commands can be used to move data between Mathcad, spreadsheets, word processors, and graphing programs—but in many instances you can also cut and paste the data between programs by using the Windows clipboard, which is generally quicker.

By using the expression `WRITE('A:\testFile.txt'):=x`, the file `testFile.txt` is created on drive `A:`, and the current value of x is written to the file. Attempting to use the `WRITE( )` function a second time to save y to the same file would cause the value of x to be lost—`WRITE( )` puts only a single value in a file, as the following code shows:

```
x := 7
WRITE('A:\testFile.txt') := x
y := 12
WRITE('A:\testFile.txt') := y
READ('A:\testFile.txt') = 12
```

For multiple values, use `WRITE( )` for the first value written to the file, and then use `APPEND( )` for additional values:

```
x := 7
WRITE('A:\testFile.txt') := x
y := 12
APPEND('A:\testFile.txt') := y
READPRN('A:\testFile.txt') = [ 7 12 ]
```

Note that `READPRN( )` was used in the second example. This is because the `READ( )` function reads only a single value, whereas testFile.txt contains two values. `READPRN( )` can read the entire file, not just the first value.

Mathcad provides a handy alternative to the file reading and writing functions called a "*file read or write component.*" When you insert a component into a worksheet, the Component Wizard dialog appears, asks a series of questions, and then performs some task. For example, to read values from a text file called A:\testFile.txt, you would do the following:

1. Start the Component Wizard using the menu commands Insert/Component.
    This causes the Component Wizard dialog to be displayed:

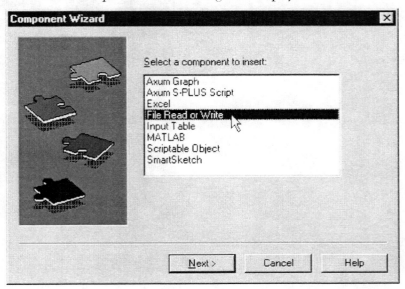

2. Select the File Read or Write component from the list, and press Next >:

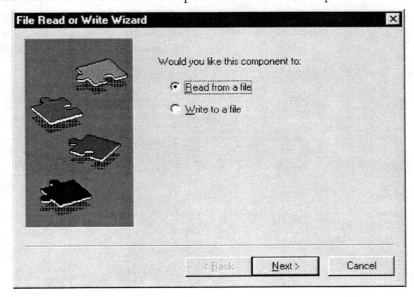

3.   Select Read from a file, and then press Next >:

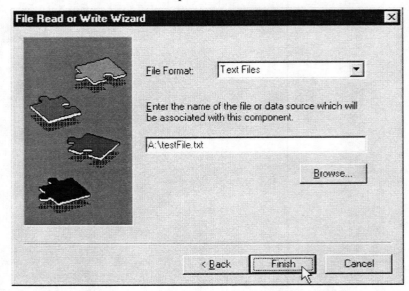

4.   Select the File Format from the drop-down list. A text file has been used in this example, but Mathcad also knows how to work with several other formats, such as spreadsheets and graphing programs.

5.   Enter the name of the file containing the data. Then click on the Finish button and Mathcad will place a picture of a disk (an icon), representing the File Read component, on your worksheet:

$$\blacksquare :=$$
$$\boxed{\blacksquare}$$
A:\testFile.txt

6.   Put a variable name in the placeholder next to the icon. The data in the file will be assigned to the variable. For example, the variable Mydata could be used:

Mydata :=
$$\boxed{\blacksquare}$$
A:\testFile.txt

Once you fill in the placeholder, Mathcad will read the values from the file (if possible) and assign them to the variable Mydata. In this example, Mydata would have two values:

Mydata :=
$$\boxed{\blacksquare}$$
A:\testFile.txt

$$\text{Mydata} = \begin{pmatrix} 7 \\ 12 \end{pmatrix}$$

The procedure for sending an array of values to a text file is essentially the same:

1.   Start the Component Wizard by using the menu commands Insert/Component.

2.   Select the File Read or Write component from the list, and press Next >.

3.   Select Write to a file, and then press Next >.

4.   Select the file format you want Mathcad to use from the drop-down list.
5.   Enter the name of the file that will receive the data, and click on the Finish button. Mathcad will then place an icon representing the File Write component on your worksheet. There will be an empty placeholder below the icon.
6.   Put the array name in the placeholder below the icon.

Mathcad will then send the values in the array to the file.

3.8   USER-WRITTEN FUNCTIONS

When Mathcad does not provide a built-in function, you can always write your own. The ability to use Mathcad's functions inside your own function definitions greatly increases the power of Mathcad to solve engineering problems and makes writing functions much simpler. Several user-written functions have been utilized in this chapter, including the following:

```
trail(x)  := |mod(x,floor(|x|))|
mantissa(x)  := x-floor(x)
state(Temp)  := if(Temp > 0,"liquid","solid")
abs(x)  := if(x ≥ 0,x,-x)
```

Each of these user-written functions has a name (e.g., `trail`) and a parameter list on the left, and a mathematical expression of some sort on the right side. In these examples, only a single argument was used in each parameter list, but multiple arguments are allowed and are very common. For example, a function to calculate the surface area of a cylinder could be written as

$$A_{cyl}(r,L) := 2 \cdot \pi \cdot r^2 + 2 \cdot \pi \cdot r \cdot L$$

Once the function has been defined, it can be used multiple times in the worksheet. In the following example, the function is employed four times, illustrating how functions can be used with and without units and with both values and variables:

```
A_cyl(7,  21)  = 1.232·10³
A_cyl(7·cm,  21·cm)  = 0.123·m²
A_cyl(7·cm,  21·cm)  = 1.232·10³°cm²
R  := 7·cm L  := 21·cm
A_cyl(R,L)  = 1.232·10³°cm²
```

Recall that the A_{cyl} function was defined using `r` and `L` for arguments. In a function definition, the arguments are dummy variables. That is, they show what argument is used in which location in the calculation, but neither `r` nor `L` needs to have defined values when the function is declared. They are just placeholders. When the function is used, the values in the `r` and `L` placeholders are put into the appropriate spots in the equation, and the computed area is returned.

In a function, you can use arguments with or without units, and the arguments can be values or defined variables. In the last calculation, `R` and `L` were used for the radius and length of the cylinder, respectively. This choice of variable names is reasonable, but entirely irrelevant to Mathcad. Variables like Q and Z would work equally well, but they would make the worksheet harder to understand. For example, we might have

```
Q  := 7·cm
Z  := 21·cm
A_cyl(Q,Z)  = 1.232·10³ ° cm²
```

PRACTICE!

Define a function for computing the volume of a rectangular box, given the height, width, and length of the box. Then use the function to compute the volumes of several boxes:

a. H = 1, W = 1, L = 1
b. H = 1, W = 1, L = 10
c. H = 1 cm, W = 1 cm, L = 10 cm
d. H = 1 cm, W = 1 m, L = 10 ft

APPLICATIONS: FIBER OPTICS

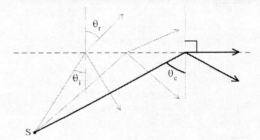

According to the *law of refraction*, the angle of incidence, θ_i, is related to the angle of refraction, θ_r, by the *index of refraction n*, for the two materials through which light passes. That is,

$$n_1 \sin(\theta_1) = n_2 \sin(\theta_2).$$

For light in a glass fiber ($n_1 \approx 1.5$) reflecting and refracting at the air ($n_2 \approx 1$) interface with an angle of incidence of 20°, what is the angle of refraction?

To solve this problem, we will use Mathcad's sin( ) and asin( ) functions and the built-in unit deg:

$$\theta_r := \text{asin}\left(\frac{1.5 \cdot \sin(20 \cdot \text{deg})}{1}\right)$$

$$\theta_r = 30.866 \circ \text{deg}$$

When the angle of reflection is 90°, the angle of incidence is called the *critical angle*. For the fiber-optic material in air, what is the critical angle?

The critical angle is

$$\theta_r := \text{asin}\left(\frac{1.5 \cdot \sin(20 \cdot \text{deg})}{1}\right)$$

$$\theta_c = 41.81 \circ \text{deg}$$

Note: The "1" in the first equation is there just to show how the index of refraction of air enters into the equation. It could be left out with no impact on the result.)

The critical angle is important because, if you keep the angle of incidence greater than the critical angle, you get total internal reflection—there is no refracted ray, and thus no light is lost because of refraction. This is extremely important if the fiber-optic material is to be used for transmitting signals, since refracted light shortens the transmission distance.

Fiber Cladding

If the medium outside the fiber is something other than air, the critical angle changes. For example, if the fiber is in water ($n_2 \approx 1.33$), the critical angle is higher:

$$\theta_r := \text{asin}\left(\frac{1.33 \cdot \sin(90 \cdot \text{deg})}{1.5}\right)$$

$$\theta_c = 62.457\text{°deg})$$

By increasing the refractive index of the material on the outside of the fiber, the angle of incidence can be closer to perpendicular to the wall of the fiber and still have total internal reflection. If the material outside the fiber has a refractive index greater than 1.5, you get total internal reflection for *any* angle of incidence. To ensure that this is the case, fiber-optic materials are often coated with a second layer of glass with a slightly higher refractive index. This process is called *cladding* the fibers.

3.8.1 Summary

In this chapter, you learned that a function is a reusable equation that accepts arguments, uses the argument values in a calculation, and returns the result(*s*). Once a function has been defined in a worksheet, it can be used multiple times in that worksheet. You have learned to write your own functions and to use Mathcad's built-in functions in the following areas:

MATHCAD SUMMARY

Logarithm and Exponentiation

exp(x)	Raises e to the power x.
ln(x)	Returns the natural logarithm of x.
log(x)	Returns the base-10 logarithm of x.

Trigonometric Functions

The units on the angle a in these functions must be radians. If you want to work in degrees, replace a by a·deg, where deg is a predefined unit for degrees:

sin(a)	Returns the sine of a.
cos(a)	Returns the cosine of a.
tan(a)	Returns the tangent of a.
sec(a)	Returns the secant of a.
csc(a)	Returns the cosecant of a.
cot(a)	Returns the cotangent of a.

Inverse Trigonometric Functions

These functions take a value between -1 and 1 and return the angle in radians. You can display the result in degrees by using deg.

asin(x)
Arcsine—returns the angle that has a sine value equal to x.

acos(x)
Arccosine—returns the angle that has a cosine value equal to x.

atan(x)
Arctangent—returns the angle that has a tangent value equal to x.

Hyperbolic Trigonometric Functions

sinh(a)   cosh(a)

tanh(a)   csch(a)

sech(a)   coth(a)

Inverse Hyperbolic Trigonometric Functions

asinh(x)
acosh(x)
atanh(x)

Round-off and Truncation Functions

floor(x)	Returns the largest integer that is less than or equal to x.
ceil(x)	Returns the smallest integer that is greater than or equal to x.
mod(x,y)	Returns the remainder after dividing x by y.

Advanced Mathematics Functions

if(cond,Tval,Fval)	Returns Tval or Fval, depending on the value of the logical condition cond.
δ(m,n)	Kronecker delta—returns 1 if m = n and returns 0 otherwise.
ϕ(x)	Heaviside step function—returns 0 if x is negative and returns 1 otherwise.
rnd(x)	Returns a random number (not an integer) between 0 and x.

Boolean (Logical) Operators

$\neg$ A	NOT Operator—returns 1 if A is zero; returns 0 otherwise.
A $\wedge$ B	AND Operator—returns 1 if A and B both have nonzero values; otherwise returns 0.
A $\vee$ B	OR Operator—returns 1 if A or B is non-zero; otherwise returns 0.
A $\oplus$ B	XOR (Exclusive OR) Operator—returns 1 if A or B, but not both, is nonzero; otherwise returns 0.

String Functions

concat(S1,S2)	Concatenates string S2 to the end of string S1. Returns a string.
strlen(S)	Determines the number of characters in the string S. Returns an integer.
substr(S,n,m)	Extracts a substring of S, starting with the character in position n and having at most m characters. The arguments m and n must be integers.
search(S,SubS,x)	Finds the starting position of the substring SubS in S, beginning from position x in S.
str2num(S)	Converts a string of numbers S into a constant.
num2str(x)	Converts the number x into a string.

File Functions

READ('file')	Reads a single value from a data file.
WRITE('file')	Writes a single value to a data file.
APPEND('file')	Appends a single value to an existing data file.
READPRN('file')	Reads an array of values from a data file.
WRITEPRN('file')	Writes an array of values to a data file.
APPENDPRN('file')	Appends an array of values to an existing data file.

KEY TERMS

ASCII text files	index of refraction	random numbers
Boolean (logical) operators	law of refraction	returns
case sensitive	logarithm	round-off
critical angle	modulo division	string-handling functions
discontinuous functions	operators	trigonometric functions
exponentiation function	parameters	truncation
function		

Problems

1. **FORCE AND PRESSURE**

    A force of 800 N is applied to a piston with a surface area of 24 cm².

    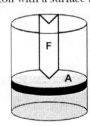

    a. What pressure (Pa) is applied to the fluid? Use

    $$P = \frac{F}{A}$$

    b. What is the diameter (cm) of a piston with a (circular) surface area of 24 cm²?

2.   CALCULATING BUBBLE SIZE

Very small gas bubbles (e.g., air bubbles less than 1 mm in diameter in water) rising through liquids are roughly spherical in shape.

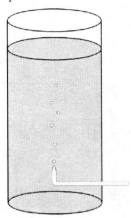

a.   What volume of air (mm^3) is contained in a spherical bubble 1 mm in diameter?

b.   What is the surface area (mm^2) of a spherical bubble 1 mm in diameter?

c.   Calculate the diameter of a spherical bubble containing 1.2×10^{-7} mole of nitrogen at 25°C at 1 atm. Use the formulas

$$V = \frac{4}{3} \pi R^3$$

and

$$A = 4 \pi R^3.$$

3.   RELATIONSHIPS BETWEEN TRIGONOMETRIC FUNCTIONS

Devise a test to demonstrate the validity of the following common trigonometric formulas:

a. $\sin(A+B) = \sin(A) \cdot \cos(B) + \cos(A) \cdot \sin(B)$

b. $\sin(2 \cdot A) = 2 \cdot \sin(A) \cdot \cos(A)$

c. $\sin^2(A) = 1/2 - 1/2 \cdot \cos(2 \cdot A)$

What values of A and B should be used to thoroughly test these functions?

(*Note:* In Mathcad, $\sin^2$(A) should be entered as `sin(A)`^{2}. This causes `sin(A)` to be evaluated first and that result to be squared.)

4.   CALCULATING ACREAGE

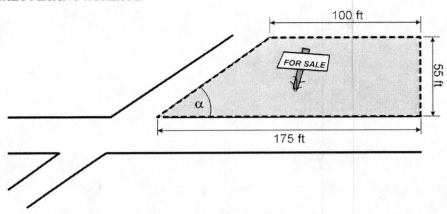

An odd-shaped corner lot is up for sale. The "going rate" for property in the area is $3.60 per square foot.

a.   Determine the corner angle, α (in degrees).
b.   What is the area of the lot in square feet? In acres?
c.   How much should the seller ask for the property?

5.   USING THE ANGLE OF REFRACTION TO MEASURE THE INDEX OF REFRACTION

A laser in air ($n_2 \approx 1$) is aimed at the surface of a liquid with an angle of incidence of 45°. A photodetector is moved through the liquid until the beam is located at an angle of refraction of 32°. What is the index of refraction of the liquid?

6.   MEASURING HEIGHTS

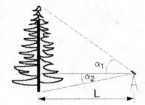

A surveyor's *transit* is a telescopelike device mounted on a protractor that allows the surveyor to sight distant points and then read the angle of the scope off the scale. With a transit it is possible to get accurate measurements of large objects.

In this problem, a transit is being used to measure the height of a tree. The transit is set up 80 feet from the base of the tree (L=80 ft), and the sights are set on the top of the tree. The angle reads 43.53° from the horizontal. Then the sights are set at the base of the tree, and the second angle is found to be 3.58°. Given this information, how tall is the tree?

7.   LADDER SAFETY

Ladders are frequently used tools, but are also the source of many injuries. Improperly positioning a ladder is a common cause of falls.

Ladders are supposed to be set against walls at an angle such that the base of the ladder stands away from the wall 1 foot for every 4 feet of working length of the ladder. So the base of a 12-foot ladder with the top resting against a wall (as shown in the foregoing figure) should be 3 feet away from the wall. At this angle, most people can stand up straight on a rung and reach out and easily grab another rung with their hands. The 1-in-4 rule is for comfort and for safety—and it is written into OSHA regulations (OSHA Standards, 29.b.5.i).

a.   What is the angle θ between the floor and the ladder if the 1-in-4 rule is used?

b.   If the 1-in-4 rule is used, at what height does the top of a 12-foot ladder touch the wall?

8.   SOLVING QUADRATIC EQUATIONS

A quadratic equation can be written in the form

$$ax2 + bx + c = 0 \ (a \neq 0).$$

These equations have two solutions, which can be found using the formula

$$x = \frac{-b \pm \sqrt{b^2 - 4ac}}{2a}$$

Find the solutions to the following equations:

a. $- 2x2 + 3x + 4 = 0.$ (Expect real roots, since $b2 - 4ac > 0$.)

b. $- 4x2 + 4x - 1 = 0.$ (Expect real, equal roots, since $b2 - 4ac = 0$.)

c. $3x2 + 2x + 1 = 0.$ (Expect imaginary roots, since $b2 - 4ac < 0$.)

9.   HEATING A HOT TUB

A 500-gallon hot tub has been unused for some time, and the water in the tub is at 65°F.

Hot water (130°F) will be added to the tub at a rate of 5 gallons per minute. The temperature in the hot tub can be calculated with the equation

$$T = T_{\text{IN}} - \left(T_{\text{IN}} - T_{\text{START}}\right)e^{\frac{-Q}{V}t},$$

where

T	is the temperature of the water already in the tub,
T_{IN}	is the temperature of the water flowing into the tub (130°F),
T_{START}	is the initial temperature of the water in the hot tub (65°F),
Q	is the hot-water flow rate (5 gpm)
V	is the volume of the tub (500 gallons), and
T	is the elapsed time since the hot water started flowing.

a. What will be the temperature of the water in the hot tub after one hour?
b. How long will it take the water in the tub to reach a temperature of 110°F?
c. If the temperature of the water flowing into the tub could be raised to 150°F, how long would it take to warm the water to 110°F?

10. VAPOR PRESSURE

Knowing the vapor pressure is important in designing equipment that will or might contain boiling or highly volatile liquids. When the pressure in a vessel is at or below the liquid's vapor pressure, the liquid will boil. If you are designing a boiler, then designing it to operate at the liquid's vapor pressure is a pretty good idea. But if you are designing a waste solvent storage facility, you want the pressure to be significantly higher than the liquid's vapor pressure. In either case, you need to be able to calculate the liquid's vapor pressure.

Antoine's equation is a common way to calculate vapor pressures for common liquids. It requires three coefficients that are unique to each liquid. If the coefficients are available, Antoine's equation[2] is easy to use. The equation is

$$\log(p_{vapor}) = A - \frac{B}{T+C},$$

where

p_{vapor}	is the vapor pressure of the liquid in mm Hg,
T	is the temperature of the liquid in °C, and
A,B,C	are coefficients for the particular liquid (found in tables).

In using Antoine's equation, keep the following important considerations in mind:

a. Antoine's equation is a *dimensional equation*; that is, specific units must be used to get correct results.
b. The log( ) function is not supposed to be used on a value with units, but that's the way Antoine's equation was written. Mathcad, however, will not allow you to take the logarithm of a value with units, so you must work without units while using Antoine's equation.
c. There are numerous forms of Antoine's equation, each requiring specific units. The coefficients are always designed to go along with a particular version of the equation. You cannot use Antoine coefficients from one text in a version of Antoine's equation taken from a different text.

Test Antoine's Equation

Water boils at 100°C at 1 atm pressure. So the vapor pressure of water at 100°C should be 1 atm, or 760 mm Hg. Check this using Antoine's equation. For water,

$$A = 7.96671 \qquad B = 1668.21 \qquad C = 228.0$$

[2] This version of Antoine's equation is from Elementary Principles of Chemical Processes, by R. M. Felder and R. W. Rousseau (New York: Wiley, 1978).

Use Antoine's Equation

a. A chemistry laboratory stores acetone at a typical room temperature of 25°C (77°F) with no problems. What would happen if, on a hot summer day, the air-conditioning failed and a storage cabinet warmed by the sun reached 50°C (122°F)? Would the stored acetone boil?

b. At what temperature would the acetone boil at a pressure of 1 atm? For acetone:

$$A = 7.02447 \qquad B = 1161.0 \qquad C = 224$$

11. CALCULATING THE VOLUME AND MASS OF A SUBSTANCE IN A STORAGE TANK

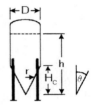

Vertical tanks with conical base sections are commonly used for storing solid materials such as grain, gravel, salt, catalyst particles, etc. The sloping sides help prevent plugging as the material is withdrawn.

If the height of solid in the tank is less than the height of the conical section, Hc, then the volume is computed by using the formula for the volume of a cone:

$$V = \frac{1}{3}\pi r^2 h$$

But if the tank is filled to a depth greater than H_c, then the volume is the sum of the filled conical section, V_{cone}, and a cylindrical section, V_{cyl}, of height $h - H_c$:

$$V = V_{cone} + V_{cyl}$$

$$V = \frac{1}{3}\pi R^2 H_C + \pi R^2(h - H_C)$$

Here, R = D/2.

The radius of the tank depends on h if $h<H_c$ but has a value of R when h = H_c. The if( ) function can be used to return the correct value of r for any h:

$$r(h) := if (h < H_c, h \cdot tan(\theta), R)$$

where θ is the angle of the sloping walls. (Variables H, R, and θ must be defined before using this function.)

When working with solids, you often want to know the mass as well as the volume. The mass can be determined from the volume using the *apparent density*, ρ_A, which is the mass of a known volume of the granular material (including the air in between the particles) divided by the known volume. Since the air between the particles is much less dense than the solid particles themselves, the apparent density of a granular solid is typically much smaller than the true density of any individual particle.

a. Use Mathcad's if( ) function to create a function that will return the volume of solids for any height.

b. Use the function from part a to determine the volume and mass of stored material (ρ_A = 20 lb/ft ^{3}) in a tank (D = 12 ft, θ = 30 °) when the tank is filled to a depth h = 21 ft.

12. FORCE COMPONENTS AND TENSION IN WIRESA

150-kg mass is suspended by wires from two hooks. The lengths of the wires have been adjusted so that the wires are each 50° from horizontal. Assume that the mass of the wires is negligible.

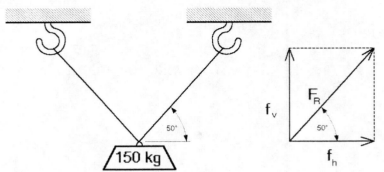

a. Since two hooks support the mass equally, the vertical component of force exerted by either hook will be equal to the force resulting from 75 kg being acted on by gravity. Calculate this vertical component of force, f_v, on the right hook. Express your result in newtons.

b. Compute the horizontal component of force, f_h, by using the result obtained in problem a. and trigonometry.

c. Determine the force exerted on the mass in the direction of the wire F_R (equal to the tension in the wire).

d. If you moved the hooks farther apart to reduce the angle from 50 ° to 30 °, would the tension in the wires increase or decrease? Why?

13. MULTIPLE LOADS

If two 150-kg masses are suspended on a wire, such that the section between the loads (wire B) is horizontal, then wire B is under tension, but is doing no lifting. The entire weight of the 150-kg mass on the right is being held up by the vertical component of the force in wire C. In the same way, the mass on the left is being supported entirely by the vertical component of the force in wire A.

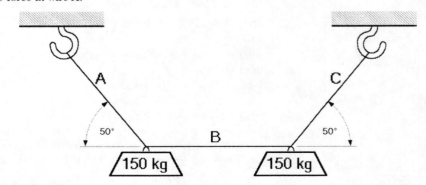

Calculate:

a. the vertical force component in wires A and C.

b. the horizontal force component in each wire.

c. the tension in wire A.

14. TENSION AND ANGLES

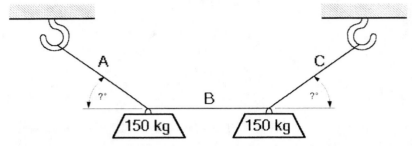

If the hooks are pulled farther apart, the tension in wire B will change, and the angle of wires A and C with respect to the horizontal will also change.

If the hooks are pulled apart until the tension in wire B is 2,000 N, determine

a. the angle between the horizontal and wire C, and

b. the tension in wire C.

How does the angle in part a change if the tension in wire B is increased to 3,000 N?

15. DESIGNING A SUSPENSION BRIDGE

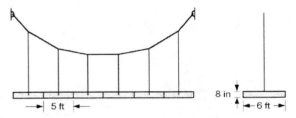

After fighting some particularly snarled traffic to get from their apartment to the pizza place across the street, some engineers decided that they should build a suspension bridge from one side of the street to the other. On the back side of a napkin, they sketched out the initial design shown in the accompanying figure. The plan calls for a single cable to be hung between the buildings, with one support wire to each deck section. The deck is to be 6 feet wide to allow pedestrian traffic on either side of the support wires. The bridge will be 30 feet long and made up of six 5-foot sections. The engineers want their design to be environmentally friendly, so the design calls for the decking to be made of a material constructed of used tires, with a density of 88 lb/ft³.

(*Note:* To help keep things straight, we use the term "wire" for the vertical wires connected to the deck sections and the term "cable" for the main suspension between the buildings.)

a. What is the mass of each deck section?

b. What force is a deck section imparting to its suspension wire?

The engineers had quite a discussion about how much tension to impose on the bridge. One wanted to minimize the stress on the buildings by keeping the tension low, but others thought that would produce a "droopy" bridge. They finally decided that the tension in the center (horizontal) section would be five times the force that any deck section put on its suspension wire.

c. What is the horizontal component of force in any of the cable sections?

d. Calculate all the forces and angles in the main cable segments.

(*Hint:* Since the center segment of the cable has only a horizontal force component and you can calculate the tension in that segment, start in the center and work your way towards the outside. Also, since the bridge is symmetrical, you only need to solve for the angles and forces in one-half of the bridge.)

At this point, the waiter walked up and made a comment that upset all of their plans. The result was a lively discussion that went on into the night, but no follow-through on the original design.

SO WHAT DID THE WAITER SAY?

"As soon as someone stands on that bridge, the deck will tip sideways and dump the person off."

The engineers spent the rest of the evening designing solutions to this problem. Do you have any ideas?

4

Working with Matrices

SECTIONS

OBJECTIVES

- know how to work with matrices in Mathcad, including Mathcad's definitions of "array", "matrix," and "vector," creating a matrix, and filling a matrix with values;
- be able to perform basic mathematical operations on matrices, including addition and subtraction, matrix multiplication, element-by-element multiplication, transposition, inversion; and finding the determinant of a matrix; and
- know how to use Mathcad's built-in functions to manipulate matrices.

4.1 TOTAL RECYCLE

NASA's Mission to Mars projects have focused attention on the idea of recovering and reusing oxygen, water, and essential nutrients on extended human excursions into space. Because the quantities of these materials that can be carried along are quite limited, the idea is to recycle everything. This is called *total recycle*. It is a great idea and an enormous engineering challenge.

The goal for NASA's Advanced Life Support Program[1] is to completely recycle water, oxygen, and food products—but not energy. Energy will be used to fuel the recycling systems. To date, water and oxygen recycle systems have been tested for up to 91 days.[2] A long-term test of a complete recycle system for food products is still many years away.

One of the many challenges of designing a total-recycle system is handling the accumulation of chemicals generated at minute levels over long periods of time. For example, traces of copper (from pipes or cooling systems) are not a serious problem, but if the copper should somehow accumulate in the water system, the concentration could increase. The microbes used to degrade organic wastes and the plants used to consume CO_2 and generate O^2 are both sensitive to copper. The loss of either of these systems would be catastrophic to the Mars mission. Special designs for handling trace contaminants and long-term testing are necessary to be sure that the total-recycle systems will work for extended missions into space.

Bringing total-recycle concepts into practice is not limited to the Mission to Mars. Just as individuals and communities are becoming increasingly involved in recycling activities, companies are also working to reduce the generation of waste products by recycling and reusing materials. There is a simultaneous push towards substituting less hazardous materials wherever possible. The separation processes required to effectively recycle materials and the equipment changes needed to allow the use of less hazardous materials will provide engineering opportunities for many years to come.

As with NASA's system, as our manufacturing facilities move towards total recycle, we may see more energy being used to fuel the separation systems that allow the materials to be recycled. During a time when there are concerns over the use of fossil fuels and global warming, using increasing amounts of energy to reduce wastes is problematic. The search for low-energy processes that simultaneously reduce waste products will be a tremendous challenge for the next generation of engineers and scientists.

4.2 MATHCAD'S MATRIX DEFINITIONS

A *matrix* is a collection of numbers that are related in some way. We commonly use matrices to hold data sets. For example, if you recorded the temperature of the concrete in a structure over time as the concrete set, the time and temperature values form a data set of related numbers. This data set would be stored in a computer as a matrix.

Common usage in mathematics calls a single column or row of values a *vector*. If the temperature and time values were stored separately, we would have both a time vector and a temperature vector. A *matrix* is a collection of one or more vectors. That is, a matrix containing a single row or column would also be a vector. On the other hand, a

---

[1] Check NASA's Web site, <http://pet.jsc.nasa.gov/alssee> for more information on the processing steps required to implement the recycle systems.

[2] The Lunar-Mars Life Support Test Project Phase III (90-Day Human Test) was completed in December 1997.

matrix containing three rows and two columns would be called a 3×2 matrix, not a vector. (But you could say the matrix is made up of three row vectors or two column vectors.) So every vector is a matrix, but only single-row or single-column matrices are called vectors.

Mathcad modifies these definitions slightly by adding the term *array*. In Mathcad, a vector has only one row or one column, and a matrix always has at least two rows or two columns. That is, there is no overlap in Mathcad's definitions of vectors and matrices. Mathcad uses the term *array* to mean a collection of related values that could be either a vector or a matrix. Mathcad uses the new term to indicate what type of parameter must be sent to functions that operate on vectors and matrices. For example, you can send either a vector or a matrix to the rows (A) function, so Mathcad's help files show an A as the function's parameter to indicate that either a vector or a matrix is acceptable.

Definitions Used in Mathcad Help Files

A	Array argument—either a matrix or a vector.
M	Matrix argument—an array with two or more rows or columns.
v	Vector argument—an array containing a single row or column.

The length (v) function requires a vector and will not accept multiple rows or columns. Mathcad indicates this vector-only restriction in its help files by showing a v as the length function's parameter. The determinant operator, $|M|$, requires a square matrix and will not work on a vector. To show that a matrix is required, Mathcad's help files display an M as the operator's parameter.

4.2.1 Array Origin

By default, Mathcad calls the first element in a vector the element zero. For a two-dimensional matrix, the *array origin* is 0,0 by default. If you would rather have Mathcad start counting elements at another value, you can change the default by using the ORIGIN function. The following example illustrates how changing the origin from 0,0 to 1,1 changes the row and column numbering of the array elements.

$$\text{MyArray} := \begin{bmatrix} 12 & 15 & 17 \\ 23 & 25 & 29 \end{bmatrix}$$

$$\text{MyArray}_{0,0} = 12 \qquad \text{MyArray}_{0,1} = 15$$

$$\text{ORIGIN} := 1$$

$$\text{MyArray} = \begin{bmatrix} 12 & 15 & 17 \\ 23 & 25 & 29 \end{bmatrix}$$

$$\text{MyArray}_{1,1} = 12 \qquad \text{MyArray}_{1,2} = 15$$

Notice that the arrays look the same, but that the array origin has been changed to 1,1 after the ORIGIN statement, so the top-left element is now element 1,1 and not 0,0. You can also change the array origin for the entire worksheet. Use the Math menu, as Math/Options, and set the new value for the Array Origin on the options dialog box. The origins for all arrays on the worksheet will be changed.

4.2.2 Maximum Array Size

There are two constraints on array sizes in Mathcad:

- If you enter the arrays from the keyboard, arrays may have no more than 100 elements. You can type in multiple arrays and join them to work around this limitation.
- The total number of elements in all arrays is dependent on the amount of memory in your computer, but will always be less than 8×10^6.

4.3   INITIALIZING AN ARRAY

Before an array can be used, it must be filled with values, or initialized. There are a number of methods for initializing an array in Mathcad. You can

- type in the values from the keyboard,
- read the values from a text file,
- compute the values by using a function or a range variable, or
- Copy and paste the values from another Windows program.

Each of these options will be discussed in turn.

4.3.1 Typing Values into an Array

You can enter a value into a particular element of an array with the use of a standard Mathcad definition. For example, typing [G][[ ] [3][,][2][:][6][4] puts the value 64 in the element at position 3,2 in the G matrix. If the G matrix has not been previously defined, then Mathcad will create a matrix large enough to a have an element at position 3,2 and will fill the undefined elements with zeroes. In the following example, notice that the array origin is 0,0, so the 64 in element 3,2 is in the fourth row, and third column:

$$G_{3,2} := 64$$

$$G := \begin{bmatrix} 1 & 1 & 1 \\ 2 & 4 & 8 \\ 3 & 9 & 27 \\ 4 & 16 & 64 \end{bmatrix}$$

Filling a matrix by defining the contents of each element would be extremely slow. Fortunately, Mathcad has provided a better way. Rather than defining each element individually, Mathcad allows you to define an entire array at one time by first creating an array of placeholders and then filling in the placeholders by typing values from the keyboard. Begin by choosing a variable name for the matrix. We will use G again and create the left side of a definition by using [G][:]:

$$G := \mathbf{|}$$

To create the array, select (click on) the placeholder on the right side of the definition, and bring up the Insert Matrix dialog box by (a) choosing Matrix from the Insert menu, (b) choosing Matrix from the Matrix Toolbox, or (c) using the keyboard shortcut [Ctrl-M]. The following figure shows what the dialog box looks like:

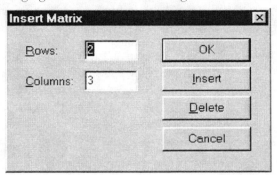

Enter the number of rows and columns you want in the G matrix:

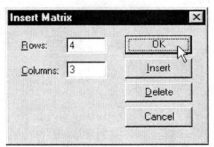

Then click the OK button to insert the matrix of placeholders, and close the dialog box. (The Insert button creates the array of placeholders and leaves the dialog box open, which is useful if you are defining several arrays.) The matrix of placeholders looks like this:

$$G := \begin{bmatrix} \blacksquare & \blacksquare & \blacksquare \\ \blacksquare & \blacksquare & \blacksquare \\ \blacksquare & \blacksquare & \blacksquare \\ \blacksquare & \blacksquare & \blacksquare \end{bmatrix}$$

To complete the definition of array G, simply click on a placeholder and enter an element value. You can move to another placeholder either by using the mouse or by pressing [Tab] after each entry. The resulting matrix might look like this:

$$G := \begin{bmatrix} 1 & 1 & 1 \\ 2 & 4 & 8 \\ 3 & 9 & 27 \\ 4 & 16 & 64 \end{bmatrix}$$

PRACTICE!

Use the Insert Matrix dialog to create the following matrices:

t := (2 4 6 8 10)

$$W := \begin{bmatrix} 1 & 2 & 3 & 4 \\ 3 & 1 & 5 & 7 \end{bmatrix}$$

$$Y := \begin{bmatrix} 1 \bullet sec & 2 \bullet min & 3 \bullet hr \\ 4 \bullet min & 5 \bullet min & 6 \bullet min \end{bmatrix}$$

4.3.2 Reading Values from a Text File

Text, or ASCII, files are commonly used to move data between programs. For example, a recording instrument or data acquisition program might collect data on the concentration of certain substances over time and save the data to a disk as a text file. You could then import the text file into Mathcad as a matrix for further analysis by using the READPRN() function.

A data file on a disk can be read and assigned to a Mathcad array variable by building the read operation into the matrix definition, like this:

$$C := \text{READPRN}(\text{``A:MyData.txt''}):$$

C =

	0	1
0	0	50
1	10	48.2
2	20	46.5
3	30	44.8
4	40	43.2
5	50	41.6
6	60	40.1
7	70	38.7
8	80	37.3
9	90	35.9

The text string sent to the READPRN( ) function tells Mathcad to read the MyData.txt file found on drive A:. This data file contains 25 rows, only part of which are displayed in the worksheet. (When only part of a matrix is displayed, Mathcad adds a shaded border at the top and on the left side of the matrix, showing which rows and columns are displayed.) To see the values that are not displayed, you would click on the portion of the C matrix that is displayed, and scroll bars would appear. You could then scroll the matrix to see the remaining values. The scroll bars will appear only when a matrix has been selected (by clicking on the displayed portion of the matrix) and when the matrix is too large to display in its entirety.

(*Note:* If you want to write the values in array C to a text file, you assign the array to the WRITEPRN( ) function:

$$\text{WRITEPRN}('A:MyData.txt') := C$$

The values in C will be assigned to file MyData.txt on drive A:.)

4.3.3 Using an Input Table to Create a Matrix

Mathcad has a *component* called an *input table* that provides a spreadsheetlike interface for entering arrays. This can be a convenient way to enter arrays by hand, but you can also automatically import values into an input table from various types of files (e.g., text files or spreadsheet files). Thus, the input table component is a convenient and flexible way of filling arrays with data from a variety of sources.

(*Note:* The read/write file component is similar to the input table component because both can read a variety of file formats. However, there is a major distinction between the two components:

- When you import values into an input table, the file is read once and the values are copied into the Mathcad worksheet. Changes to values in the file are not reflected in the worksheet.)

- A read/write file component reads the file each time the Mathcad worksheet is calculated, so changes to the values in the file *are* reflected in the worksheet.)

To use an input table component to create and fill a matrix, do the following:

1. Insert the input table component by selecting Insert/Component and then Input Table from the list on the Component Wizard:

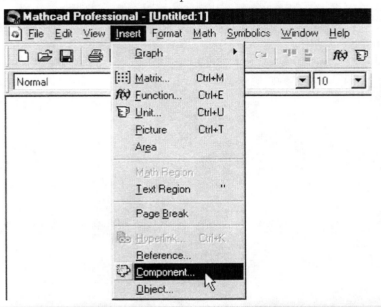

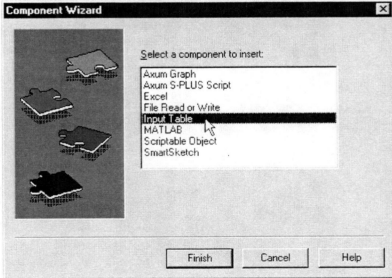

2. Enter the name of the array to be created in the placeholder at the top-left corner of the input table. In this example, the array will be called "A":

A :=

	0	1
0	0	
1		

Now you can simply start typing values into the table, or you can follow the remaining steps to import values from a file.

3. Click anywhere on the input table to select it.

4. Right-click on the table and select Import from the pop-up menu:

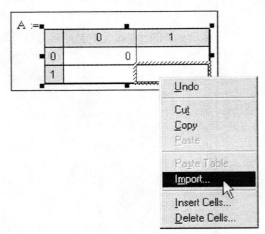

5. A standard Open File dialog (titled Read from File) will be displayed. Select the type of file (e.g., Excel file) to be imported, and then browse for the file.

Once the input table has been filled (shown on the left), you can use array "A" for other calculations. Here, the filled array has simply been displayed as a matrix.

A :=

	0	1
0	1	1
1	2	2.46
2	3	4.17
3	4	6.06
4	5	8.1
5	6	10.27
6	7	12.55
7	8	14.93
8	8	17.4
9	10	19.95

$$A = \begin{pmatrix} 1 & 1 \\ 2 & 2.462 \\ 3 & 4.171 \\ 4 & 6.063 \\ 5 & 8.103 \\ 6 & 10.271 \\ 7 & 12.55 \\ 8 & 14.929 \\ 9 & 17.399 \\ 10 & 19.953 \end{pmatrix}$$

4.3.4 Units on Matrix Elements

If all of the elements of an array have the same units, you can multiply the entire array by the units. If not, each element can have its own units. The two time vector definitions

$$\text{time} := \begin{bmatrix} 0 \\ 10 \\ 20 \\ 30 \end{bmatrix} \cdot \text{min}$$

and

$$time := \begin{bmatrix} 0 \bullet min \\ 10 \bullet min \\ 20 \bullet min \\ 0.5 \bullet hr \end{bmatrix}$$

are functionally equivalent.

4.3.5 Computing Array Element Values by Using Range Variables

Mathcad provides an unusual type of variable that takes on a whole series, or range, of values. This type of variable is called a *range variable* and can be used with arrays to identify particular elements of an array. For example, the first of the preceding time vectors could have been created using a range variable. The range variable needs to take the values 0, 1, 2, and 3, as it will be used to indicate each element of the time vector in turn. The range variable can have any name, but i and j are often employed, since range variables are commonly used as index variables. The range variable is defined as [i][:][0][;][3], or

```
i := 0..3
```

Note that you indicate the range by pressing [;] (semicolon), but Mathcad displays a series of dots (called an *ellipsis*). The range variable we've defined has four values, and anytime you use this variable in an equation, the equation will be evaluated four times, once with i = 0, once with i = 1, etc. Range variables can be very handy, but they do take a little getting used to.

Once the range variable has been defined, the elements of the time vector can be calculated with the use of the range variable, like this:

```
time_i := (i·10)·min
```

$$time = \begin{bmatrix} 0 \\ 10 \\ 20 \\ 30 \end{bmatrix} \bullet min$$

The range variable has been used as an index subscript (left-square-bracket subscript) on the left side of the definition, to indicate which element of the time vector is being computed, and is also used on the right side as part of the calculation itself. As the value of the range variable changes from 0 to 3, the computed element values change from 0 to 30 minutes.

PRACTICE!

What will the matrix M look like when defined by the following expressions:

a. i := 0..4
   Mi := 2·i
b. i := 0..4
   j := 0..3
   $M_{i,j}$:= (3+2·i−j)·ft

4.3.6 An Example of a Two-Dimensional Array

In the following equations, range variables r and c are defined to indicate the row and column of the element of the matrix S being computed, and the value of the element depends on the values of r and c:

```
r := 0..4     c := 0..2
S_{r,c} := r²+c²
```

$$S = \begin{bmatrix} 0 & 1 & 4 \\ 1 & 2 & 5 \\ 4 & 5 & 8 \\ 9 & 10 & 13 \\ 16 & 17 & 20 \end{bmatrix}$$

4.3.7 Computing Array Element Values Using the Matrix( ) Function

Mathcad's `matrix( )` function allows you to fill an array with computed values without explicitly declaring range variables. In effect, Mathcad declares the range variables on the basis of the information you send to the `matrix( )` function. The `matrix(r, c, f)` function creates a matrix with r rows and c columns in which the value of the i,jth element is computed using the function `f()`. This function must be a function of two variables and must be declared before calling the `matrix( )` function. The function `f(i,j)` is evaluated repeatedly to fill the matrix, with i ranging from 0 to r−1 and j ranging from 0 to c−1.

The S matrix could be created using the `matrix( )` function as follows:

```
myFunc(r,c) := r²+c²
S := matrix(5, 3, myFunc)
```

$$S = \begin{bmatrix} 0 & 1 & 4 \\ 1 & 2 & 5 \\ 4 & 5 & 8 \\ 9 & 10 & 13 \\ 16 & 17 & 20 \end{bmatrix}$$

PRACTICE!

What would the matrix returned by `matrix(4,4,f)` look like, if `f(r,c)` were defined as

  a. `f(r,c) := 2+r+c`

  b. `f(r,c) := 0.5·r+c²`

The following matrix was created using the matrix( ) function:

```
M := matrix(3, 5, f)
```

$$M = \begin{bmatrix} 0 & 3 & 6 & 9 & 12 \\ 1 & 4 & 7 & 10 & 13 \\ 2 & 5 & 8 & 11 & 14 \end{bmatrix}$$

What did `f(r,c)` look like?

4.3.8 Copying and Pasting Arrays from Other Windows Programs

A convenient way to move values from another program into Mathcad is to copy the values in the other program (e.g., a spreadsheet) and then paste them into an array definition in Mathcad. If the values already exist in another Windows program, this can save a lot of typing.

In the next example, two columns of values are displayed in an Excel spreadsheet. The values shown in column B are computed by raising the values in column A to the third power. (You do not need to convert the spreadsheet formulas to values before moving the data to Mathcad.)

B1		▾	× ✓ =	=A1^3	
	A	B	C	D	
1	1	1			
2	2	8			
3	3	27			
4	4	64			
5	5	125			
6					

To create a 5×2 array in Mathcad containing these values, select the 10 values in cells A1..B5, and copy them to the Windows clipboard (using the spreadsheet's menu commands Edit/Copy, for example). Then begin an array definition in Mathcad:

$$C := \blacksquare$$

Click on the placeholder, and paste the contents of the clipboard into the placeholder by using Mathcad's Edit/Paste menu commands.

The values displayed in the spreadsheet are now a Mathcad array:

$$C := \begin{bmatrix} 1 & 1 \\ 2 & 8 \\ 3 & 27 \\ 4 & 64 \\ 5 & 125 \end{bmatrix}$$

(*Note:* The formulas used in the spreadsheet did not come across to Mathcad; just the displayed values were pasted.)

PROFESSIONAL SUCCESS

Let your software do the work.

Retyping data, equations, and results into a report is tedious and tends to introduce errors. The past few generations of software products have had the ability to exchange data, and the capabilities of the products are improving with every new version. Mathcad can share information with other mathematics packages, such as Excel and Matlab (data), and word processors, such as Microsoft Word (values, equations, graphs).[1] If you find yourself frequently reentering the same information into multiple software packages, you might want to see if there's a better way.

---

[1]Microsoft Word and Excel are products of the Microsoft Corporation, Redmond, WA.

4.3.9 Creating an Identity Matrix

An *identity matrix* is a square matrix filled with ones along the diagonal and zeroes everywhere else. Mathcad's `identity( )` function creates identity matrices. Since the number of rows is always equal to the number of columns in an identity matrix, you need to specify just one or the other, so the `identity( )` function takes only a single parameter indicating the number of rows (or columns). Here's an example of the use of the `identity()` function to create a 5×5 identity matrix called `ID`:

```
ID := identity(5)
```

$$ID = \begin{bmatrix} 1 & 0 & 0 & 0 & 0 \\ 0 & 1 & 0 & 0 & 0 \\ 0 & 0 & 1 & 0 & 0 \\ 0 & 0 & 0 & 1 & 0 \\ 0 & 0 & 0 & 0 & 1 \end{bmatrix}$$

4.4   MODIFYING AN ARRAY

Suppose you have just entered a large array from the keyboard and notice that you accidentally left out one row. You don't have to start all over again; you can insert a row or column into an existing array. You can also delete one or more rows or columns. In addition, Mathcad allows you to join arrays either side to side [`augment( )`] or one on top of the other [`stack( )`]. Finally, Mathcad lets you assign portions of an array to a new variable by using the `submatrix( )` function.

4.4.1 Inserting a Row or Column into an Existing Array

Suppose that you have just entered a massive array by hand and discovered that you left out a row. Don't worry; all is not lost. Mathcad will allow you to insert one or more rows into an existing array. Mathcad inserts the row after the currently selected row, so click on the row immediately above where you want the new row to be inserted. For example, to insert a new row just after the row containing 3, 9, and 27, click on the 3, 9, or 27 to indicate where the new row should be placed:

$$G := \begin{bmatrix} 1 & 1 & 1 \\ 2 & 4 & 8 \\ 3 & 9 & 27 \\ 4 & 16 & 64 \end{bmatrix}$$

Then bring up the Insert Matrix dialog box by pressing [Ctrl-M]. Indicate the number of rows to be added (and zero columns!), and then press the Insert or OK button:

Insert Matrix ✕

Rows: `1`   OK

Columns: `0|`   Insert

        Delete

        Cancel

A row of placeholders is inserted into the matrix:

$$G := \begin{bmatrix} 1 & 1 & 1 \\ 2 & 4 & 18 \\ 3 & 9 & 27 \\ \blacksquare & \blacksquare & \blacksquare \\ 4 & 16 & 64 \end{bmatrix}$$

Click on the placeholders to enter values.

For example, to add two columns at the right side of the original G matrix, do the following:

1. Click on any element in the third column. Mathcad will insert the new columns to the right of the column you select:

$$G := \begin{bmatrix} 1 & 1 & 1| \\ 2 & 4 & 8 \\ 3 & 9 & 27 \\ 4 & 16 & 64 \end{bmatrix}$$

2. Bring up the Insert Matrix dialog box by pressing [Ctrl-M]. Indicate the number of columns to be added (and zero rows), and then press the Insert button:

Insert Matrix ✕

Rows: `0`   OK

Columns: `2`   Insert

        Delete

        Close

The result will be

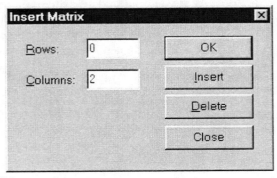

$$G := \begin{bmatrix} 1 & 1 & 1 & \blacksquare & \blacksquare \\ 2 & 4 & 8 & \blacksquare & \blacksquare \\ 3 & 9 & 27 & \blacksquare & \blacksquare \\ 4 & 16 & 64 & \blacksquare & \blacksquare \end{bmatrix}$$

To add rows at the top of the array or columns at the left, select the entire array, rather than a single element, before inserting rows or columns:

$$G := \begin{bmatrix} 1 & 1 & 1 \\ 2 & 4 & 8 \\ 3 & 9 & 27 \\ 4 & 16 & 64 \end{bmatrix}$$

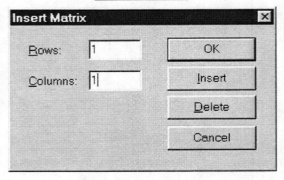

The matrix should now look like this:

$$G := \begin{bmatrix} \blacksquare & \blacksquare & \blacksquare & \blacksquare \\ \blacksquare & 1 & 1 & 1 \\ \blacksquare & 2 & 4 & 8 \\ \blacksquare & 3 & 9 & 27 \\ \blacksquare & 4 & 16 & 64 \end{bmatrix}$$

The preceding example illustrates that Mathcad will allow the addition of both rows and columns in a single operation.

4.4.2 Deleting Rows and Columns

The procedure for deleting rows and columns is similar to that used to insert columns. To delete one or more rows, select an element in the first row or column to be deleted. If you want to delete three rows, the rows will include the row containing the selected element and the two rows immediately below it. Similarly, to delete two columns, select an element in the leftmost column to be removed. The deleted columns will include the column containing the selected element and the column to the right of it. For example, to delete the middle two rows of the original G array, do the following:

1. Select an element in the second row of the array:

$$G := \begin{bmatrix} 1 & 1 & 1 \\ 2 & 4 & 8 \\ 3 & 9 & 27 \\ 4 & 16 & 64 \end{bmatrix}$$

2.   Bring up the Insert Matrix dialog box. Set the number of rows to be deleted to 2 and the number of columns to 0. Click the Delete button on the dialog box:

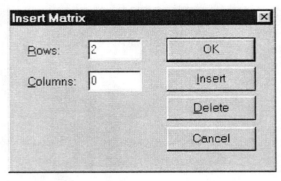

The middle two rows of the G matrix have been deleted:

$$G := \begin{bmatrix} 1 & 1 & 1 \\ 4 & 16 & 64 \end{bmatrix}$$

4.4.3 Selecting a Portion of an Array

There are times when you need just a portion of an array. Mathcad provides a column operator, [Ctrl-^], that allows you to select a single column and a submatrix( ) function that allows you to select an arbitrary subsection of an array.

Selecting a Single Column   Mathcad's *column operator* allows you to take a single column (vector) of a multicolumn array and assign that column to a new variable. The column operator is available on the Matrix Toolbar or by pressing [Ctrl-6]. To see how the column operator is used, consider the time and concentration data that were read from the MyData.txt file:

C := READPRN("A:MyData.txt")

		0	1
	0	0	50
	1	10	48.2
	2	20	46.5
	3	30	44.8
C =	4	40	43.2
	5	50	41.6
	6	60	40.1
	7	70	38.7
	8	80	37.3
	9	90	35.9

The first column actually contains time information in minutes, and the second column contains concentration data in units of mg/L. Because the units on the columns are different, we can't just multiply the entire array by a set of units. But if we separate the time and concentration vectors, then we can put units on each vector.

We can use the column operator to extract the left column (column 0) and assign the values to a new variable, called time. We can build in units at the same time:

time := $C^{<0>} \cdot$ min

time =

	0
0	0
1	10
2	20
3	30
4	40
5	50
6	60
7	70
8	80
9	90

$\cdot$ min

Similarly, we can pull out the concentration data and assign it to a new variable, conc:

conc := $C^{<1>} \cdot \dfrac{mg}{L}$

conc =

	0
0	50
1	48.2
2	46.5
3	44.8
4	43.2
5	41.6
6	40.1
7	38.7
8	37.3
9	35.9

$\cdot \dfrac{mg}{L}$

This is an easy way to get units on values read in from text files. The column operator is also useful in getting vectors ready for plotting, since Mathcad allows you to plot one vector against another simply by entering the vector names in the placeholders on the x- and y-axes of an $x - y$ plot:

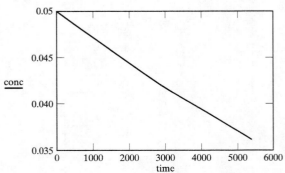

The values on the axes may surprise you, but remember that Mathcad always displays graphs in base units, so the concentrations are in kg/m³ , and the times are in seconds.

[*Note:* You can "trick" Mathcad into displaying values in the other units by dividing the vector names (on the axes) by the desired units. The resulting graph appears to display the correct values (but the axis labels can be quite misleading)]:

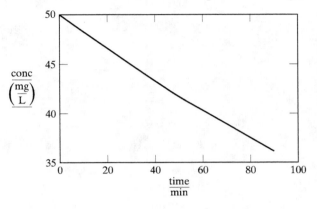

PRACTICE!

Create a 5 ×5 identity matrix by using

```
ID := identity(5)
```

Then use the column operator to pull out the center column of matrix ID (column number 2). What would change when you used the column operator to extract the column number 2 if the identity matrix were created like this:

```
ORIGIN := 1
ID := identity(5)
```

Selecting a Single Row   Mathcad does not provide a mechanism for selecting a single row, but you can get the job done by turning the array sideways (i.e., transposing the array) and selecting a column by means of the column operator. Going back to the G matrix that we used before, suppose we want to select the third row and assign it to a new variable, R3. We have

$$G := \begin{bmatrix} 1 & 1 & 1 \\ 2 & 4 & 8 \\ 3 & 9 & 27 \\ 4 & 16 & 64 \end{bmatrix}$$

We need to turn the G array around by using the *transpose* operator from the Matrix Toolbar:

$$G_{tr} := G^T$$

$$G_{tr} = \begin{bmatrix} 1 & 2 & 3 & 4 \\ 1 & 4 & 9 & 16 \\ 1 & 8 & 27 & 64 \end{bmatrix}$$

Then we can select what is now the third column (Mathcad's column number 2, since it starts counting at zero) by using the column operator:

$$R3_{tr} := G_{tr}^{<2>}$$

$$R3_{tr} = \begin{bmatrix} 3 \\ 9 \\ 27 \end{bmatrix}$$

Finally, we turn the result back into a row vector by transposing the $R3_{tr}$ vector:

$$R3 := R3_{tr}^{T}$$
$$R3 = [3 \ 9 \ 27]$$

This multistep operation can be carried out in a single command, thereby eliminating some variables:

$$R3 := [(G^T)^{<2>}]^T$$
$$R3 = [3 \ 9 \ 27]$$

If you need to extract a row frequently, you might want to create a function that operates like a "row operator":

$$\text{row\_operator}(A,r) := (A^T)^{<r>T}$$

This function can then be used to extract the third row of the G matrix:

$$R3 := \text{row\_operator}(G,2)$$
$$R3 = [3 \ 9 \ 27]$$

Choosing a Subset of an Array   An alternative to all of the transposing that was done in the preceding example is Mathcad's submatrix(A, r_{start}, r_{stop}, c_{start}, c_{stop}) function. This function takes a number of parameters and allows you to specify exactly which part of a matrix to extract. The first parameter, A, is the name of the array from which the submatrix is to be taken. The starting and stopping row and column numbers must be integers. Remember that, by default, Mathcad calls the top left element, $A_{0,0}$. If you wanted to start with that element, then r_{start} and c_{start} would both be zero, not one.

To choose the third row of the G matrix, the submatrix( ) function could be used with the following arguments:

$$R3 := \text{Submatrix}(G, 2, 2, 0, 2)$$

These arguments tell the submatrix( ) function to start with the G array and pull out rows 2 through 2 (using Mathcad's way of counting rows) and columns 0 through 2:

$$R3 := \text{submatrix}(G,2,2,0,2)$$
$$R3 = [3 \ 9 \ 27]$$

The submatrix( ) function can also return portions of an array that are not complete rows or columns. For example, the function could be used to extract the four elements in the top left corner of the G matrix:

TL4 := submatrix(G,0,1,0,1)

$$TL4 = \begin{bmatrix} 1 & 1 \\ 2 & 4 \end{bmatrix}$$

4.4.4 Combining Two Arrays

Mathcad provides two functions for combining arrays: augment ( ) and stack( ). Whereas the stack( ) function stacks matrices, augment ( ) connects them side by side. Here are a couple of simple examples:

$$B := \begin{bmatrix} 7 & 8 & 9 \\ 8 & 9 & 10 \\ 9 & 10 & 11 \end{bmatrix}$$

Aug := augment(A,B)

$$Aug := \begin{bmatrix} 1 & 2 & 3 & 7 & 8 & 9 \\ 2 & 3 & 4 & 8 & 9 & 10 \\ 3 & 4 & 5 & 9 & 10 & 11 \end{bmatrix}$$

Stk := stack(A,B)

$$Stk = \begin{bmatrix} 1 & 2 & 3 \\ 2 & 3 & 4 \\ 3 & 4 & 5 \\ 7 & 8 & 9 \\ 8 & 9 & 10 \\ 9 & 10 & 11 \end{bmatrix}$$

PRACTICE!

In what order would you use the stack( ) and augment( ) functions to create the following matrix from the matrices A and B in the previous section?

$$T = \begin{bmatrix} 1 & 2 & 3 & 1 & 2 & 3 \\ 2 & 3 & 4 & 2 & 3 & 4 \\ 3 & 4 & 5 & 3 & 4 & 5 \\ 7 & 8 & 9 & 1 & 2 & 3 \\ 8 & 9 & 10 & 2 & 3 & 4 \\ 9 & 10 & 11 & 3 & 4 & 5 \end{bmatrix}$$

How would the submatrix( ) function be used to extract matrix

$$T_{sub} = \begin{bmatrix} 5 & 3 & 4 \\ 9 & 1 & 2 \\ 10 & 2 & 3 \\ 11 & 3 & 4 \end{bmatrix}$$

from the T matrix?

4.5 ARRAY OPERATIONS

Array operations such as addition and multiplication require that certain conditions be met and that certain procedures be followed. For each of the standard array operations that follow, the requirements and the procedures are listed.

4.5.1 Array Addition and Subtraction

Requirement: The arrays to be added or subtracted must be the same size.
   Procedure: Element-by-element addition.
   Array addition and subtraction in Mathcad are handled just like scalar addition and subtraction:

$$B := \begin{bmatrix} 7 & 8 & 9 \\ 8 & 9 & 10 \\ 9 & 10 & 11 \end{bmatrix}$$

$$Sum := A+B$$

$$Sum = \begin{bmatrix} 8 & 10 & 12 \\ 10 & 12 & 14 \\ 12 & 14 & 16 \end{bmatrix}$$

$$Dif := Sum-B$$

$$Dif = \begin{bmatrix} 1 & 2 & 3 \\ 2 & 3 & 4 \\ 3 & 4 & 5 \end{bmatrix}$$

(*Note:* Array subtraction is not a standard array operation; you usually have to multiply by −1 and then add. Array subtraction, however, is defined in Mathcad.)

4.5.2 Matrix Multiplication

Requirement: The inside dimensions of the arrays to be multiplied must be equal. The outside dimensions determine the size of the product matrix. Thus, we might have

$D_{2\times3}\times E_{3\times2}$ inner dimensions are equal (3)
                product dimensions will be 2×2

Procedure: Working across the columns of the first array and down the rows of the second array, multiply elements and add the results. Mathematically, *matrix multiplication* is summarized as:

```
Prod_{0,0} = [(1×10) + (2+12) + (3×14)] = 76
Prod_{0,1} = [(1×11) + (2×13) + (3×15)] = 82
Prod_{1,0} = [(4×10) + (5×12) + (6×14)] = 184
Prod_{1,1} = [(4×11) + (5×13) + (6×15)] = 199
```

$$D := \begin{bmatrix} 1 & 2 & 3 \\ 4 & 5 & 6 \end{bmatrix}$$

$$Prod := D\cdot E$$

$$Prod = \begin{bmatrix} 76 & 82 \\ 84 & 199 \end{bmatrix}$$

PRACTICE!

The order in which the matrices are multiplied makes a difference. What is the result of the following matrix multiplication?

    Prod$_2$:= E·D

4.5.3 Element-by-Element Multiplication

Sometimes you don't want true matrix multiplication, but rather, you want each element of the first matrix multiplied by the corresponding element of the second matrix.

Element-by-element multiplication is available in Mathcad by means of the *vectorize* operator on the Matrix Toolbar.

Requirement: The arrays must be the same size for element-by-element multiplication.

Procedure: Multiply each individual element of the first matrix by the corresponding element of the second matrix:

$$B := \begin{bmatrix} 7 & 8 & 9 \\ 8 & 9 & 10 \\ 9 & 10 & 11 \end{bmatrix}$$

$$ElemMult = \overrightarrow{(A \bullet B)}$$

$$ElemMult = \begin{bmatrix} 7 & 16 & 27 \\ 16 & 27 & 40 \\ 27 & 40 & 55 \end{bmatrix}$$

PRACTICE!

Compare the results of the following matrix multiplications:

    A•B
    $\overrightarrow{(A \bullet B)}$

4.5.4 Transposition

Requirement: Any array can be transposed.

Procedure: Interchange row and column elements, $\text{Trans}_{j,1} = C_{i,j}$:

$$C := \begin{bmatrix} 1 & 1 \\ 2 & 8 \\ 3 & 27 \\ 4 & 64 \\ 5 & 125 \end{bmatrix}$$

$$\text{Trans} := C^T$$

$$\text{Trans} = \begin{bmatrix} 1 & 2 & 3 & 4 & 5 \\ 1 & 8 & 27 & 64 & 125 \end{bmatrix}$$

4.5.5 Inversion

When you invert a scalar, you divide 1 by the scalar, and the result is a value that, when multiplied by the original value, yields 1 as a product. Similarly, when you multiply an inverted matrix by the original matrix, you obtain an identity matrix as a result.

Requirement: Only square matrices can be inverted, and the matrix must be nonsingular.

Procedure: The procedure for *inverting* a matrix is quite involved. You first augment the matrix with an identity matrix and then use row operations by multiplying by scale factors and then adding and subtracting rows to convert the original matrix into an identity matrix. The same row operations will transform the original identity matrix into the inverse matrix. (For more details, see any text on matrix mathematics.) Suffice it to say that, for large matrices, the inversion process requires many calculations, and there can be significant round-off error associated with the process. How big is a "large" matrix? That depends on how accurate you want your solutions to be, but when matrices get above about 20×20, you should start trying to find solution methods that avoid inversion.

Inverting a matrix in Mathcad is easy; you simply raise the matrix to the −1 power:

$$F := \begin{bmatrix} 2 & 3 & 5 \\ 7 & 2 & 4 \\ 8 & 11 & 6 \end{bmatrix}$$

$$F^{-1} = \begin{bmatrix} -0.1517 & 0.1754 & 0.0095 \\ -0.0474 & -0.1327 & 0.128 \\ 0.2891 & 0.0095 & -0.0806 \end{bmatrix}$$

If Mathcad cannot invert the matrix, it will tell you that the matrix is singular.

(*Note:* A system of linear equations can be written in matrix form, consisting of a coefficient matrix, an unknown vector, and a right-hand-side vector:

$$[C] [x] = [r]$$

One common solution method requires that the coefficient matrix be inverted and multiplied by the right-hand-side vector to calculate the values of the unknowns:

$$[x] = [C]^{-1} [r]$$

If the coefficient matrix is singular—that is, if it cannot be inverted—then there is no unique solution to the original set of equations. If there is a solution to the equations, you should be able to invert the coefficient matrix.

APPLICATIONS: REMOVAL OF CO_2 FROM A GAS STREAM

Solutions of various ethanolamines [(e.g., monoethanolamine (MEA) or diethanolamine (DEA)] or potassium carbonate in water are commonly used to remove CO_2 from gas streams. The solution contacts the gas stream in a tall tower. The liquid flows down while the gas flows up, and the tower is designed to provide good contact between the liquid and the gas.

One hundred moles of a gas stream containing 10% CO_2 and 90% other combustion products (OCP) is fed at the bottom of the tower, and a solution (SOLN) containing 2% CO_2 and 98% MEA is fed at the top (s_1).

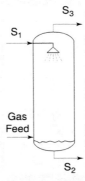

The exiting streams are analyzed and found to contain the following products:

liquid out (s_2):	12% CO_2	1% OCP	87% SOLN
gas out (s_3):	1% CO_2	99% OCP	

How many moles are in each of the unknown streams s_1, s_2, and s_3?

Solution

This problem can be solved by writing material balances. The material balance for CO_2, for example, simply states that the CO_2 going into the process (10% of the 100 moles of gas in and 2% of the liquid in) must come out again (1% of the gas out and 12% of the liquid out). In mathematical terms, we have

$$CO_2 \text{ Balance:} \quad 10 + 0.02 \cdot s_1$$
$$= 0.12 \cdot s_2 + 0.01 \cdot s_3$$

The idea that the CO_2 entering the tower must leave again is true if the process operates at steady state (CO_2 is not accumulating in the tower) and if there is no chemical reaction involving CO_2 taking place in the tower. Similar balances can be written for OCP and SOLN:

$$OCP \text{ Balance:} \quad 90 \eth \; 0.01 \cdot s_2 \quad 0.99 \cdot s_3$$
$$SOLN \text{ Balance:} \quad 0.98 \cdot s_1 \eth \; 0.87 \cdot s_2$$

To solve for the moles in s_1, s_2, and s_3, we first collect all the terms involving an 's' on one side and all the constants on the other:

$$0.02 \cdot s_1 \; -0.12 \cdot s_2 \; -0.01 \cdot s_3 \; = \; -90$$
$$-0.01 \cdot s_2 \; -0.99 \cdot s_3 \; = \; -90$$
$$0.98 \cdot s_1 \; -0.87 \cdot s_2 \qquad = \; 0$$

This set of equations can be written in matrix form as a coefficient matrix C and a right-hand-side vector r. Using Mathcad, we define the matrices as follows:

$$r := \begin{bmatrix} -10 \\ -90 \\ 0 \end{bmatrix}$$

We solve for the s vector (the numbers of moles in the unknown streams) by inverting the C matrix and multiplying the result with the r vector:

$$C_{inv} := C^{-1} \quad C_{inv} = \begin{bmatrix} -8.691 & 0.088 & 1.198 \\ -9.79 & 0.099 & 0.2 \\ 0.099 & -1.011 & -2.018 \cdot 10^{-3} \end{bmatrix}$$

$$s := C_{inv} \cdot r \quad s = \begin{bmatrix} 79 \\ 89 \\ 90 \end{bmatrix}$$

Stream s_1 contains 79 moles (77.4 moles SOLN, 1.6 moles CO_2), stream s_2 contains 89 moles, and stream s_3 contains 90 moles.

(*Note:* This is a way to get CO_2 out of a combustion gas, but it doesn't get it out of the environment. The CO_2 is still present. It has simply been moved from one stream to another. Still, a process like this might be used as part of a solution to the global warming problem. By heating up the MEA solution, the CO_2 comes out of solution. This process is a way to obtain concentrated CO_2 , which might then be used for another purpose. For example, it could be used by growing plants or perhaps turned into ethanol and used as a fuel to replace fossil fuels.)

4.5.6 Determinant

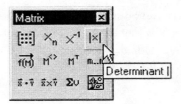

The *determinant* is a scalar value that can be computed from a square matrix. The process for computing a determinant is fairly straightforward, but tedious for matrices larger than 3×3. Fortunately, Mathcad will compute determinants automatically. The determinant operator is found on the Matrix Toolbar.

For a 1×1 matrix (a single value), the determinant of the matrix is simply the value of the matrix. Vertical bars are used to indicate the determinant. For example.

$$|4| = 4$$

For a 2×2 matrix, the determinant is computed by multiplying diagonal elements and subtracting the results:

$$A := \begin{bmatrix} A_{00} & A_{01} \\ A_{10} & A_{11} \end{bmatrix}$$

$$D = |A| = A_{00} \cdot A_{11} - A_{10} \cdot A_{01}$$

For larger matrices, the determinants are found by breaking down the matrix into smaller units called *cofactors*, calculating the determinants for each cofactor, and summing the results. The general equation for computing a determinant is

$$D = A_{i0} + C_{i0} + A_{i1}\ C_{i1} + \ldots + A_{i(n-1)}\ C_{i(n-1)} \qquad i = 0\ \ldots\ (n-1)$$

where the C's are the cofactors. For a 3×3 matrix, the cofactors are computed as follows:

- The cofactor for element A_{00} is computed from the shaded terms in the following matrix and is $C_{00} = +(A_{11} \cdot A_{22} - A_{21} \cdot A_{12})$ (*note the plus sign before this cofactor*):

$$\begin{array}{ccc} \boxed{A_{00}} & A_{01} & A_{02} \\ A_{10} & A_{11} & A_{12} \\ A_{20} & A_{21} & A_{22} \end{array}$$

- For element A_{10}, the cofactor is $C_{10} = -(A_{01} \cdot A_{22} - A_{21} \cdot A_{02})$ (*note the minus sign before this cofactor*):

$$\begin{array}{ccc} A_{00} & A_{01} & A_{02} \\ \boxed{A_{10}} & A_{11} & A_{12} \\ A_{20} & A_{21} & A_{22} \end{array}$$

- For element A_{20}, the cofactor is $C_{20} = +(A_{01} \cdot A_{12} - A_{11} \cdot A_{02})$ (*note the plus sign before this cofactor*):

$$\begin{array}{ccc} A_{00} & A_{01} & A_{02} \\ A_{10} & A_{11} & A_{12} \\ \boxed{A_{20}} & A_{21} & A_{22} \end{array}$$

- The sign in front of the cofactor equation alternates between plus and minus, depending on the position of the cofactor in the matrix, with C_{00} (the top-left element) always taking the plus sign:

$$\begin{array}{ccc} \boxed{+} & - & + \\ - & + & - \\ + & - & + \end{array}$$

With numbers, the process looks like this:

$$F := \begin{bmatrix} 2 & 3 & 4 \\ 7 & 2 & 5 \\ 8 & 11 & 6 \end{bmatrix}$$

$$
\begin{aligned}
C_{0,0} &:= 2 \cdot 6 - 11 \cdot 4 & C_{0,0} &= -32 \\
C_{1,0} &:= -(3 \cdot 6 - 11 \cdot 5) & C_{1,0} &= 37 \\
C_{2,0} &:= 3 \cdot 4 - 2 \cdot 5 & C_{2,0} &= 2 \\
D &:= F_{0,0} \cdot C_{0,0} + F_{1,0} \cdot C_{1,0} + F_{2,0} \cdot C_{2,0} & D &= 211
\end{aligned}
$$

Or, using the determinant operator from the Matrix Toolbox, we obtain

$$|\ F\ | = 211$$

(*Note:* In the preceding example, the determinant was computed using cofactors for elements in the left column. Actually, you can use cofactors for the elements in any column or row to compute the determinant.)

4.5.7 How Is the Determinant Used?

The determinant shows up in a number of engineering calculations, but one of the most straightforward applications is using a determinant to find out whether a system of simultaneous linear equations has a unique solution. If the determinant of the coefficient matrix is nonzero, then the system has a unique solution. For example, we could have checked whether the coefficient matrix in the last Application example could be solved by calculating its determinant:

$$C := \begin{bmatrix} 0.02 & -0.12 & -0.01 \\ 0 & -0.01 & -0.99 \\ 0.98 & -0.87 & 0 \end{bmatrix} \qquad |C| = 0.099$$

Because the determinant is nonzero, there should be a solution, and there is.

(*Note:* The calculation of determinants suffers from the same problem encountered with matrix inversion: For a large matrix, the number of calculations required leads to round-off errors on digital computers.)

PRACTICE!

Each of the two systems of equations that follow has no unique solution. Verify this statement by calculating the determinant of the coefficient matrix.

a. The second and third equations are identical:
$$2 \cdot x_1 + 3 \cdot x_2 + 1 \cdot x_3 = 12$$
$$1 \cdot x_1 + 4 \cdot x_2 + 7 \cdot x_3 = 16$$
$$1 \cdot x_1 + 4 \cdot x_2 + 7 \cdot x_3 = 16$$

b. The third equation is the sum of the first and second equations:
$$2 \cdot x_1 + 3 \cdot x_2 + 1 \cdot x_3 = 12$$
$$1 \cdot x_1 + 4 \cdot x_2 + 7 \cdot x_3 = 16$$
$$3 \cdot x_1 + 7 \cdot x_2 + 8 \cdot x_3 = 28$$

PRACTICE!

The following two systems of equations might have solutions. Use the determinant to find out for sure if they do.

a.
$$2 \cdot x_1 + 3 \cdot x_2 + 1 \cdot x_3 = 12$$
$$1 \cdot x_1 + 4 \cdot x_2 + 7 \cdot x_3 = 16$$
$$4 \cdot x_1 + 1 \cdot x_2 + 3 \cdot x_3 = 9$$
b.
$$2 \cdot x_1 + 3 \cdot x_2 + 1 \cdot x_3 = 12$$
$$1 \cdot x_1 + 4 \cdot x_2 + 7 \cdot x_3 = 16$$
$$7 \cdot x_1 + 18 \cdot x_2 + 23 \cdot x_3 = 48$$

4.6   ARRAY FUNCTIONS

Several functions are sometimes useful when one is working with arrays. The min(A) and max(A) functions find the minimum and maximum values in the array specified as the function's parameter:

$$C := \begin{bmatrix} 1 & 1 \\ 2 & 8 \\ 3 & 27 \\ 4 & 64 \\ 5 & 125 \end{bmatrix}$$

$$\max(C) = 125$$
$$\min(C) = 1$$

$$a := \begin{bmatrix} 3 \\ 2 \\ 7 \\ 4 \end{bmatrix}$$

$$\max(a) = 7$$
$$\min(a) = 2$$

Four additional functions return information on the size of an array or a vector. The cols(A) function returns the number of columns in array A, while the rows(A) function returns the number of rows in A. For vectors, there is a length(v) function that returns the number of elements in the vector and a last(v) function that returns the index of the last element of the vector. For example, we might have

$$C := \begin{bmatrix} 1 & 1 \\ 2 & 8 \\ 3 & 27 \\ 4 & 64 \\ 5 & 125 \end{bmatrix}$$

$$\text{rows}(C) = 5$$
$$\text{cols}(C) = 2$$

$$a := \begin{bmatrix} 3 \\ 2 \\ 7 \\ 4 \end{bmatrix}$$

$$\text{rows}(a) = 4$$
$$\text{cols}(a) = 1$$
$$\text{length}(a) = 4$$
$$\text{last}(a) = 3$$

$$a_3 = 4$$

Note that the rows(A) and cols(A) functions work with either matrices or vectors, but the length(v) and last(v) functions operate only on vectors. The value returned by last(v) will be one less than that returned by length(v) as long as the matrix ORIGIN is zero.

4.6.1 Sorting

There are three functions for sorting vectors and arrays in Mathcad. The sort(v) function arranges the elements of a (v) vector in increasing order. You can combine the sort(v) function with the reverse(v) function to get the elements of a vector arranged in decreasing order:

$$a_1 := \text{sort}(a)$$

$$a_1 := \begin{bmatrix} 2 \\ 3 \\ 4 \\ 7 \end{bmatrix}$$

$$a_2 := \text{reverse}(a1)$$

$$a_2 := \begin{bmatrix} 7 \\ 4 \\ 3 \\ 2 \end{bmatrix}$$

Note that the `reverse(v)` function is not a sorting function: It doesn't perform a sort, but just reverses the order of the elements in a vector.

There are two sorting functions for arrays: `csort(A,n)` and `rsort(A,n)`. The `csort(A,n)` function arranges the rows of array A such that the elements in column n will be in increasing order. To sort array H on the left column, use the command `csort(H,0)`, as shown here:

$$H := \begin{bmatrix} 7 & 9 & 2 \\ 4 & 8 & 1 \\ 8 & 2 & 0 \\ 3 & 7 & 4 \end{bmatrix}$$

$$H_1 := \text{csort}(H, 0) \qquad H_1 = \begin{bmatrix} 3 & 7 & 4 \\ 4 & 8 & 1 \\ 7 & 9 & 2 \\ 8 & 2 & 0 \end{bmatrix}$$

To sort array H on the rightmost column, use the command `csort(H,2)`:

$$H_2 := \text{csort}(H, 2) \qquad H_2 = \begin{bmatrix} 8 & 2 & 0 \\ 4 & 8 & 1 \\ 7 & 9 & 2 \\ 3 & 7 & 4 \end{bmatrix}$$

To rearrange the columns so that the elements in the top row are in increasing order, use the `rsort(A,0)` command:

$$H_3 := \text{rsort}(H, 0) \qquad H_3 = \begin{bmatrix} 2 & 7 & 9 \\ 1 & 4 & 8 \\ 0 & 8 & 2 \\ 4 & 3 & 7 \end{bmatrix}$$

APPLICATIONS: TOTAL RECYCLE

One of the many tests performed during NASA's Lunar-Mars Life Support Test Project III (LMLSTP III) was the cultivation of wheat to consume CO_2, produce O_2, and contribute to the food requirements of the crew. The gas that flows between the crew's cabin and the plant growth center passes through two concentrators, one for oxygen and the other for carbon dioxide:

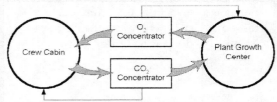

Let us take a look at how Mathcad's matrix-handling features can help us determine the flow rates through the plant growth center and the O_2 concentrator. In the following figure, the unknown streams have been labeled S_1 through S_3:

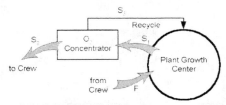

The feed to the plant growth center, F, will be treated as a known commodity. NASA's Web site[1] states that the concentration of CO_2 in stream F is 85 to 95% pure CO_2. (We'll assume 85% on a molar basis.) The amount of CO_2 entering the plant growth center must be equal to the amount of CO_2 being generated by the crew. The LMLSTP III had a crew of four, and a typical rate of CO_2 production for a resting person is 200 ml/min.[2]

With the understanding that the crew is working, not resting, we'll assume a CO_2 generation rate of 1000 ml/min. This is the rate at which CO_2 enters the plant growth center, and it is 85% of F. The remainder of F is assumed to contain O_2 and N_2 in the ratio commonly found in air: 21:79 (21 moles of O_2 for every 79 moles of N_2). With these (numerous) assumptions, the contents of stream F can be summarized as follows:

F Contains:	0.0444 moles (per minute)
mole fractions:	0.8500 or 85 mole % CO_2
	0.0313 or 3.13 mole % O_2
	0.1187 or 11.87 mole % N_2

From other statements in the NASA Web site and a good healthy assumption about how the O_2 concentrator works, the compositions of the other streams are expected to be something like the following:

MOLE FRACTION	S_1	S_2	S_3
CO_2	0.00079	0	0.00080
O_2	0.20983	0.85000	0.20665
N_2	0.78938	0.15000	0.79255

With these compositions, we can write material balances to find the molar flow rates in streams S_1 through S_3.

Since CO_2 is being consumed and O_2 is being produced in the growth center, the simplest balance we can write is on N_2 (no reaction term is needed):N_2 balance around the plant growth center:

$$N_2 \text{ in F} + N_2 \text{ in } S_3 = N_2 \text{ in } S_1$$

$$0.1187 \cdot 0.0444 \text{ mole} + 0.79255 \cdot S_3 = 0.78938 \cdot S_1$$

There is no reaction in the O_2 concentrator, so simple material balances could be written on any component. However, the very small amounts of CO_2 and the very small change in CO_2 composition across the O_2 concentrator make a CO_2 balance a poor choice, because these low-precision values can turn into large errors. So we write O_2 and N_2 balances around the concentrator:O_2 balance around the O_2 concentrator:

$$O_2 \text{ in } S_1 = O_2 \text{ in } S_3 - O_2 \text{ in } S_3$$

$$0.20983 \cdot S_1 = 0.20665 \cdot S_3 - 0.85 \cdot S_2$$

N_2 balance around the O_2 concentrator:

$$N_2 \text{ in } S_1 = N_2 \text{ in } S_3 - N_2 \text{ in } S_2 2$$

$$0.78938 \cdot S_1 = 0.79255 \cdot S_3 - 0.15 \cdot S_2$$

In matrix form, the coefficient matrix and right-hand-side vector for these three equations look like this:

$$F := 0.0444 \cdot \text{mole}$$

$$C := \begin{bmatrix} 0.78938 & -0.15 & -0.79255 \\ -0.78938 & 0 & 0.79255 \\ 0.20983 & -0.85 & -0.20665 \end{bmatrix}$$

$$r := \begin{bmatrix} 0 \\ -0.1187 \cdot F \\ 0 \end{bmatrix} \cdot \text{mol}$$

The coefficient matrix C can then be inverted and multiplied by the right-hand-side vector r to find the flow rates in the three unknown streams:

$$C^{-1} = \begin{bmatrix} -1.414 \cdot 10^3 & -1.349 \cdot 10^3 & 249.591 \\ -6.667 & -6.667 & 0 \\ -1.409 \cdot 10^3 & -1.343 \cdot 10^3 & 248.593 \end{bmatrix}$$

$$S := C^{-1} \cdot r \begin{bmatrix} 7.111 \\ 0.035 \\ 7.076 \end{bmatrix} \cdot \text{mol}$$

So the flow rates are $S_1 = 7.111$ mole, (per minute), $S_2 = 0.035$ mole, and $S_3 = 7.076$ moles.

[1]<http://pet.jsc.nasa.gov/alssee>.
[2]This value is from the "standard man data" in R. C. Seagrave *Biomedical Applications of Heat and Mass Transfer*. Iowa State (Ames, IA: Iowa State University Press, 1971.)

4.6.2 Summary

In this chapter, we learned about how to work with matrices in Mathcad. Matrix values can be entered from the keyboard, computed from equations, read from data files, or copied from other programs. Once a matrix exists, there are a variety of ways it can be modified and manipulated to insert or delete rows or columns or to choose a portion of the matrix and assign it to another variable.

The standard array operations were described, including addition, multiplication, transposition, and inversion. The way Mathcad handles these operations is summarized in the following two lists:

MATHCAD SUMMARY

Matrix Fundamentals

ORIGIN	Changes the starting value of the first array element (0 by default).
[Ctrl-M]	Opens the matrix dialog to create a matrix and to insert or delete rows or columns.
Matrix(r,c,f)	Creates a matrix with r rows and c columns, using function f. Function f is user defined and must be a function of two variables.
Identity(c)	Creates an identity matrix with c rows and columns.
[Ctrl-6]	Selects a single column of a matrix.
Submatrix(A, r_{start}, r_{stop}, c_{start}, cstop)	Extracts a portion of matrix A.
Augment(A$_1$, A$_2$)	Combines arrays A$_1$ and A$_2$ side by side
Stack(A$_1$, A$_2$)	Stacks array A1 on top of array A$_2$.
READPRN(*path*)	Reads array values from a text file.
WRITEPRN(*path*)	Writes array values to a text file.

Matrix Operations

+	Addition of matrices.
[Shift-8]	Matrix multiplication.
→	Vectorize (from the Matrix Toolbar)—used when you want element-by-element multiplication instead of matrix multiplication.
T	Transpose (from the Matrix Toolbar).
[Shift-6]	Invert a matrix.
|M|	Determinant (from the Matrix Toolbar).
sort(v)	Sorts vector v into ascending order.
reverse(v)	Reverses the order of vector v—this operation is used after sort(v) to get a vector sorted into descending order.
csort(A,n)	Sorts array A so that the values in column n are in ascending order.
rsort(A,n)	Sorts array A so that the values in row n are in ascending order.

KEY TERMS

array	identity matrix	range variable
array origin	inverting	transpose
determinant	matrix	vector
Element-by-element multiplication	matrix multiplication	vectorize

Problems

1. MATRIX OPERATIONS

    Given the matrices and vectors

    $$I = \begin{bmatrix} 1 & 0 & 0 & 0 \\ 0 & 1 & 0 & 0 \\ 0 & 0 & 1 & 0 \\ 0 & 0 & 0 & 1 \end{bmatrix}, \quad a = \begin{bmatrix} 1 \\ 2 \\ 3 \\ 4 \end{bmatrix}, \quad b = \begin{bmatrix} 2 & 4 & 6 & 8 \end{bmatrix}, \text{ and } C = \begin{bmatrix} 2 & 3 & 7 & 11 \\ 1 & 4 & 3 & 9 \\ 0 & 6 & 5 & 1 \\ 1 & 8 & 4 & 2 \end{bmatrix},$$

    which of the following matrix operations are allowed? For each operation that can be performed, what is the result?

    a. I^T transpose the identity matrix

    b. $|a|$ find the determinant of vector a

    c. a^{-1} invert the a vector

    d. $|C|$ find the determinant of matrix C

    e. C^{-1} invert the C matrix

    f. $I \cdot a$ multiply the identity matrix by vector

    g. $a \cdot b$ multiply the a vector by vector b

    h. $b \cdot a$ multiply the b vector by vector a

    i. $C^{-1} \cdot a$ multiply the inverse of the C matrix by vector a

2. SIMULTANEOUS EQUATIONS

    The arrays that follow represent coefficient matrices and right-hand-side vectors for sets of simultaneous linear equations written

    [C] [x] = [r]

    in matrix form. Calculate the determinant of these coefficient matrices to see whether each set of simultaneous equations can be solved, and if so, solve for the solution vector [x].

    $$C = \begin{bmatrix} 3 & 1 & 5 \\ 2 & 3 & -1 \\ -1 & 4 & 0 \end{bmatrix}, \qquad r = \begin{bmatrix} 20 \\ 5 \\ 7 \end{bmatrix};$$

    $$C = \begin{bmatrix} 4 & 2 & 1 \\ 2 & 3 & 0 \\ 0 & 4 & -1 \end{bmatrix}, \qquad r = \begin{bmatrix} 18 \\ 6 \\ -2 \end{bmatrix};$$

    $$C = \begin{bmatrix} 7 & 3 & 1 \\ 2 & -5 & 6 \\ 1 & 5 & 1 \end{bmatrix}, \qquad r = \begin{bmatrix} 108 \\ -62 \\ 56 \end{bmatrix};$$

    $$C = \begin{bmatrix} 4 & 2 & 1 & 0 \\ 2 & 3 & 0 & 1 \\ 0 & 4 & -1 & 3 \\ 2 & 1 & 4 & 2 \end{bmatrix}, \qquad r = \begin{bmatrix} 13 \\ 8 \\ 4 \\ 19 \end{bmatrix}.$$

3. SIMULTANEOUS EQUATIONS, II
    Write the following sets of simultaneous equations in matrix form, and solve (if possible):

    a. $3x_1 + 1x_2 + 5x_3 = 20$
        $2x_1 + 3x_2 - 1x_3 = 5$
        $- 1x_1 + 4x_2 = 7$

    b. $6x_1 + 2x_2 + 8x_3 = 14$
        $x_1 + 3x_2 + 4x_3 = 5$
        $5x_1 + 6x_2 + 2x_3 = 7$

    c. $4y_1 + 2y_2 + 1y_3 + 5y_4 = 52.9$
        $3y_1 + y_2 + 4y_3 + 7y_4 = 74.2$
        $2y_1 + 3y_2 + y_3 + 6y_4 = 58.3$
        $3y_1 + y_2 + y_3 + 3y_4 = 34.2$

4. ELEMENT-BY-ELEMENT MATRIX MATHEMATICS
    In the following heat exchanger, cold fluid flows through the inside tube and is warmed from T_{C_in} to T_{C_out} by energy from the hot fluid surrounding the inside tube:

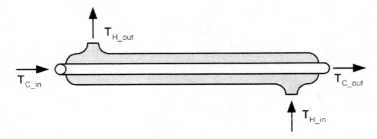

The temperature change of the cold fluid depends on the amount of energy the fluid picks up during the time it is flowing through the exchanger, that is, the rate at which energy is acquired by the cold fluid. The energy and the change in temperature are, respectively,

$$q_{COLD} = \dot{m}\, C_p\, \Delta T_{COLD}$$

$$\Delta T_{COLD} = T_{C\_out} - T_{C\_in}.$$

If you performed a series of experiments on this heat exchanger, you might vary the flow rate of the cold fluid to determine the effect on the energy acquired by the cold fluid. Suppose you did this and got the following results:

Experiment	ColdFluid Rate	Heat Capacity	T_{C_in}	$T_{C\_out}q_{COLD}$	q_{COLD}
	kg/ minute	joule/ kg K	°C	°C	watts
1	2	4187	6	62	
2	5	4187	6	43	
3	10	4187	6	26	
4	15	4187	6	20	
5	20	4187	6	14	

You could solve for the five q_{COLD} values one at a time, but if you create vectors containing the cold fluid rate values and the δT_{COLD} values, Mathcad can solve for all of the q_{COLD} values at once by using element-by-element matrix mathematics.

Create two matrices like the following:

$$\text{flow} := \begin{bmatrix} 2 \\ 5 \\ 10 \\ 15 \\ 20 \end{bmatrix} \cdot \frac{kg}{min} \qquad \Delta T_{COLD} := \begin{bmatrix} 62-6 \\ 43-6 \\ 26-6 \\ 20-6 \\ 14-6 \end{bmatrix} \cdot K$$

Then solve for all five Q_{COLD} values using element-by-element matrix mathematics. The equations is

$$q_{COLD} := \overrightarrow{\text{flow} \cdot C_p \cdot \Delta T_{COLD}}$$

The arrow over the right side of the equation is the *vectorize* operator (from the Matrix Toolbar). It is used to tell Mathcad to multiply element by element and is required for this problem.

(*Note:* Degrees Celsius is not a defined unit in Mathcad, but a temperature change of one degree Celsius is equal to a temperature change of one degree on the kelvin scale—so kelvins can be specified for the δT_{COLD} matrix.)

5.   ELEMENT-BY-ELEMENT MATRIX MATHEMATICS

The preceding problem considered only the energy acquired by the cold fluid as it passed through the heat exchanger. This problem considers the energy transferred from the hot fluid to the cold fluid (the energy passing across the tube of the heat exchanger.) The diagram is the same as before:

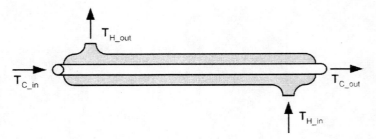

The rate at which energy crosses a heat exchanger tube is predicted with the use of a heat transfer coefficient h. The equation is

$$q_{HX} = h\,A\,\Delta T_{LM}$$

where A is the area through which the energy passes (the surface area of the tube) and δT_{LM} is the *log mean temperature difference*, defined, for the heat exchanger shown, as

$$\Delta T_{LM} = \frac{(T_{H\_out} - T_{C\_in}) - (T_{H\_in} - T_{C\_out})}{\ln\left[\dfrac{(T_{H\_out} - T_{C\_in})}{(T_{H\_in} - T_{C\_out})}\right]} = \frac{\Delta T_{left} - \Delta T_{right}}{\ln\left[\dfrac{\Delta T_{left}}{\Delta T_{right}}\right]}$$

Given the data that follow, use element-by-element matrix mathematics to determine all of the q_{HX} values with one calculation.

Experiment	H	A	T_{C_in}	T_{C_out}	T_{H_in}	T_{H_out}	q_{HX}
	W/m² K	m²	°C	°C	°C	°C	watts
1	300	0.376	6	36	75	54	
2	450	0.376	6	48	73	51	
3	600	0.376	6	52	71	47	
4	730	0.376	6	57	77	40	
5	1200	0.376	6	60	74	35	

(*Note:* The natural logarithm is not defined for matrices, so element-by-element mathematics is required for this problem. Use the *vectorize* operator (from the Matrix Toolbar) over the entire right side of defining equations to tell Mathcad to use element-by-element mathematics.)

6. MATERIAL BALANCES ON AN EXTRACTOR

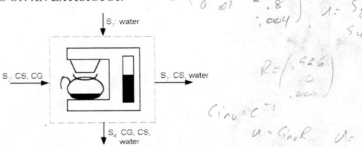

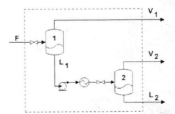

This problem focuses on a low-cost, high-performance chemical extraction unit: a drip coffeemaker. The ingredients are water, coffee solubles (CS), and coffee grounds (CG). Stream S_1 is water only, and the coffeemaker is designed to hold 1 liter. Stream S_2 is the dry coffee placed in the filter and contains 99% grounds and 1% soluble ingredients. The product coffee contains 0.4% CS and 99.6% water. Finally, the waste product (S_3) contains 80% CG, 19.6% water, and 0.4% CS. (All percentages are on a volume basis.)

Write material balances on water, CS, and CG, and then solve the material balances for the volumes S_2 through S_4.

7. FLASH DISTILLATION

When a hot, pressurized liquid is pumped into a tank (flash unit) at a lower pressure, the liquid boils rapidly. This rapid boiling is called a *flash*. If the liquid contains a mixture of chemicals, the vapor and liquid leaving the flash unit will have different compositions, and the flash unit can be used as a separator. The physical principle involved is vapor-liquid equilibrium: The vapor and the liquid leaving the flash unit are in equilibrium. This allows the composition of the outlet streams to be determined from the operating temperature and pressure of the flash unit. Multiple flash units can be used together to separate multicomponent mixtures.

A mixture of methanol, butanol, and ethylene glycol is fed to a flash unit operating at 165°C and 7 atm. The liquid from the first flash unit is recompressed, reheated, and sent to a second flash unit operating at 105°C and 1 atm. The compositions of the feed stream F and the three product streams are listed in the following table:

| | MASS FRACTION IN STREAM | | | |
COMPONENT	FEED	V_1	V_2	L_2
Methanol	0.300	0.716	0.533	0.086
Butanol	0.400	0.268	0.443	0.388
Ethylene Glycol	0.300	0.016	0.024	0.526

The mixture is fed to the process at a rate of 10,000 kg/h. Write material balances for each chemical, and then solve for the mass flow rate of each product stream (V_1, V_2, L_2). A material balance is simply a mathematical statement that all of the methanol (for example) going into the process has to come out again (assuming a steady state and no chemical reactions.) The methanol balance is as follows:

$$\text{methanol in the feed} = \text{methanol in } V_1 + \text{methanol in } V_2 + \text{methanol in } L_2;$$

$$0.300 \cdot (10{,}000 \text{ kg/h}) = 0.716 \cdot V_1 + 0.533 \cdot V_2 + 0.086 \cdot L_2.$$

8. **FINDING THE MEDIAN GRADE**

It is common for instructors to report the average grade on an examination. An alternative way to let students know how their scores compare with the rest of the class is to find the *median* score. If the scores are sorted, the median score is the value in the middle of the data set.

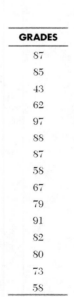

GRADES

87
85
43
62
97
88
87
58
67
79
91
82
80
73
58

a.   Use the `sort( )` function to sort the 15 scores (elements 0 to 14) listed at the left, and then display the value of element 7 in the sorted array. Element 7 will hold the median score for the sorted grades.

b.   Check your result by using Mathcad's `median( )` function on the original vector of grades.

9.   **CURRENTS IN MULTILOOP CIRCUITS**

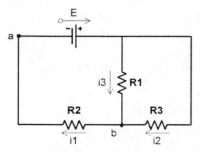

Multiloop circuits are analyzed using Kirchhoff's voltage law, and Kirchhoff's current law, namely,

At any junction in a circuit, the input current(s) must equal the output current(s).

The latter is simply a statement of conservation of current: All of the electrons entering a junction have to leave again, at least at steady state.

Applying the current law at point b in the accompanying diagram yields

$$i_3 + i_2 = i_1.$$

Applying the voltage law to the left loop and the overall loop provides two more equations:

$$E - i_3 R_1 - i_1 R_2 = 0;$$
$$E - i_2 R_3 - i_1 R_2 = 0.$$

We thus have three equations in the unknowns i_1, i_2, i_3.

Use the following resistance values, and solve the system of simultaneous equations to determine the current in each portion of the circuit:

$$E = 9 \text{ volts};$$
$$R1 = 20 \text{ ohms};$$
$$R2 = 30 \text{ ohms};$$
$$R3 = 40 \text{ ohms}.$$

10. THE WHEATSTONE BRIDGE

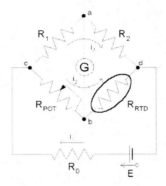

Resistance temperature devices (RTDs) are often used as temperature sensors. As the temperature of the device changes, its resistance changes. If you can determine an RTD's resistance, you can look on a table to find the temperature. A circuit known as a Wheatstone bridge can be used to measure unknown resistances. In the preceding figure, an RTD has been built into the bridge as the unknown resistance.

To use the Wheatstone bridge, the adjustable resistor R_{POT} (called a potentiometer) is adjusted until the galvanometer G shows that points a and b are at the same potential. Once the bridge has been adjusted so that no current is flowing through the galvanometer (because there is no difference in potential between a and b), the reading on the potentiometer and the known resistances R_1 and R_2 can be used to compute the resistance of the RTD.

How Does It Work?

Because resistors R_1 and R_{POT} come together at point c, and we know that the voltages at a and b are the same, there must be the same voltage drop across R_1 and R_{POT} (not the same current), so

$$i_3 \cdot R_1 = i_2 \cdot R_{POT}.$$

Similarly, because R_2 and R_{RTD} are connected at point d, we can say that

$$i_3 \cdot R_2 = i_2 \cdot R_{RDT}.$$

If you solve for $i3$ in one equation and substitute into the other, you get

$$R_{RDT} = R_{POT} \frac{R_2}{R_1}.$$

In this way, if you know R_1 and R_2 and have a reading on the potentiometer, you can calculate R_{RDT}.

a. Given the following resistances, what is R_{RDT}? Assume that a 9-volt battery is used for E.

$$R_0 = 20 \text{ ohms};$$
$$R_1 = 10 \text{ ohms};$$
$$R_2 = 5 \text{ ohms};$$
$$R_{POT} \text{ adjusted to } 12.3 \text{ ohms}.$$

b. Use Kirchhoff's current law at either point c or d, and Kirchhoff's voltage law to determine the values of i_1, i_2, and i_3.

11. STEADY-STATE CONDUCTION, II

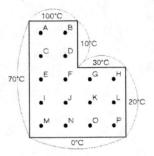

In the previous problem, Laplace's equation was applied to steady-state conduction in a square region. Actually, the equation can be applied to any region composed of rectangles or any shape that can be approximated with rectangles. Again, the final version of the equation presented in the last problem does require that the distance between the points be the same in the x and y directions.

Apply Laplace's equation to the foregoing L-shaped region, and determine the temperatures at points A through P.

12. TRAFFIC FLOW, part II

Since the number of vehicles entering and leaving an intersection must be equal, the four intersections in the following road pattern allow four vehicle balances to be written that can be solved for four unknown vehicle counts.

   a.   Write vehicle balances for each of the four intersections.

   b.   Solve for the four unknown traffic counts using matrix methods.

   c.   Is there any evidence that people are making U-turns in the intersections?

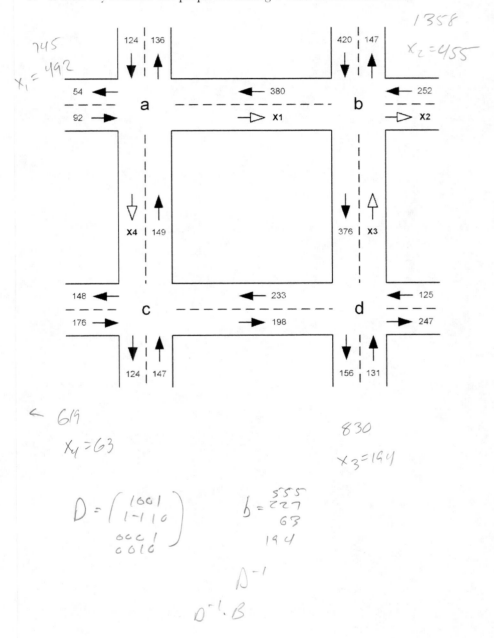

$$745$$
$$x_1 = 492$$

$$1358$$
$$x_2 = 455$$

$$\leftarrow 619$$
$$x_4 = 63$$

$$830$$
$$x_3 = 194$$

$$D = \begin{pmatrix} 1 & 0 & 0 & 1 \\ 1 & -1 & 1 & 0 \\ 0 & 0 & 0 & 1 \\ 0 & 0 & 1 & 0 \end{pmatrix}$$

$$b = \begin{matrix} 555 \\ 227 \\ 63 \\ 194 \end{matrix}$$

$$D^{-1}$$

$$D^{-1} \cdot B$$

5

Data Analysis Functions

OBJECTIVES

- know how to create graphs in Mathcad, including element-by-element graphing using range variables, graphing one vector against another; and producing quickPlots of functions-letting Mathcad automatically evaluate a function over a range of values and plot the result;
- understand Mathcad's built-in functions for statistical analysis;
- know how to use Mathcad's interpolation functions, including: linear interpolation and spline interpolation; and
- know how to fit linear regression curves to data.

5.1   RISK ANALYSIS

Each year, we read in the newspapers of earthquakes with terrible consequences in terms of lost lives and damaged property. There have also been serious earthquakes in highly populated areas in California, with, relatively speaking, considerably less damage. The difference is due to *risk analysis* and *risk management*. Because of the serious threat earthquakes pose in many parts of California, the state has spent a great deal of time and effort trying to learn what might happen in an earthquake (risk analysis) and has invested heavily in trying to minimize the consequences of a major earthquake (risk management).

Because engineers work on projects that can affect large numbers of people, safety and risk management are a standard practice. What happens if a device fails? If a power line fails, can we get power to the hospital from another direction? Can we use an inflatable bag to improve passenger safety in an automobile accident? But what about the safety of small children in automobiles with air bags? These questions are all related to risk analysis and management.

Understanding the potential risks associated with a process or product requires a thorough knowledge of the process or product, as well as the ability and willingness to consider what might go wrong. What would happen if that pipe leaving that vessel of toxic material were to break? There's usually someone who will say, "It'll never happen. Pipes don't just break." While it's true that pipes don't spontaneously give way, they do corrode with time, and back hoe can break a pipe instantly. The idea is that you have to be willing to think outside of normal operating procedure to perform a risk analysis.

It takes a lot of work to anticipate how a process or product might fail and to quantify the outcome of a potential failure. If that pipe breaks, how far will the toxin, flame, or explosion spread? There are models to help quantify risk, but they require good data on the products and processes involved. Getting the data into a form that the models can use requires a lot of analysis. That's why risk analysis is a good lead-in to a chapter on Mathcad's data analysis functions.

5.2   GRAPHING WITH MATHCAD

Engineers spend a lot of time analyzing data. By looking at data from a current design, you can learn what can be changed to make the device, system, or process work better. Mathcad's data analysis functions can provide a lot of help in understanding and evaluating data sets.

One of the most fundamental steps in analyzing data is visualizing the data, usually in the form of a graph. Mathcad provides a variety of graphing options.

5.2.1   Plotting Vector against Vector

The easiest way to create a graph in Mathcad is simply to plot one vector against another. For example, a vector of temperature values can be plotted against a vector of time values. This method works well for many data analysis situations, because the data are often already available in vector form, as in the following example:

Time =

	0
0	0
1	1
2	2
3	3
4	4
5	5
6	6
7	7
8	8
9	9

• min   Temp =

	0
0	298
1	299
2	301
3	304
4	306
5	309
6	312
7	316
8	319
9	322

• K

When you plot one vector against another, the vectors must each have the same number of elements. The preceding vectors each have 10 elements, so they can be plotted against each other. To create an x-y graph, use the Graph Toolbox and click on the X-Y Plot button, or use the keyboard shortcut [Shift-2]. The result is as follows:

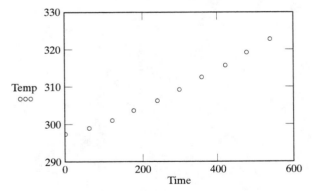

Note that the temperature values look fine, but the time values are not the same as those shown in the Time vector. Mathcad always plots values in its default (base) units. The base unit for temperature (in the default SI unit system) is kelvins, so the temperature values were unaffected. The time values were plotted as Mathcad saved them, in seconds. There is a trick that is sometimes used to get the right values to display on the graph: You can get the values in minutes by dividing the Time on the x-axis by minutes, as shown in the following figure:

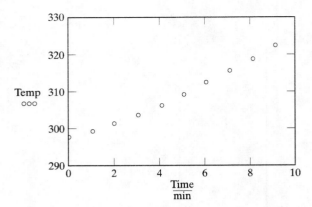

Now the right values are displayed, but the axis labels are hard to interpret. An alternative is to remove the units from the Time and Temp vectors and then plot the values. Then you can add your own axis labels to indicate the units. (Double-click on the graph to add axis labels.) Note that removing the units from the Temp values is not really necessary in this example, but it was done to demonstrate a general approach to graphing values with units. Using this approach, we obtain

$$Time_{plot} := \frac{Time}{min}$$

$$Temp_{plot} := \frac{Temp}{K}$$

The plotted result is

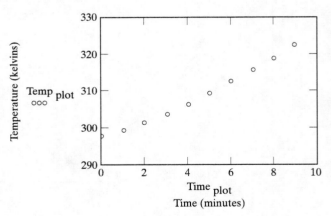

The process of removing the units and plotting only values is exactly what is being accomplished with the "trick" used to plot time on the previous graph. Hopefully, making the process more explicit and including units with the axis labels makes the graph easier to read.

5.2.2 Plotting Multiple Curves

Mathcad allows up to 16 curves on a single graph. If you have two vectors of y values corresponding to the same set of x values, you plot the second curve to the graph as follows:

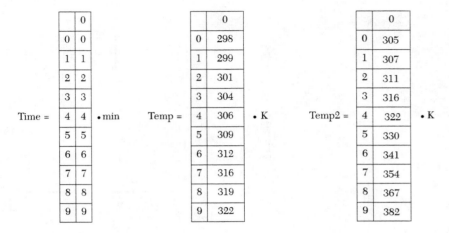

Time = (matrix, column labeled 0)

	0
0	0
1	1
2	2
3	3
4	4
5	5
6	6
7	7
8	8
9	9

· min

Temp =

	0
0	298
1	299
2	301
3	304
4	306
5	309
6	312
7	316
8	319
9	322

· K

Temp2 =

	0
0	305
1	307
2	311
3	316
4	322
5	330
6	341
7	354
8	367
9	382

· K

1. Click on the placeholder on the y-axis.
2. Press [Comma]:

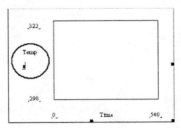

3. Enter the names of the vectors of y values in the placeholders on the y-axis.

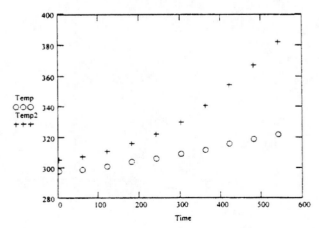

If the vectors you want to plot do not share the same x values, you need to have two vectors indicated on each axis. For example, the following x vectors contain different values, but span nearly the same range, and each x vector has a corresponding y vector (x1 and y1 are related, as are x2 and y2):

$$x1 := \begin{pmatrix} 1 \\ 3 \\ 5 \\ 7 \\ 9 \end{pmatrix} \qquad y1 := \begin{pmatrix} 2 \\ 5 \\ 9 \\ 16 \\ 28 \end{pmatrix} \qquad x2 := \begin{pmatrix} 1 \\ 2 \\ 3 \\ 4 \\ 5 \\ 6 \\ 7 \end{pmatrix} \qquad y2 := \begin{pmatrix} 3 \\ 6 \\ 8 \\ 13 \\ 20 \\ 27 \\ 35 \end{pmatrix}$$

These vectors can be plotted on the same graph by putting two placeholders on each axis. The extra placeholders are created by clicking on the existing placeholders and then pressing [Comma]. (This must be done on both the x-axis and the y-axis.) The result is

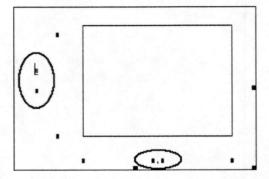

Then fill in the placeholders with the vector names to create the graph:

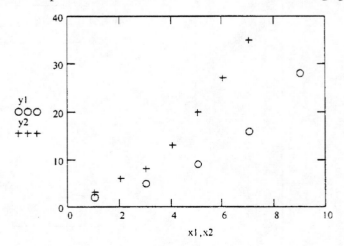

5.2.3 Element-by-Element Plotting

In older versions of Mathcad, the standard method for graphing was to plot one element of one vector against one element of another vector. This method is still available and can sometimes be convenient. To plot the temperature and time vectors element by element, we must define a range variable containing as many elements as each of the vectors. This is easily done using the `last (v)` function as follows:

```
i := 0 .. last(Time)
```

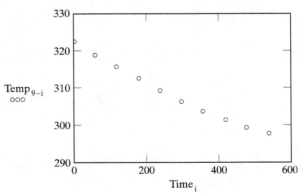

The index of the last element of the `Time` vector was 9, so the range variable, `i`, was defined over the range 0 to 9. The range indicator ("..", or ellipsis) is entered by using the [;] (semicolon) key. The subscripts on the `Temp` and `Time` vectors are array index subscripts, entered by using the [[ ] (left square bracket) key. While this plot looks the same as that created by plotting the vectors directly, the use of the range variable gives you a lot of control over how the elements are plotted. For example, you could change the order of the plotted elements by changing the subscript on the `Temp` vector. The graph will then look like this:

5.2.4 QuickPlots

The final method for creating a graph using Mathcad is a *QuickPlot*, which is used when you want to see what a function looks like. You start by creating an *x-y graph* and then entering the function on the *y*-axis. Functions always have one or more parameters, such as the x in the function sin(x). Next, enter the parameter on the *x*-axis. By default, Mathcad will automatically evaluate the function for a range of parameter values, from -10 to +10. For sin(x), the results will look like this:

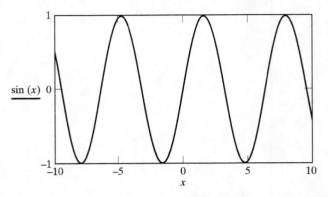

To plot a different range, simply click on the *x*-axis of the graph and change the displayed axis limits:

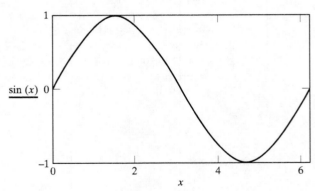

Here, the *x*-axis limits were changed to 0 and 2π to plot one complete *sine wave*.

PRACTICE!

   a. Try QuickPlots of other common functions, like ln(x) and exp(x).

   b. See what Quickplots of the following functions look like (the Φ function is available on the Greek Toolbar, the absolute value operator on the Calculator Toolbar):

      • if (sin(x)>0, -sin(x), sin(x))

      • $\Phi(|\text{mod}(x,2)| -1)$—*this uses the Heaviside step function* Φ *to generate a square wave*

5.2.5 Modifying Graphical Display Attributes

You can change the appearance of a graph by double-clicking anywhere on the graph. This will bring up the graph-formatting dialog box. From this dialog box, you can change the

- axis characteristics (linear or logarithmic plots, for example, and whether grid lines are displayed),
- trace (curve) characteristics, such as the symbol and line style, and
- text and position of labels.

For example, we can use the formatting dialog box to show a curve by using a dashed line and adding grid lines and labels to the sine graph. The necessary changes to the dialog boxes are circled in the figures that follow:

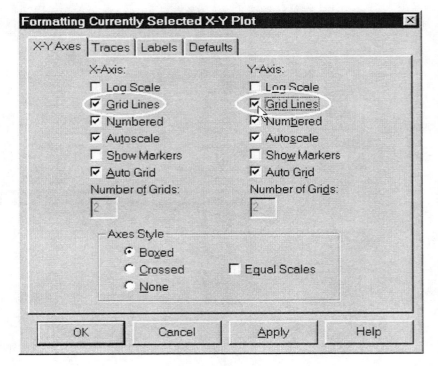

To change a graph's format, double-click in the middle of the graph to open the formatting dialog box. Then turn on the grid lines by using the check boxes on the X-Y Axes panel. Next, switch to the Traces panel and choose a dashed line for trace 1 (there is only one trace, or curve, displayed on this graph):

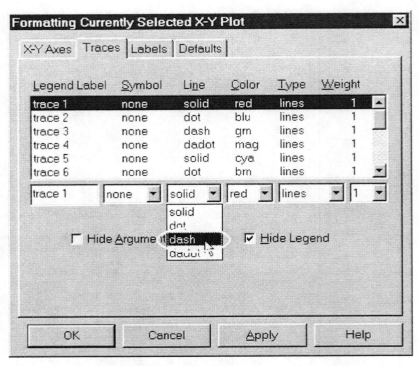

Finally, add a title and axis labels to the graph by using the Labels panel. The screen should look like this:

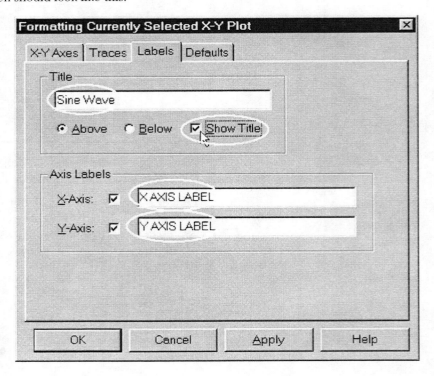

Then, click on the dialog's OK button to make the changes to the graph. The graph will look like this:

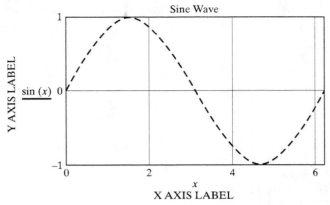

5.3   STATISTICAL FUNCTIONS

Mathcad provides several functions for commonly used statistical calculations, including mean(A), stdev(A), and var(A) to calculate, respectively, the *mean*, *standard deviation*, and *variance* of a population. As the following examples illustrate, these functions work with vectors or matrices, and they can handle units:

APPLICATION: SAMPLES AND POPULATIONS

- The transparency of each windshield on an assembly line might be measured before the windshield is installed. Since every windshield is included in the data set, the data set is called a *population*.
- One out of every thousand windshields might be tested for impact strength (i.e., it might be broken). The results from the broken windshields are used to represent the impact strength of all the windshields. Since the data set does not include all of the windshields, it is called a *sample*. Any time you use a sample, you need to be careful to try to get a *representative sample* (usually a random sample).

$$C = \begin{bmatrix} 1 & 1 \\ 2 & 8 \\ 3 & 27 \\ 4 & 64 \\ 5 & 128 \end{bmatrix} \qquad a = \begin{bmatrix} 3 \\ 2 \\ 7 \\ 4 \end{bmatrix}$$

$C_{avg} := \text{mean}(C)$ $C_{avg} = 24$

$a_{avg} := \text{mean}(a)$ $a_{avg} = 4$

$\text{Temp}_{avg} := \text{mean}(\text{Temp})$ $\text{Temp}_{avg} = 308.733 \bullet K$

$\text{Temp}_{std} := \text{stdev}(\text{Temp})$ $\text{Temp}_{std} = 7.961 \bullet K$

$\text{Temp}_{var} := \text{var}(\text{Temp})$ $\text{Temp}_{var} = 63.377 \bullet K^2$

The functions for the standard deviation and variance of a sample are $\text{Stdev}(v)$ and $\text{Var}(v)$, respectively. The uppercase S and V are used to differentiate these functions for samples from those for populations.

PRACTICE!

The standard deviation lets you know far a typical value is from the mean value of the data set. The data sets shown here have approximately the same mean value. Which has the greatest standard deviation? Use Mathcad's `stdev( )` function to check your result.

$$Set_1 = \begin{bmatrix} 2.5 \\ 2.5 \\ 2.5 \\ 2.5 \\ 2.5 \end{bmatrix} \quad Set_2 = \begin{bmatrix} 2.2 \\ 2.6 \\ 2.6 \\ 2.5 \\ 2.4 \end{bmatrix} \quad Set_3 = \begin{bmatrix} 1.6 \\ 1.6 \\ 2.8 \\ 2.1 \\ 3.8 \end{bmatrix}$$

5.4 INTERPOLATION

If you have a data set—for example, a set of temperature values at various times—and you want to predict a temperature at a new time, you could fit a function to the data and calculate the predicted temperature at the new time. Or you can interpolate between data set values. Mathcad provides a number of functions for linear interpolation and cubic spline interpolation. The *linear interpolation* function, $\text{linterp}(vx, vy, x_{new})$, predicts a new y value at the new x value (specified in the function's argument list) by using a linear interpolation and by using the x values in the data set nearest to the new x value.

As an example, consider the temperature and time data presented at the beginning of this chapter.

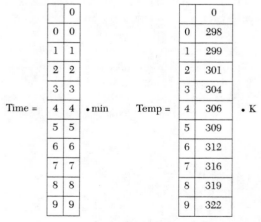

$$Time = \begin{bmatrix} & 0 \\ 0 & 0 \\ 1 & 1 \\ 2 & 2 \\ 3 & 3 \\ 4 & 4 \\ 5 & 5 \\ 6 & 6 \\ 7 & 7 \\ 8 & 8 \\ 9 & 9 \end{bmatrix} \cdot min \qquad Temp = \begin{bmatrix} & 0 \\ 0 & 298 \\ 1 & 299 \\ 2 & 301 \\ 3 & 304 \\ 4 & 306 \\ 5 & 309 \\ 6 & 312 \\ 7 & 316 \\ 8 & 319 \\ 9 & 322 \end{bmatrix} \cdot K$$

The temperature vector includes temperatures at 2 and 3 minutes, but not at 2.3 minutes. We can use the `linterp( )` function to interpolate between the temperature values at 2 and 3 minutes to predict the temperature at 2.3 minutes:

$Temp_{interp} := \text{linterp (Time, Temp, 2.3·min)}$
$Temp_{interp} = 302.165·K$

You can also use `linterp( )` to extrapolate beyond the limits of a data set, although extrapolation is always risky. The previous temperature data were collected from time 0 to 9 minutes. We can extrapolate to a time of 20 minutes by using `lint-erp( )`:

```
Temp_interp := linterp (Time, Temp, 20·min)
Temp_interp = 360.398·K
```

Extrapolation will give you a result, but there is no guarantee that it is correct. Since the result is outside the range of the data set, the result is uncertain. For this data set, the heater might have been turned off after 9 minutes, and the temperatures might have started to decrease with time. Because the data set includes only temperatures between 0 and 9 minutes, we cannot know what happened at later times.

An alternative to linear interpolation is *cubic spline interpolation*. This technique puts a curve (a cubic polynomial) through the data points, which results in a curve that passes through each data point with continuous first and second derivatives. Interpolation for values between points can be done using the cubic polynomial. To use cubic spline interpolation in Mathcad, you first need to fit the cubic polynomial to the data by using the `cspline(vx, vy)` function. This function returns a vector of second-derivative values, vs, that is then used in the interpolation, which is performed with the `interp(vs, vx, vy, x_new)` function:

```
vs := cspline (Time, Temp)
Temp_interp := interp (vs, Time, Temp, 2.3·min)
Temp_interp = 302.136 ·K
```

You can also extrapolate with the cubic spline, but doing so is risky. Because the cubic spline technique fits three adjacent points with a cubic polynomial, it runs into trouble at each end of the data set, since the first and last points do not have another point on each side. Hence, the cubic spline method must do something special for these endpoints. Mathcad provides three methods for handling the endpoints:

- `cspline( )`—creates a spline curve that is cubic at the endpoints.
- `pspline( )`—creates a spline curve that is parabolic at the endpoints.
- `lspline( )`—creates a spline curve that is linear at the endpoints.

These spline functions will all yield the same interpolated results for interior points, but can give widely varying results if you extrapolate your data set:

```
vs := cspline (Time, Temp)    interp (vs, Time, Temp, 20· min)
                              = 365.401·K
vs := pspline (Time, Temp)    interp (vs, Time, Temp, 20· min)
                              = 368.65·K
vs := lspline (Time, Temp)    interp (vs, Time, Temp, 20· min)
                              = 325.525·K
```

CAUTION!

1. Extrapolation (predicting values outside the range of the data set) should be avoided whenever possible. The temperatures used in the foregoing example were recorded for times ranging from 0 to 9 minutes. Predicting a temperature at 9.2 minutes is safer than predicting one at 90 or 900 minutes, but you are still making an assumption that nothing changed between 9.0 and 9.2 minutes. (The researcher might have turned off the heater, and the temperatures might have started falling.)
2. Cubic spline fits to noisy data can produce some amazing results. In the accompanying graph, an outlier at x = 5 was included in the data set to demonstrate how this single bad point affects the spline curve for adjacent points

as well. Interpolation using these curves is a very bad idea. Regression to find the "best fit" curve and then using the regression result to predict new values is a better idea for noisy data.

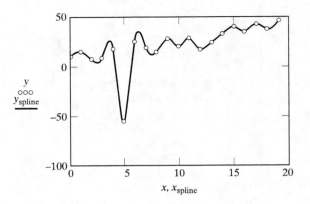

5.4.1 Using a QuickPlot to Plot the Spline Curve

If you want to see what the spline curve looks like, Mathcad's QuickPlot feature will allow you to see the curve with little effort. Since a QuickPlot will evaluate a function multiple times over a range of values, simply let Mathcad evaluate the `interp( )` function many times and display the result. For the temperature-time data presented earlier, this means calculating the second-derivative values by using `cspline( )` (or `pspline( )` or `lspline( )`) and then creating the QuickPlot.

In the figure that follows, the t in the `interp( )` function and on the x-axis is a dummy variable. Mathcad evaluates the `interp( )` function for values of t between -10 and 10 (by default) and displays the result. We need to change the limits on the x-axis to coincide with the time values in the data set, 0 to 9 minutes. To change the axis limits, click on the x-axis and then edit the limit values:

```
vs := cspline (Time, Temp)
```

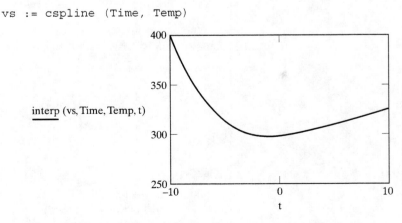

Note: The graph also demonstrates why it is not a good idea to extrapolate by using the `interp( )` function. The data set gives no evidence that the temperatures were very high before the experiment started (negative times), but that is what the `cspline( )` fit predicts. The results obtained by using `lspline( )` would be very different. (Check them out!)

The spline fit of the actual data set (not extrapolated) with the *x*-axis limits changed is shown in the following graph:

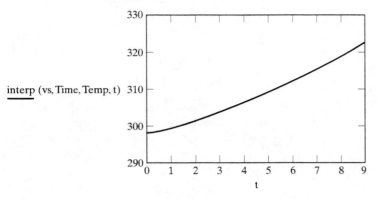

interp (vs, Time, Temp, t)

The curve looks well behaved in this range of times, typical of a spline fit to clean data.

PRACTICE!

The following "noisy" data were created by adding random numbers to the "clean" data set.

$$
x = \begin{bmatrix} 0.0 \\ 0.5 \\ 1.0 \\ 1.5 \\ 2.0 \\ 2.5 \\ 3.0 \end{bmatrix} \quad y_{clean} = \begin{bmatrix} 0.00 \\ 0.48 \\ 0.84 \\ 1.00 \\ 0.91 \\ 0.60 \\ 0.14 \end{bmatrix} \quad y_{noisy} = \begin{bmatrix} 0.24 \\ 0.60 \\ 0.69 \\ 1.17 \\ 0.91 \\ 0.36 \\ 0.18 \end{bmatrix}
$$

a. Compare the cubic spline fit of each data set by plotting the cubic spline interpolation for each.

b. Use the `interp( )` function to predict the *y*-value corresponding to x = 1.7 for each data set.

5.5   CURVE FITTING

5.5.1 Simple Linear Regression

Mathcad provides a number of functions to fit curves to data and to use fitted curves to predict new values. One of the most common curve-fitting applications is *linear regression*. Simple linear regression is carried out in Mathcad by using two or three of the following functions: `slope(vx, vy)`, `intercept(vx, vy)`, and `corr(vx, vy)`. These functions respectively return the *slope*, *intercept*, and *correlation coefficient* of the best fit straight line through the data represented by the x and y vectors. For example, for the time-temperature data of the preceding section,

```
b := intercept (Time,          b = 296.369·K
Temp)

m := slope (Time, Temp)
                               m = 2.756• K/min
```

The temperature values predicted by the model equation can be calculated from the slope and intercept values by using a range variable to keep track of the times. Then the quality of the fit can be determined by using the corr ( ) function:

```
i := 0 .. last(Time)

Temp_pred_i := b+m•Time_1

R2 := corr(Temp, Temp_pred)^2    R2 = 0.98904
```

Here, the correlation coefficient was squared to calculate the *coefficient of determination* (usually called the R^2 value) for the regression. An R^2 value of 1 implies that the regression line is a perfect fit to the data. The value 0.98904 suggests that the regression line is a pretty good fit to the data, but it is always a good idea to plot the original data together with the regression line. The result looks like this:

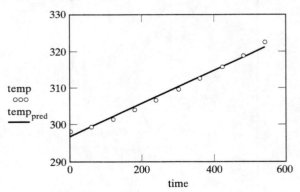

With this plot, we can clearly see that the actual curve of temperature versus time is not linear. This becomes quite apparent if you plot the *residuals*:

$$Residual_i := Temp_i - Temp_{pred_i}$$

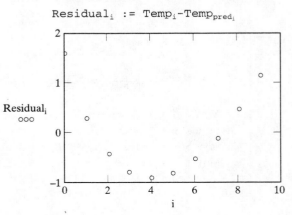

A residual plot should show randomly scattered points. Obvious trends in such a plot, such as the "U" shape in the preceding one, suggest that the equation used to fit the data was a poor choice. Here, it is saying that the linear equation is not a good choice for fitting these nonlinear data.

The foregoing example was included as a reminder that, while you can perform a simple (straight-line) linear regression on any data set, it is not always a good idea to do so. Nonlinear data require a more sophisticated curve-fitting approach.

PRACTICE!

Two sets of y values are shown. The noisy data were calculated from the clean data by adding random values. Try linear regression on these data sets. What is the impact of noisy data on the calculated slope, intercept, and R^2 value?

$$ x = \begin{bmatrix} 0.0 \\ 0.5 \\ 1.0 \\ 1.5 \\ 2.0 \\ 2.5 \\ 3.0 \end{bmatrix} \quad y_{\text{clean}} = \begin{bmatrix} 0.00 \\ 0.48 \\ 0.84 \\ 1.00 \\ 0.91 \\ 0.60 \\ 0.14 \end{bmatrix} \quad y_{\text{noisy}} = \begin{bmatrix} 0.24 \\ 0.60 \\ 0.69 \\ 1.17 \\ 0.91 \\ 0.36 \\ 0.18 \end{bmatrix} $$

PROFESSIONAL SUCCESS

Visualize your data and results.

Numbers, such as those in the following data set, are a handy way to store information:

x	y	x	y
-1.0000	-0.5478	0.1367	0.0004
-0.9900	-0.4252	0.1543	0.3042
-0.9626	-0.3277	0.2837	0.5407
-0.9577	-0.7865	0.4081	0.0122
-0.9111	-0.2327	0.4242	0.7593
-0.8391	-0.9654	0.5403	0.0304
-0.7597	-0.1030	0.6469	0.0565
-0.7481	-0.9997	0.6603	0.9821
-0.6536	-0.9791	0.7539	0.0999
-0.5477	-0.0319	0.8439	0.9617
-0.5328	-0.8888	0.9074	0.2277
-0.4161	-0.0130	0.9147	0.8781
-0.2921	-0.0043	0.9602	0.7795
-0.2752	-0.5260	0.9887	0.4184
-0.1455	-0.0005	0.9912	0.6536
0.0044	0.0088	1.0000	0.5403

For most of us, howevers, a data set is hard to visualize. A quick glance at the data at the left suggests that the y values get bigger as the x values get bigger. To try to describe there data, linear regression could be performed to calculate a slope and an intercept:

$$m := \text{slope}(x,y) \qquad\qquad m = 0.653$$

$$b := \text{intercept}(x,y) \qquad\qquad b = 1.211 \cdot 10^{-3}$$

$$r2 := \text{corr}(x,y)^2 \qquad\qquad r2 = 0.667$$

But by graphing the data, it becomes clear that simple linear regression is not appropriate for this data set:

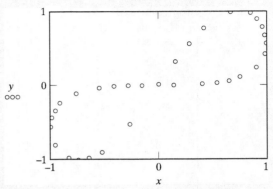

5.5.2 Generalized Linear Regression

The $\text{linfit}(vx, \ vy, \ vf)$ function performs a linear regression with an arbitrary linear model. For example, we might try to improve the fit of the regression line to the earlier temperature-time data by using a second-order polynomial, such as

$$\text{Temp}_{pred} = b_0 + b_1 \, \text{time} + b_2 \, \text{time}^2$$

The $\text{linfit}(\ )$ function will find the coefficients b_0, b_1, and b_2 that best fit the model to the data. However, the $\text{linfit}(\ )$ function does not handle units, so we first remove the units from the Time and Temp vectors:

$$\text{time} := \frac{\text{Time}}{\text{min}} \qquad\qquad \text{temp} := \frac{\text{Temp}}{\text{K}}$$

Then we define the linear model. The second-order polynomial has three terms: a constant, a term with time raised to the first power, and a term with time raised to the second power. We define this functionality in the vector function $f(\ )$ and then perform the regression by using the $\text{linfit}(\ )$ function. The coefficients computed by $\text{linfit}(\ )$ are stored in the vector b. For example, for the aforesaid time-temperature data,

$$f(x) := \begin{bmatrix} 1 \\ x \\ x^2 \end{bmatrix}$$

$$b := \text{linfit}(\text{time}, \text{temp}, f)$$

$$b = \begin{bmatrix} 297.721 \\ 1.742 \\ 0.113 \end{bmatrix}$$

We can then use the coefficients with the second-order polynomial to compute predicted temperature values at each time. A range variable, i, was used to compute a predicted value at each time value.

$$temp_{pred_i} := b_0 + b_1 \bullet time_i + b_2 \bullet (time_i)^2$$

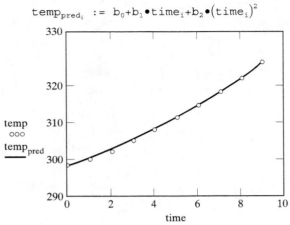

A range variable was used to predict a temperature value for each time value. Then the graph was produced by plotting the resulting temperature vector against the associated time vector.

As the preceding graph shows, the second-order polynomial appears to do a much better job of fitting the data than the linear model does. We can quantify the "goodness of fit" using the corr ( ) function:

```
r2 := corr (temp, temp_pred)²
r2 = 0.99961
```

The R^2 value is closer to 1 than the R^2 we obtained by using simple slope-intercept linear regression, indicating that the polynomial is a better fit than the straight line obtained via simple linear regression.

PRACTICE!

Look at the following data, and decide whether or not to include an intercept in the regression model:

$$x = \begin{bmatrix} 0.0 \\ 0.5 \\ 1.0 \\ 1.5 \\ 2.0 \\ 2.5 \\ 3.0 \end{bmatrix} \qquad Y_{clean} = \begin{bmatrix} 0.00 \\ 0.48 \\ 0.84 \\ 1.00 \\ 0.91 \\ 0.60 \\ 0.14 \end{bmatrix}$$

Note: These are the same data used in the "Practice!" box for the spline fit (to save typing).

Now try using the following polynomial models to fit the data with the linfit () function:

a. $y_p = b_0 + b_1 x + b_2 x^2$ or, $y_p = b_0 x + b_1 x^2$

b. $y_p = b_0 + b_1 x + b_2 x^2 + b_3 x^3$ or, $y_p = b_0 x + b_1 x^2 + b_2 x^3$

5.5.3 Other Linear Models

The models used in the earlier examples, namely,

$$\text{temp}_{\text{pred}} = b + m \cdot \text{time}$$

and

$$\text{temp}_{\text{pred}} = b_0 + b_1 \cdot \text{time} + b_2 \cdot \text{time}^2$$

are both linear models (linear in the coefficients, not in `time`). Since `linfit( )` works with any linear model, you could try fitting an equation such as

$$\text{temp}_{\text{pred}} = b_0 + b_1 \cdot \sinh(\text{time}) + b_2 \cdot \text{atan}(\text{time}^2)$$

or

$$\text{temp}_{\text{pred}} = b_0 \cdot \exp(\text{time}^{0.5}) + b_1 \cdot \ln(\text{time}^3)$$

These equations are linear in the coefficients (the b's) and are compatible with `linfit( )`. The `F(x)` functions for the respective equations would look like this:

$$F(x) := \begin{bmatrix} 1 \\ \sinh(x) \\ \text{atan}(x) \end{bmatrix} \qquad F(x) := \begin{bmatrix} \exp(x^{0.5}) \\ x^3 \end{bmatrix}$$

There is no reason to suspect that either of these last two models would be a good fit to the temperature-time data. In general, you choose a linear model either from some theory that suggests a relationship between your variables or from looking at a plot of the data set.

PRACTICE!

A plot of the data used in the spline fit and polynomial regression "Practice!" boxes has a shape something like half a sine wave. Try fitting the data with a linear model such as

a. $y_p = b_0 + b_1 \sin(x)$

b. $y_p = b_0 + b_1 \cos(x)$

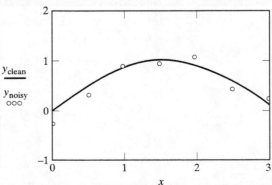

Do the following data suggest that the model should include an intercept?

$$x = \begin{bmatrix} 0.0 \\ 0.5 \\ 1.0 \\ 1.5 \\ 2.0 \\ 2.5 \\ 3.0 \end{bmatrix} \qquad y_{\text{clean}} = \begin{bmatrix} 0.00 \\ 0.48 \\ 0.84 \\ 1.00 \\ 0.91 \\ 0.60 \\ 0.14 \end{bmatrix} \qquad y_{\text{noisy}} = \begin{bmatrix} -0.25 \\ 0.33 \\ 0.88 \\ 0.92 \\ 1.07 \\ 0.44 \\ 0.25 \end{bmatrix}$$

APPLICATIONS: FITTING PHYSICAL PROPERTY DATA

Silane is an interesting chemical that is being increasingly employed in the manufacture of silicon wafers and chips used in the electronics industry. It is highly flammable and, under the right conditions, will ignite spontaneously upon contact with air. The manufacturers of silane must take special precautions to minimize the risks associated with this gas.

The following table gives the vapor pressure of silane, in pascals, at various temperatures, in kelvins.

Silane

Vapor	Pressure (Pa)
$T_{MIN}(K)$	88.48
$T_{MAX}(K)$	269.7
TEMP	P_{VAPOR}
88.48	21
97.54	167
106.60	640
115.66	2227
124.72	6110
133.79	14144
142.85	30318
151.91	57430
160.97	100078
170.03	163913
179.09	254015
188.15	378009
197.21	541607
206.27	754829
215.33	1027536
224.40	1372259
233.46	1804187
242.52	2341104
251.58	3006269
260.64	3827011
269.70	4838992

Analyzing the risks associated with possible accidents is an important part of a chemical facility's safety program and a big part of some chemical engineers' jobs. There are computer programs to help perform risk analyses, but they require some knowledge of the chemical, physical, and biomedical properties of the chemicals involved. Risk analysis programs have been written to use standardized fitting equations, so if you add your own information, it must be in a standard form. The accompanying silane vapor pressure data were calculated by using the ChemCad Physical Properties Database.[1]

Standard Fitting Equation for Vapor Pressure[2]

The standard equation for fitting a curve to vapor pressure p° is

$$\ln(p^{\circ}) = a + b/T + c\ln(T) + dT^{e}.$$

You must specify a and b; a, b. and c; or a, b, c, d. and e. If e is used, the equation becomes nonlinear, and other techniques are used to estimate the value of e. For silane, the value of e is expected to be 1.

To try fitting these data by using the first three terms (a, b. and c), we would use the `lin-fit( )` function, with the `f( )` vector defined as

$$f(x) := \begin{bmatrix} 1 \\ \dfrac{1}{x} \\ \ln(x) \end{bmatrix}$$

The coefficients themselves would be computed by `linfit( )` by using the *vectorize* operator (from the Matrix Toolbar) to take the natural logarithm of each element of the P_{vapor} vector:

$$\text{coeffs} := \text{linfit}(\text{Temp}, \overrightarrow{\ln(P_{vapor})}, f)$$

$$\text{coeffs} = \begin{bmatrix} 30.303 \\ -1.802 \bullet 10^{3} \\ -1.494 \end{bmatrix}$$

Finally, we can plot the original data and the predicted vapor pressures by using the computed coefficients, just to make sure that the process worked and to verify that the last term is not required:

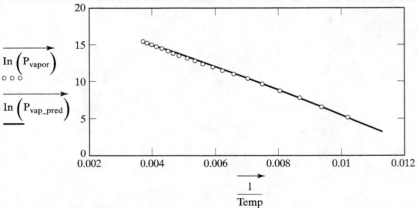

[1]ChemCad is a product of Chemstations, Inc., Houston, TX.
[2]*ChemCad User Guide*. version III, p. 11.64.

5.5.4 Specialized Regression Equations

Mathcad provides functions for finding coefficients for a number of commonly used fitting equations. These functions use iterative methods to find the coefficients that best fit the data, so a set of initial guesses for the coefficients must be provided.

As an example, consider fitting the data shown here with an *exponential curve*:

$$x = \begin{pmatrix} 0 \\ 1 \\ 2 \\ 3 \\ 4 \\ 5 \\ 6 \\ 7 \\ 8 \\ 9 \\ 10 \end{pmatrix} \qquad y = \begin{pmatrix} 5.32 \\ 5.83 \\ 6.09 \\ 7.12 \\ 7.62 \\ 9.15 \\ 9.95 \\ 11.8 \\ 13.39 \\ 15.19 \\ 18.12 \end{pmatrix}$$

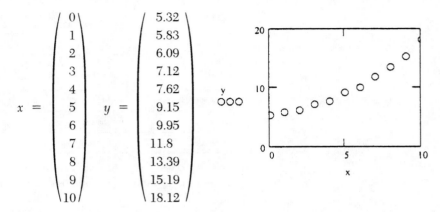

The data have been plotted, and the y values do seem to increase exponentially (albeit, weakly), so an exponential curve may be a good choice.

The expfit( ) function finds values for a, b, and c that best fit the following equation to the data:

$$y_{pred} = a\, e^{bx} + c$$

In order to use expfit( ) a vector of initial guesses for a, b, and c must be provided:

$$guesses := \begin{pmatrix} 1 \\ 1 \\ 1 \end{pmatrix}$$

Then the vector of x values, the vector of y values, and the guesses are sent to expfit( ). The coefficients of the exponential equation are returned:

```
coeffs := expfit (x, y, guesses)
```

$$coeffs = \begin{pmatrix} 2.398 \\ 0.184 \\ 2.854 \end{pmatrix}$$

These coefficients can be used with the known x values in the fitting equation to predict values:

```
a := coeffs₀          a = 2.398
b := coeffs₁          b = 0.184
c := coeffs₂          c = 2.854
```

$$y_{pred} := a \cdot e^{b \cdot x} + c$$

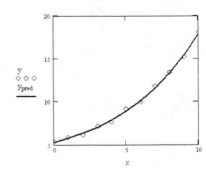

The following table summarizes the specialized fitting equations available in Mathcad:

	FUNCTION	EQUATION OF CURVE
Exponential	expfit(vx, vy, vg)	$y_{pred} = a\, e^{bx} + c$
Logistic	lgsfit(vx, vy, vg)	$y_{pred} = \dfrac{a}{(1 + b\, e^{-cx})}$
Logarithmic	logfit(vx, vy, vg)	$y_{pred} = a\, \ln(x)^{bx} + c$
Power	pwrfit(vx, vy, vg)	$y_{pred} = a\, x^{b} + c$
Sine	sinfit(vx, vy, vg)	$y_{pred} = a\, \sin(x + b) + c$

Note that the parameters for each function are the same: a vector of x values, a vector of y values, and a vector of initial guesses for the three coefficients (a, b, c).

SUMMARY

In this chapter, you learned to use Mathcad's built-in functions for data analysis. You learned to make X-Y graphs from data, to calculate statistical values from data, to interpolate between data set values, and to fit curves (linear models) to data. You also learned about the risk associated with extrapolating data, especially with nonlinear methods like cubic splines.

KEY TERMS

coefficient of determination	mean	sample
correlation coefficient	population	sine wave
cubic spline interpolation	QuickPlot	slope
exponential curve	representative sample	standard deviation
intercept	residuals	variance
linear interpolation	risk analysis	Visualize
linear regression	risk management	x-y graph

MATHCAD SUMMARY

X-Y Graphs Vector Against Vector:

1. Select X-Y Plot from the Graph Toolbar.
2. Enter the name of your vector of independent values on the x-axis.
3. Enter the name of your vector of dependent values on the y-axis.

Element By Element:

1. Declare a range variable starting at 0 and going to last(v), where v is one of your data set vectors.
2. Select X-Y Plot from the Graph Toolbar.
3. Enter the name of your vector of independent values on the x-axis—with an index subscript containing the range variable.
4. Enter the name of your vector of dependent values on the y-axis—with an index subscript containing the range variable.

Quickplot:

1. Select X-Y Plot from the Graph Toolbar.
2. Enter your function name on the y-axis, with a dummy variable as an argument.
3. Enter the dummy variable on the x-axis.
4. Adjust the x-axis limits to change the displayed range.

Statistical Functions:

mean(A)	Returns the mean (arithmetic average) of the values in A.
stdev(A)	Returns the population standard deviation of the values in A.
var(A)	Returns the population variance of the values in A.
stdev(A)	Returns the sample standard deviation of the values in A.
var(A)	Returns the sample variance of the values in A.

Interpolation:

linterp(vx, vy, x_{new})	Returns the y value corresponding to $x = x_{new}$, computed by using linear interpolation on the x and y data.
cspline(vx, vy)	Returns the vector of second derivatives that specify a spline curve that is cubic at the endpoints.
pspline(vx, vy)	Returns the vector of second derivatives that specify a spline curve that is parabolic at the endpoints.
lspline(vx, vy)	Returns the vector of second derivatives that specify a spline curve that is linear at the endpoints.
interp(vs, vx, vy, x_{new})	Uses the vector of second derivatives from any of the spline functions previously listed and returns the y value corresponding to $x = x_{new}$, which is computed by using spline interpolation on the x and y data.

Regression:

slope (vx, vy)	Returns the slope of the best fit (minimum total squared error) straight line through the data in vx and vy.
intercept(vx, vy)	Returns the intercept of the best fit straight line through the data in vx and vy.
corr(vx, vy)	Returns the coefficient of correlation (usually called R) of the best fit straight line through the data in vx and vy. The coefficient of determination, R^2, can be computed from R and is more commonly used.
linfit(vx, vy, vf)	Returns the coefficients that best fit the linear model described by vf to the data in vx and vy. The vector vf is a vector of functions you provide that describes the linear model you want to use to fit to the data.

Specialized Fitting Functions:

expfit(vx, vy, vg)	Fits an exponential curve ($y_{pred} = a\,e^{bx} + c$) to the data in the vx and vy vectors. A three-element vector of guessed values for the coefficients (a, b, c) must be provided.
lgsfit(vx, vy, vg)	Fits a *logistic curve* $y_{pred} = \dfrac{a}{(1 + b\,e^{-cx})}$ to the data in the vx and vy vectors. A three-element vector of guessed values for the coefficients (a, b, c) must be provided.
logfit(vx, vy, vg)	Fits a *logarithmic curve* ($y_{pred} = a\ln(x)^b + c$) to the data in the vx and vy vectors. A three-element vector of guessed values for the coefficients (a, b, c) must be provided.
pwrfit(vx, vy, vg)	Fits a *power curve* ($y_{pred} = a\,x^b + c$) to the data in the vx and vy vectors. A three-element vector of guessed values for the coefficients (a, b, c) must be provided.
sinfit(vx, vy, vg)	Fits an exponential curve ($y_{pred} = a\sin(x + b) + c$) to the data in the vx and vy vectors. A three-element vector of guessed values for the coefficients (a, b, c) must be provided.

Problems

1. STATISTICS: COMPETING COLD REMEDIES

   Two proposed cold remedies, CS1 (cough syrup) and CS2 (chicken soup), have been compared in a hospital study. The objective was to determine which treatment caused patients to recover more quickly. The duration of sickness was defined as the time (days) between when patients reported to the hospital requesting treatment and when they requested to leave the hospital. The results are tabulated as follows:

CS1		CS2	
PATIENT	DURATION	PATIENT	DURATION
1	8.10	1	5.79
2	7.25	2	2.81
3	5.89	3	3.27
4	7.12	4	4.87
5	5.60	5	5.49
6	1.85	6	6.60
7	4.00	7	2.63
8	5.58	8	4.64
9	9.92	9	6.96
10	4.25	10	5.83

   a. Determine the mean recovery time for each medication.

   b. Which remedy caused the fastest recoveries?

2. USING X-Y TRACE WITH GRAPHS

   Create a QuickPlot of the function

   $$f(x) = 1 - e^{-x}.$$

   Use Mathcad's X-Y Trace dialog to evaluate this function at $x = 1, 2$, and 3. (Click on the graph, and then use the menu commands Format/Graph/Trace.)

3. USING QUICKPLOTS TO SOLVE PROBLEMS

   The equation describing the process of warming a hot tub by adding hot water is

   $$T = T_{IN} - (T_{IN} - T_{START})e^{\frac{-Q}{V}t},$$

where

T	is the temperature of the water in the hot tub,
T_{IN}	is the temperature of the water flowing into the hot tub, (130°F)
T_{START}	is the initial temperature of the water in the hot tub (65°F),
Q	is the hot-water flow rate (5 gpm),
V	is the volume of the hot tub (500 gallons), and
t	is the elapsed time since the hot water started flowing.

a. Use QuickPlot to see how long it will take the hot tub to reach 110°F. (You may want to work this problem without units, since °F is not defined in Mathcad.)

b. If the hot-water flow rate was increased to 10 gpm, how long would it take for the water temperature in the tub to reach 110°F?

4. FITTING AN EXPONENTIAL CURVE TO DATA

The equation describing the process of warming a hot tub by adding hot water is

$$T = T_{IN} - (T_{IN} - T_{START})e^{\frac{-Q}{V}t},$$

where

T	is the temperature of the water in the hot tub,
T_{IN}	is the temperature of the water flowing into the hot tub, (130°F)
T_{START}	is the initial temperature of the water in the hot tub (65°F),
Q	is the hot-water flow rate (5 gpm),
V	is the volume of the hot tub (500 gallons), and
t	is the elapsed time since the hot water started flowing.

If you have experimental temperature vs. time data taken as the hot tub warms up, Mathcad's expfit( ) function could be used to fit an exponential function to the experimental data. The general form of an exponential curve is

$$y_{pred} = a \cdot e^{b \cdot x} + c$$

Suppose the hot-tub warming data are as follows:

TIME (minutes)	Water Temperature(°F)
0	65
15	75
30	82
45	89
60	95
75	99
90	102

a. Let

$$\text{guesses} := \begin{bmatrix} 1 \\ -0.01 \\ 10 \end{bmatrix}$$

be the initial estimates of the exponential function coefficients. Use expfit( ) to find the coefficients of the exponential curve that fits the experimental data.

b. Plot the experimental values and the exponential curve on the same graph. Does the curve fit the data?

5. CHECKING THERMOCOUPLES

Two thermocouples have the same color codes on the wires, and they appear to be identical. But when they were calibrated, they were found to give somewhat different output voltages. The calibration data are shown in the following table:

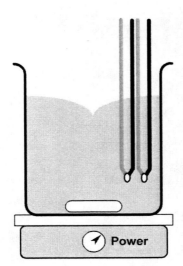

WATER TEMP.	TC 1 OUTPUT	TC 2 OUTPUT
(°C)	(mV)	(mV)
20.0	1.019	1.098
30.0	1.537	1.920
40.0	2.059	2.526
50.0	2.585	2.816
60.0	3.116	2.842
70.0	3.650	4.129
80.0	4.187	4.266
90.0	4.726	4.340

Plot the output voltages (y-axis) against temperature (x-axis) for each thermocouple. Which thermocouple would you want to use in an experiment? Why?

6. THERMOCOUPLE CALIBRATION

Thermocouples are made by joining two dissimilar metal wires. Contact between the two metals results in a small, but measurable, voltage drop across the junction. This voltage drop changes as the temperature of the junction changes; thus, the thermocouple can be used to measure temperature if you know the relationship between temperature and voltage. Equations for common types of thermocouples are available, or you can simply take a few data points and prepare a calibration curve. This is especially easy for thermocouples because, for small temperature ranges, the relationship between temperature and voltage is nearly linear.

T(°C)	V(mV)
10	0.397
20	0.796
30	1.204
40	1.612
50	2.023
60	2.436
70	2.851
80	3.267
90	3.662

Q FT³/MIN	DP PSI
3.9	0.13
7.9	0.52
11.8	1.18
15.7	2.09
19.6	3.27
23.6	4.71
27.5	6.41
31.4	8.37
35.3	10.59
39.3	13.08

a. Use the slope( ) and intercept( ) functions to find the coefficients of a straight line through the data at the left.
(*Note:* The thermocouple voltage changes because the temperature changes—that is, the voltage *depends* on the temperature. For regression, the independent variable (temperature) should always be on the *x*-axis, and the dependent variable (voltage) should be on the *y*-axis.)

b. Calculate a predicted voltage at each temperature, and plot the original data and the predicted values together to make sure that your calibration curve actually fits the data.

7. ORIFICE METER CALIBRATION

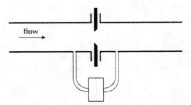

Orifice meters are commonly used to measure flow rates, but are highly nonlinear devices. Because of this nonlinearity, special care must be taken when one prepares calibration curves for these meters. The equation relating the flow rate Q to the pressure drop across the orifice δP (the measured variable) is

$$Q = \frac{A_0 C_0}{\sqrt{1 - \beta^4}} \sqrt{\frac{2g_c \Delta P}{\rho}}$$

For purposes of creating a calibration curve, the details of the equation are unimportant (as long as the other terms stay constant). What is necessary is that we see the theoretical relationship between Q and δP, namely, that

$$Q \propto \sqrt{\Delta P}$$

Also, the pressure drop across the orifice plate depends on the flow rate, not the other way around. So $\sqrt{\Delta P}$ should be regressed as the dependent variable (y values) and Q as the independent variable (x values).

a. Using the accompanying data, regress Q and $\sqrt{\Delta P}$ to create a calibration curve for the orifice meter.

b. Calculate and plot predicted values together with the original data to check your results.

Note that if you use the slope( ) and intercept( ) functions in this problem, you will need to use the *vectorize* operator as well, because taking the square root of an entire matrix is not defined. The vectorize operator tells Mathcad to perform the calculations (taking the square root, for example) on each element of the matrix. The slope( ) function might then look like this:

$$m := \text{slope}(Q, \overrightarrow{\sqrt{\Delta P}})$$

8. VAPOR-LIQUID EQUILIBRIUM

When a liquid mixture is boiled, the vapor that leaves the vessel is enriched in the more volatile component of the mixture. The vapor and liquid in a boiling vessel are in equilibrium, and vapor-liquid equilibrium (VLE) data are available for many mixtures. The data are usually presented in tabular form, as in the accompanying table, which represents VLE data for mixtures of methanol and *n*-butanol boiling at 12 atm. From the VLE data, we see that if a 50:50 liquid mixture of the alcohols is boiled, the vapor will contain about 80% methanol.

VLE data are commonly used in designing distillation columns, but an equation relating vapor mass fraction to liquid mass fraction is a lot handier than tabulated values.

Use the `linfit( )` function and the tabulated VLE data to obtain an equation relating the mass fraction of methanol in the vapor (y) to the mass fraction of vapor in the liquid (x). Test different linear models (e.g., polynomials) to see which gives the best fit to the experimental data. For your best model, calculate predicted values using the coefficients returned by `linfit( )`, and plot the predicted values and the original data values on the same graph.

x	y
0.000	0.000
0.022	0.066
0.046	0.133
0.071	0.201
0.098	0.269
0.126	0.335
0.156	0.399
0.189	0.461
0.224	0.519
0.261	0.574
0.302	0.626
0.346	0.674
0.393	0.720
0.445	0.762
0.502	0.802
0.565	0.839
0.634	0.874
0.710	0.907
0.796	0.939
0.891	0.970
1.000	1.000

Methanol / n-Butanol VLE

Note: The VLE data shown were generated from version 4.0 of Chemcad.[1] The x column represents the mass fraction of methanol in the boiling mixture. (The mass fraction of *n*-butanol in the liquid is calculated as 1-x for any mixture.) The mass fraction of methanol in the vapor leaving the solution is shown in the y column.

9. FITTING PHYSICAL PROPERTY DATA

In an earlier Applications example, experimental data on the vapor pressure of silane were fit to a standard equation. Try fitting a curve to data for silane's liquid heat capacity. The standard fitting equation for this property is

$$C_P = a + bT + cT^2 + dT^3 + eT^4$$

Not all coefficients need to be used. (That is, any order of polynomial is acceptable.)

SILANE	
Tmin(K)	88.48
Tmax(K)	161.00

TEMP	C_P	TEMP	C_P
88.48	59874	124.74	61026
92.11	60174	128.37	61231
95.73	60676	131.99	61289
99.36	60156	135.62	61655
102.98	60358	139.24	61160
106.61	60863	142.87	61658
110.24	60604	146.50	62038
113.86	60784	150.12	62085
117.49	61037	153.75	61864
121.11	61215	157.37	61712

Note: The data set for the liquid heat capacity (J/kmol K) of silane is shown. Find the coefficients for the best fitting model for the data.

[1] Chemcad is a chemical process simulation package produced by Chemstations, Inc. in Houston, Texas, USA.

10. **INTERPOLATION**

Use linear interpolation with the thermocouple calibration data in Problem 5.8 to predict

a. the thermocouple voltage at a temperature of 85°C.

b. the temperature of the junction when the thermocouple voltage is 2.500 mV.

Use a cubic spline interpolation with the orifice meter calibration data in Problem 5.9 to predict

a. the flow rate corresponding to a pressure drop of 9.5 psi.

b. the pressure drop to be expected at a flow rate of 15 ft³/min.

11. **INTERPOLATING TABULATED DATA**

In the past, a lot of useful information was provided in the form of tables and graphs. Much of this information is now available in equation form (see the note at the end of this problem), but occasionally it is still necessary to read values from tables. Consider the following *compound amount factor* table:

COMPOUND AMOUNT FACTORS

Year	2%	4%	6%	8%	10%	12%	14%	16%	18%
0	1.000	1.000	1.000	1.000	1.000	1.000	1.000	1.000	1.000
2	1.040	1.082	1.124	1.166	1.210	1.254	1.300	1.346	1.392
4	1.082	1.170	1.262	1.360	1.464	1.574	1.689	1.811	1.939
6	1.126	1.265	1.419	1.587	1.772	1.974	2.195	2.436	2.700
8	1.172	1.369	1.594	1.851	2.144	2.476	2.853	3.278	3.759
10	1.219	1.480	1.791	2.159	2.594	3.106	3.707	4.411	5.234
12	1.268	1.601	2.012	2.518	3.138	3.896	4.818	5.936	7.288
14	1.319	1.732	2.261	2.937	3.797	4.887	6.261	7.988	10.147
16	1.373	1.873	2.540	3.426	4.595	6.130	8.137	10.748	14.129
18	1.428	2.026	2.854	3.996	5.560	7.690	10.575	14.463	19.673
20	1.486	2.191	3.207	4.661	6.727	9.646	13.743	19.461	27.393
22	1.546	2.370	3.604	5.437	8.140	12.100	17.861	26.186	38.142
24	1.608	2.563	4.049	6.341	9.850	15.179	23.212	35.236	53.109

The table can be used to determine the future value of an amount deposited at a given interest rate. One thousand dollars invested at 10% (annual percentage rate) for 20 years would be worth 6.727 × $1,000 = $6,727 at the end of the 20th year. The 6.727 is the compound amount factor for an investment held 20 years at 10% interest.

Interest tables such as the preceding provided useful information, but it was frequently necessary to interpolate to find the needed value.

a. Use linear interpolation to find the compound amount factor for 6% interest in year 15.

b. Use linear interpolation to find the compound amount factor for 11% interest in year 10.

Note: Mathcad 2000 provides the `fv()` function, that can be used to calculate future values directly, eliminating the need for an interest table. The `fv(rate,N,pmt,pv)` function finds the future value of an amount deposited at time zero (`pv`, include a negative sign to indicate out-of-pocket expenses), plus any periodic payments (`pmt`), invested at a specified interest `rate`, for N periods. The example that was worked out earlier in this problem looks like this in Mathcad:

```
F := fv(10%, 20, 0, -1000)
F = 6727
```

12. **RELATING HEIGHT TO MASS FOR A SOLIDS STORAGE TANK**

Solids storage tanks are sometimes mounted on *load cells* (large scales, basically) so that the mass of solids in the tank is known, rather than the height of the solids. To make sure they do not overfill the tank, the operators might ask for a way to calculate the height of material in the tank, given the mass reading from the load cells.

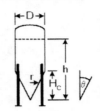

h(ft)	m(lb)
0	0
2	56
4	447
6	1508
8	3574
10	6981
12	11470
14	16000
16	20520
18	25040
20	29570
22	34090
24	38620

The values shown in the accompanying table relate height and mass in the tank and are the starting point for this problem. The tank has a conical base section ($\theta=30°$) and a diameter of 12 feet. The apparent density of the solids in the tank is 20 lb/ft^3.

Use a cubic spline to fit a curve to the mass (as x) and height (as y) data, and then use the `interp( )` function to predict the height of solids in the tank when the load cells indicate 3200 kg solids.

Note: The load cells actually measure the mass of the tank and the stored solids, but adjusting the display to read 0 kg before adding any solids effectively causes the load cells to display only the mass of the solids. This is called setting the *tare weight* for the load cells.

6

Mathcad's Symbolic Math Capabilities

OBJECTIVES

- know how to use Mathcad's symbolic math capabilities to solve for a particular variable in an equation
- know how to use Mathcad's symbolic math capabilities to manipulate mathematical expressions (e.g., substituting and factoring expressions, and expanding terms)
- understand how Mathcad can perform matrix operations symbolically
- be able to use symbolic math to integrate and differentiate functions

6.1 COMPOSITE MATERIALS

The field of composite materials has already had an impact on most of us in the developed world. The sporting goods industry, for example, has found that the lighter and stronger composite materials allow sports enthusiasts to go faster and farther. Composites are common in modern aircraft for the same reasons. But the field of composite materials is just getting started.

Material scientists have long analyzed the behavior of materials under various stresses. Concrete, for example, is known to perform well under compression, but doesn't hold up under tension. Cables are designed for holding loads under tension, but do nothing under compression. (You can't push a rope!) The analytical skills of the materials scientists are still required to understand composite materials, but they now go a step further: It has become possible to talk about designing materials for specific purposes. If a part needs to perform better under tension, you might change the type of fibers used in the composite. If the part needs better resistance to compression, the type of matrix used to surround the fibers might be changed. For better bending performance, the bonding between the fibers and the matrix might be improved. But in order to design a better composite material, you have to know how each element of the composite works, as well as how all the elements interact with each other. You also need to understand the chemical and physical natures of the elements of the composite, in addition to the properties imparted to the elements and the final composite by the manufacturing processes. This is a field that will require the skills of a wide range of scientists and engineers working together.

In the past, composites have been used primarily to improve the structural performance of a system. The mechanical properties of composites are still an important research area, but these materials also have interesting potential for improving electrical, chemical, and thermal properties of systems. Some years back, there was talk of room-temperature superconductors that could revolutionize power distribution systems. The excitement in that area has died down, but the research continues. Strong bone replacements could be made of composites that are biologically inert to reduce the risk of rejection. Composite engines and furnaces could operate more efficiently at higher temperatures. Some success has already been seen in each of these areas, and the future for these materials appears to be especially bright.

6.2 SYMBOLIC MATH USING MATHCAD

Scientists and engineers commonly want a numerical value as the result of a calculation, and Mathcad's numerical math features provide this type of result. However, there are times when you need a result in terms of the mathematical symbols themselves, and you can use Mathcad's *symbolic math* capability for that type of calculation. A symbolic result may be required when

- you want to know how Mathcad obtained a numerical result by seeing the equation solved symbolically,
- you want greater precision on a matrix inversion, so you have Mathcad invert the matrix symbolically, rather than numerically, or
- you want to integrate a function symbolically and use the result in another function.

Mathcad provides symbolic math functions in two locations: the *Symbolics menu* at the top of the window and the *Symbolic Keyword Toolbar*. Both locations provide access to essentially the same symbolic capabilities, with one important distinction: The Symbolic Keyword Toolbar uses the *live symbolic operator*, or → symbol. This is called a "live" operator because it automatically recalculates the value of an expression whenever information to the left of or above the operator changes.

The results of calculations carried out using the Symbolics menu are not live. That is, once a symbolic operation has been performed using commands from the Symbolics menu, the result will not be automatically updated, even if the input data change. Thus, to update a result using the Symbolics menu, you must repeat the calculation.

The Symbolics menu is a bit more straightforward than the Symbolic Keyword Toolbar for solving for a particular variable and for factoring an expression. The Symbolic Keyword Toolbar is simpler for substitution. Both approaches will be demonstrated.

6.2.1 Symbolics Menu

The Symbolics menu is on the menu bar at the top of the Mathcad window. One of the first considerations in using the symbolic commands is how you want the results to be displayed. You can set this feature by using the Evaluation Style dialog box from the Symbolics menu:

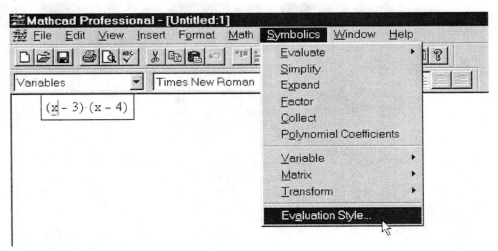

The Evaluation Style dialog box controls whether the results of a symbolic operation are presented to the right of the original expression or below the original expression. When results are placed below the original expression, the new equation regions can start running into existing regions. This can be avoided by having Mathcad insert blank lines before displaying the results. By default, Mathcad places the results below the original expression and adds blank lines to avoid overwriting other equation regions:

Evaluation Style

Show evaluation steps

⊙ Vertically, inserting lines

○ Vertically, without inserting lines

○ Horizontally

OK

Cancel

☐ Show Comments

☐ Evaluate In Place

(*Note:* If you select "Evaluate in Place," your original expression will be replaced by the computed result.)

As an example of using the Symbolics menu, we will find the solutions of the equation:

$$(x - 3) \cdot (x - 4) = 0.$$

This equation has two obvious solutions $(x = 3, x = 4)$, so it is easy to see whether Mathcad is finding the correct ones.

PROFESSIONAL SUCCESS

Keep test expressions as simple as possible.

When you are choosing mathematical expressions to test the features of a software package or to validate your own functions, try to come up with a test that

- is just complex enough to demonstrate that the function is (or is not) working correctly and
- has an obvious, or at least known, solution, so that it is readily apparent whether the test has succeeded or failed.

Since we want to find the values of x that satisfy the equation, click on the equation and select either one of the x variables. Note that symbolic equality (=) was used in the equation:

$$(x - 3) \bullet (x - 4) = 0$$

To solve for the variable x, use Symbolics/Variable/Solve:

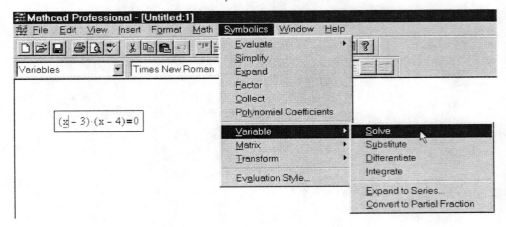

The solutions—the two values of x that satisfy the equation—are presented as a two-element vector:

$$(x- 3) \cdot (x- 4) = 0$$

$$\begin{bmatrix} 3 \\ 4 \end{bmatrix}$$

Symbolic operations are often performed on expressions, rather than complete equations. If you solve the expression $(x- 3) \cdot (x- 4)$ for x, Mathcad will set the expression to zero before finding the solutions. Thus, we would have

$$(x- 3) \cdot (x- 4)$$

$$\begin{bmatrix} 3 \\ 4 \end{bmatrix}$$

6.2.2 Symbolic Keyword Toolbar

The Symbolic Keyword Toolbar is available from the Math Toolbar. Click on the button showing a mortarboard icon to open the Symbolic Keyword Toolbar. When opened, the Symbolic Keyword Toolbar looks like this:

Symbolic		
$\rightarrow$	$\blacksquare \rightarrow$	Modifiers
float	complex	assume
solve	simplify	substitute
factor	expand	coeffs
collect	series	parfrac
fourier	laplace	ztrans
invfourier	invlaplace	invztrans
$M^T \rightarrow$	$M^{-1} \rightarrow$	$|M| \rightarrow$

To use the features on this Toolbar, first enter an expression, and then select the expression and click one of the buttons on the Toolbar to perform a symbolic operation on the expression. For instance, the preceding example, we know that the equation

$$(x - 3) \cdot (x - 4) = 0$$

has two solutions: $x = 3$ and $x = 4$. Mathcad can also find those solutions using the [solve] button on the Symbolic Keyword Toolbar. This will be demonstrated in the next section.

6.3 SOLVING AN EQUATION SYMBOLICALLY

If you enter an incomplete equation, such as the left-hand side of the previous equation, Mathcad will set the expression equal to zero when the solve operation is performed. To solve the equation in this manner, enter the expression to be solved and select it:

$$(x - 3) \cdot (x - 4)$$

Then click on the [solve] button on the Symbolic Keyword Toolbar:

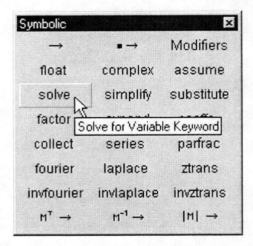

The word "solve" appears after the expression, with an empty placeholder. Mathcad needs to be told which variable to solve for. Enter an x in the placeholder and then press [enter]:

$$(x-3) \bullet (x-4) \quad \text{solve,} \quad \blacksquare \rightarrow$$

Mathcad returns the result. In this case, since there are two solutions, the solutions are returned as a two-element vector:

$$(x-3) \bullet (x-4) \quad \text{solve, } x \rightarrow \begin{bmatrix} 3 \\ 4 \end{bmatrix}$$

(*Note:* When using the Symbolic Keyword Toolbar, you tell Mathcad which variable to solve for by typing the variable name into the placeholder. When using the Symbolics menu to solve for x, you tell Mathcad to solve for x by first selecting one of the x variables in the expression and then choosing "solve" from the menu.)

If Mathcad cannot solve an expression symbolically, nothing will be displayed on the right side of the arrow operator, and the expression will be displayed in red to indicate that an error has occurred:

$$(x- 3) \cdot (x- 4) \quad \text{solve,} y \rightarrow$$

If you click on the expression, Mathcad will display an error message indicating that no solution was found.

6.4   MANIPULATING EQUATIONS

A number of algebraic manipulations, such as factoring out a common variable, are frequently used when one is working with algebraic expressions, and Mathcad implements these through the Symbolic Keyword Toolbar. These routine manipulations include the following:

- *Expanding* a collection of variables (e.g., after factoring).
- *Factoring* a common variable out of a complex expression.

PRACTICE!

Use Mathcad to solve the following equations (you can leave off the zero when entering the expressions into Mathcad):

a. $(x - 1) \cdot (x + 1) = 0.$
b. $x^2 - 1 = 0.$
c. $(y - 2) \cdot (y + 3) = 0$
d. $.3z^2 - 2z + 8 = 0.$
e. $\dfrac{x + 4}{x^2 + 6x - 2} = 0.$

- *Substituting* one variable or expression for another variable.
- *Simplifying* a complex expression.
- *Collecting terms* on a designated variable.

A *partial-fraction expansion* in which a complex expression is expanded into an equivalent expression consisting of products of fractions is a somewhat more complex operation, but one that can be helpful in finding solutions. This procedure will not work on all fractional expressions, but can be very useful in certain circumstances.

Examples of each of the preceding manipulations follow.

6.4.1   Expand

Expanding the expression $(x- 3) \cdot (x- 4)$ yields a polynomial in x. To expand an expression using the Symbolics menu, select the expression, and then choose Symbolics/Expand:

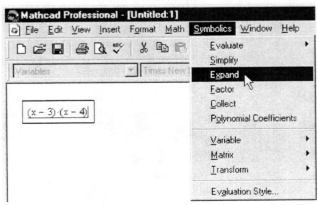

After expansion, the result is placed below the original expression:

$(x- 3) \cdot (x- 4)$
$x^2- 7 \cdot x + 12$

Alternatively, select the expression, and then press the [expand] button on the Symbolic Keyword Toolbar. In the placeholder, tell Mathcad to expand on x:

$(x- 3) \cdot (x- 4) \text{ expand, } x \rightarrow x^2- 7 \cdot x + 12$

6.4.2 Factor

Factoring reverses the expand operation, pulling an x out of the polynomial:

$x^2- 7 \cdot x + 12 \text{ factor, } x \rightarrow (x- 3) \cdot (x- 4)$

Probably a more common usage of the factor operation is to pull a similar quantity out of a multiterm expression. For example, $2\pi r$ appears in both terms in the expression for the surface area of a cylinder. To factor this expression, select the terms to be factored (the entire expression in this case), and then use Symbolics/Factor. The result is placed below the original expression:

$2 \cdot \pi \cdot r^2 + 2 \cdot \pi \cdot r \cdot L$
$2 \cdot r \cdot \pi \cdot (r+L)$

You can also factor only a portion of an expression. For example, we could factor only the right-hand side of the following equation:

$$A_{cyl} = \underline{2 \cdot \pi \cdot r^2 + 2 \cdot \pi \cdot r \cdot L}$$

To factor only the right-hand side, select that side, and then use Symbolics/Factor:

$A_{cyl} = 2 \cdot r \cdot \pi \cdot (r+L)$

PRACTICE!

Try using the Symbolics menu to factor the *x* out of these expressions:

a. $6x^2 + 4x$.
b. $3xy + 4x - 2y$. (Select only part of this expression before factoring.)

6.4.3 Substitute

The *substitute operation* replaces a variable by another expression. Substitution is a bit simpler using the Symbolic Keyword Toolbar buttons, so that approach will be shown first.

SUBSTITUTION USING THE SYMBOLIC KEYWORD TOOLBAR

A simple replacement, such as replacing all the x's in an expression with y's, is easily carried out using the [substitute] button on the Symbolic Keyword Toolbar:

$(x- 3) \cdot (x- 4) \text{ substitute, } x=y \rightarrow (y- 3) \cdot (y- 4)$

But you can also replace a variable with a more complicated expression. For example, suppose you wanted to replace the x's with an exponential expression, such as

$e^{-t/\tau}$. The [substitute] button can handle this: simply enter the complete exponential expression into the placeholder in the substitute command:

$$(\text{x-3})\bullet(\text{x-4}) \text{ substitute, } x = e^{\frac{-t}{\tau}} \rightarrow \left(\exp\left(\frac{-t}{\tau}\right)-3\right)\bullet\left(\exp\left(\frac{-t}{\tau}\right)-4\right)$$

SUBSTITUTION USING THE SYMBOLICS MENU

If you want to use the Symbolics menu to carry out a substitution, there are two things to keep in mind:

1. The new expression (the expression that will be substituted into the existing expression) must be copied to the Windows clipboard before performing the substitution.
2. You must select the variable to be replaced before performing the substitution.

To repeat the last example, the $e^{-t/\pi}$ would be entered into the Mathcad worksheet, selected, and copied to the Windows clipboard using Edit/Copy:

Then one of the x variables in $(\text{x}-\ 3) \cdot (\text{x}-\ 4)$ would be selected. (This tells Mathcad to replace all of the x's in the expression with the contents of the Windows clipboard.) Finally, the substitution is performed using Symbolics/Variable/Substitute, and the results are placed below the original expression. The final Mathcad worksheet now looks like this (with the added comments):

$e^{\frac{-t}{}}$ *entered on worksheet, the copied to Windows clipboard*

$(\text{x-3}) \bullet (\text{x-4})$ *one x selected before substitution*

$\left(\exp\left(\frac{-t}{}\right)-3\right)\bullet\left(\exp\left(\frac{-t}{}\right)-4\right)$ *the result of the substitution*

6.4.4 Simplify

According to the Mathcad help files, the *Simplify menu command* "performs arithmetic, cancels common factors, uses basic trigonometric and inverse function identities, and simplifies square roots and powers." If we try to simplify $(\text{x}-\ 3) \cdot (\text{x}-\ 4)$ using Symbolics/Simplify, the expression is returned unchanged: Mathcad thinks that $(\text{x}-3) \cdot (\text{x}-\ 4)$ is as simple as this expression gets. In order to demonstrate the Simplify operation, we need to complicate the example a little. Consider this modification:

$$\left(\text{x-}\sqrt{9}\right)\bullet\left(\text{x-}2^2\right)$$

If we try to simplify this expression using Symbolics/Simplify, the original expression is returned:

$$\left(\text{x-}\sqrt{9}\right)\bullet\left(\text{x-}2^2\right)$$
$$(\text{x-3})\bullet(\text{x-4})$$

The Simplify operation simplified the square root (selecting the positive root) and power. Perhaps a more significant use of the operation is obtaining a common denominator. For example, by selecting the entire expression

$$\frac{a}{(x-3)} + \frac{b}{(x-4)}$$

and then using the Symbolics/Simplify function, the terms will combine over a common denominator:

$$\frac{(a \bullet x - 4 \bullet a + b \bullet x - 3 \bullet b)}{((x-3) \bullet (x-4))}$$

You can also factor the numerator to see the process used to obtain the common denominator. First, you factor the a out of the first two terms in the numerator by selecting those two terms:

$$\frac{(a \cdot x - 4 \cdot a + b \cdot x - 3 \cdot b)}{[(x-3) \cdot (x-4)]}$$

Then you use Symbolics/Factor8. Next, you choose the last two terms in the new numerator:

$$\frac{(a \cdot x - 4 \cdot a + b \cdot x - 3 \cdot b)}{[(x-3) \cdot (x-4)]}$$

Again, you use Symbolics/Factor. The final result is

$$\frac{(a \bullet (x-4) + b \bullet (x-3))}{((x-3) \bullet (x-4))}$$

PRACTICE!

Use the Symbolics menu to simplify these expressions:

a. $\dfrac{x}{x+4} - \dfrac{12}{x+2}$.

b. $\dfrac{1}{x} + \dfrac{x}{x-7} - \dfrac{x+6}{x^2}$.

c. $\sqrt{\dfrac{4x}{y^2}}$.

6.4.5 Collect

The Collect operation is used to rewrite a set of summed terms as a polynomial in the selected variable (if it is possible to do so). For example, the Expand function, operating on the x in $(x-3) \cdot (x-4)$, returned a polynomial. So we know that that expression can be written as a polynomial in x. The Collect function should also return that polynomial, and in the following example, we observe that it does:

$$(x-3) \cdot (x-4) \quad \text{collect}, x \rightarrow x^2 - 7 \cdot x + 12$$

What is the difference between the Collect and Expand operations if they both return a polynomial? The Expand operation evaluates all powers and products of sums in the selected expression. For the expression $(x- 3) \cdot (x- 4)$, the result was a polynomial, but this is not always true. The Collect operation attempts to return a polynomial in the selected variable. For example, using the Expand operation on the result of a sum of terms with a common denominator yields a different result from that obtained using the Collect operation on the same sum, as is shown in these examples:

$$\frac{(a\bullet x-4\bullet a+b\bullet x-3\bullet b)}{((x-3)+(x-4))} \text{ expand, } x \rightarrow \frac{1}{((x-3)\bullet(x-4))}\bullet a\bullet x-$$

$$\frac{4}{((x-3)\bullet(x-4))}\bullet a + \frac{1}{((x-3)\bullet(x-4))}\bullet b\bullet x - \frac{3}{((x-3)\bullet(x-4))}\bullet b$$

$$\frac{(a\bullet x-4\bullet a+b\bullet x-3\bullet b)}{((x-3)+(x-4))} \text{ collect, } x \rightarrow \frac{((a+b)\bullet x-4\bullet a-3\bullet b))}{(x-3)\bullet(x-4)}$$

6.4.6 Partial-Fraction Expansion

A partial-fraction expansion on a variable is a method for expanding a complex expression into a sum of (hopefully) simpler expressions with denominators containing only linear and quadratic terms and no functions of the variable in the numerator. As a first example, a partial-fraction expansion, based upon x, on

$$\frac{\left(a\bullet(x-4)+b\bullet(x-3)\right)}{((x-3)\bullet(x-4))}$$

gives back the original function,

$$\frac{a}{(x-3)} + \frac{b}{(x-4)}$$

This was accomplished by selecting an x (any of them) and then choosing Symbolics/Variable/Convert to Partial Fraction from the Symbolics menu.

A slightly more complex example is to take the ratio of two polynomials and expand it by using partial fractions. The process is the same as described in the preceding example: Select the variable upon which you want to expand (z in this example), and then choose Symbolics/Variable/Convert to Partial Fraction from the Symbolics menu. The result will look like this:

$$\frac{\left(9\bullet z^2-40\bullet z+23\right)}{\left(z^3-7\bullet z^2+7\bullet z+15\right)}$$

$$\frac{2}{(z-3)} + \frac{3}{(z+1)} + \frac{4}{(z-5)}$$

An expanded example involving two variables illustrates how the partial fraction expansion depends on the variable selected . The starting expression now involves both z and y.

$$\frac{\left(7\bullet z^3+19\bullet z^2-43\bullet z^2\bullet y-100\bullet z\bullet y+9\bullet z-33\bullet y+60\bullet y^2\bullet z+105\bullet y^2\right)}{\left(z^4+4\bullet z^3-8\bullet z^3\bullet y-32\bullet z^2\bullet y+3\bullet z^2-24\bullet z\bullet y+15\bullet y^2\bullet z^2+60\bullet y^2\bullet z+45\bullet y^2\right)}$$

A partial fraction expansion on z requires that each denominator be linear or quadratic in z and precludes any function of z from every numerator. The result is

$$\frac{5}{(2\bullet(z+3))} + \frac{3}{(2\bullet(z+1))} - \frac{2}{(-z+5\bullet y)} - \frac{1}{(-z+3\bullet y)}$$

On the other hand, a partial fraction expansion on y precludes functions of y in the numerators, but allows functions of z. The result of a partial fractions expansion on y is

$$\frac{(4 \bullet z + 7)}{(z^2 + 4 \bullet z + 3)} - \frac{2}{(-z + 5 \bullet y)} - \frac{1}{(-z + 3 \bullet y)}$$

6.5   POLYNOMIAL COEFFICIENTS

If you have an expression that can be written as a polynomial, Mathcad will return a vector containing the coefficients of the polynomial. This operation is available from the Symbolics menu using Symbolics/Polynomial Coefficients.

The coefficients of the polynomial $x^2 - 7x + 12$ are pretty obvious. If you select any x in the expression, say,

$$\boxed{x^2 - 7 \cdot x + 12}$$

and then ask for the vector of *polynomial coefficients* as Symbolics/Polynomial Coefficients, the coefficients are returned as a vector.

$x^2 - 7 \cdot x + 12$

$$\begin{bmatrix} 12 \\ -7 \\ 1 \end{bmatrix}$$

[*Note:* While Mathcad's symbolic math functions typically display the higher powers first (i.e., the x^2 before the $7x$), the first polynomial coefficient in the returned vector is the constant, 12.]

When your expression is written as a polynomial, the coefficients are apparent. However Mathcad's symbolic processor can return the polynomial coefficients of expressions that are not displayed in standard polynomial form. For example, we know that $x^2 - 7x + 12$ is algebraically equivalent to $(x - 3) \cdot (x - 4)$. Using Symbolics/ Polynomial Coefficients on $(x - 3) \cdot (x - 4)$ returns the same polynomial coefficients as in the standard-form case:

$(x - 3) \cdot (x - 4)$

$$\begin{bmatrix} 12 \\ -7 \\ 1 \end{bmatrix}$$

6.6   SYMBOLIC MATRIX MATH

Mathcad provides symbolic matrix operations from either the Symbolics menu or the Symbolic Keyword Toolbar. These are very straightforward operations and only summarized in this section.

6.6.1 Tranpose

To transpose a matrix, select the entire matrix and then choose Symbolics/Matrices/ Transpose. The original and transposed matrices are, respectively,

$$\begin{bmatrix} 1 & 1 \\ 2 & 8 \\ 3 & 27 \\ 4 & 64 \\ 5 & 125 \end{bmatrix}$$

and

$$\begin{bmatrix} 1 & 2 & 3 & 4 & 5 \\ 1 & 8 & 27 & 64 & 125 \end{bmatrix}$$

6.6.2 Inverse

To invert a matrix symbolically, select the entire matrix and then choose Symbolics/ Matrices/Invert. The original and inverted matrices are, respectively,

$$\begin{bmatrix} 2 & 3 & 5 \\ 7 & 2 & 4 \\ 8 & 11 & 6 \end{bmatrix}$$

and

$$\begin{bmatrix} \dfrac{-32}{211} & \dfrac{37}{211} & \dfrac{2}{211} \\[2mm] \dfrac{-10}{211} & \dfrac{-28}{211} & \dfrac{27}{211} \\[2mm] \dfrac{61}{211} & \dfrac{2}{211} & \dfrac{-17}{211} \end{bmatrix}$$

If you want to see the inverted matrix represented as values rather than fractions, select the entire inverted matrix, then choose Symbolics/Evaluate/Floating Point..., and, finally, enter the number of digits to display. Twenty digits is the default, but that is often excessive. Here, the result is displayed with a floating-point precision of 4 digits:

$$\begin{bmatrix} -.1517 & .1754 & .009479 \\ -.04739 & -.1327 & .128 \\ .2891 & .009479 & -.08057 \end{bmatrix}$$

6.6.3 Determinant

Mathcad will also symbolically calculate the determinant of a matrix. To do so, select the entire matrix and then choose Symbolics/Matrices/Determinant. In this example, the determinant is found to be 211:

$$\begin{bmatrix} 2 & 3 & 5 \\ 7 & 2 & 4 \\ 8 & 11 & 6 \end{bmatrix}$$

211

6.7   SYMBOLIC INTEGRATION

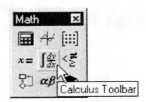

Mathcad provides a number of ways to integrate and differentiate functions. In this chapter, we focus on symbolic, or analytic integration, leaving numerical integration for the next chapter. The *integration* and *differentiation* operators are found on the *Calculus Toolbar*, which is available from the Math Toolbar.

In this section, we use a simple polynomial as a demonstration function and the same polynomial throughout to allow us to compare the various integration and differentiation methods, except where multiple variables are required to demonstrate multivariate integration. The polynomial is $12+3x-4x^2$, and a multivariable function, the formula for the volume of a cylinder, $\iiint r\, dr\, d\theta\, dl$ (with $0 \leq r \leq R$, $0 \leq \theta \leq 2\pi$, $0 \leq 1 \leq L$), is used to demonstrate multivariable integration and differentiation.

6.7.1   Indefinite Integrals

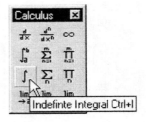

SYMBOLIC
INTEGRATION
USING THE
INDEFINITE
INTEGRAL
OPERATOR

The most straightforward of Mathcad's integration methods uses the *indefinite integral operator* from the Calculus Toolbar. When you click on the button for the indefinite integral operator, the operator is placed on your worksheet with two empty placeholders, the first for the function to be integrated and the second for the integration variable:

$$\int \blacksquare d\blacksquare$$

To integrate the sample polynomial, enter the polynomial in the first placeholder and an *x* in the second:

$$\int (12+3 \bullet x - 4 \bullet x^2)dx$$

Complete the integration using the "evaluate symbolically" symbol, the →. This symbol is entered by pressing [Ctrl-.] (Hold down the Control key while pressing the period key.) The result is

$$\int (12+3 \bullet x - 4 \bullet x^2)dx \;\rightarrow\; 12 \bullet x + \frac{3}{2} \bullet x^2 - \frac{4}{3} \bullet x^3$$

Note that the integration variable is a dummy variable. You can put any variable you want in that placeholder. However, if you write the polynomial as a function of x and integrate with respect to y, Mathcad will perform the integration, but the result will not be very interesting:

$$\int (12+3 \bullet x-4 \bullet x^2)dx \rightarrow (12+3 \bullet x-4 \bullet x^2) \bullet y$$

Alternatively, you can select the entire expression and then choose Simplify from the Symbolics menu:

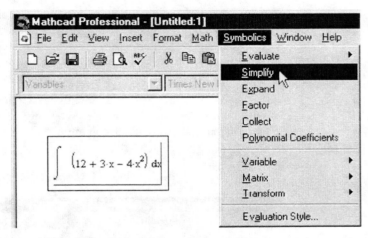

By default, the result will be placed below the integral operator:

$$\int (12+3 \bullet x-4 \bullet x^2)dx$$

$$12 \bullet x + \frac{3}{2} \bullet x^2 - \frac{4}{3} \bullet x^3$$

You can modify the placement of the result by using the Symbolics/Evaluation style menu options.

Observe that Mathcad does not add the constant of integration you might expect when integrating without limits. Mathcad shows the functional form of the integrated expression, but you have to add your own integration constant if you want to evaluate the result. The integrated result is an editable equation region, so adding the constant is no problem:

$$12 \bullet x + \frac{3}{2} \bullet x^2 - \frac{4}{3} \bullet x^3 + C$$

SYMBOLIC INTEGRATION WITH MULTIPLE VARIABLES

You can use the indefinite integration operator to integrate over multiple variables. Simply use one indefinite operator symbol for each integration variable. The second integration operator goes in the first operator's function placeholder, and so on. To integrate over three variables say, r, θ , and 1, we'll use three integration operators:

$$\int \int \int \blacksquare \; d\blacksquare \; d\blacksquare \; d\blacksquare$$

Note that there is now only one function placeholder (before the first d), but three integration variable placeholders. In the computation of the volume of a cylinder, the function placeholder contains only an r:

$$\int \int \int r \; d\blacksquare \; d\blacksquare \; d\blacksquare$$

And the integration variables are r, θ, and 1:

$$\int\int\int r\,dr\,d\theta\,dl$$

You instruct Mathcad to evaluate the integral with the $\rightarrow$ operator:

Not quite the result you anticipated, perhaps? The expression was integrated as an indefinite integral. The π that you normally see in the formula for the volume of a cylinder comes from the *integration limits* on θ. This will become apparent later, when we integrate this function with limits (using the definite integral operator).

SYMBOLIC INTEGRATION USING THE SYMBOLICS MENU

Symbolic integration using the Symbolics menu is an alternative method for integrating with respect to a *single variable*. Symbolic integration does not use the indefinite integral operator at all. Instead, you enter your function, e.g.,

$$12+3\cdot x-\ 4\cdot x^2$$

and then select the variable of integration, one of the x's in this example:

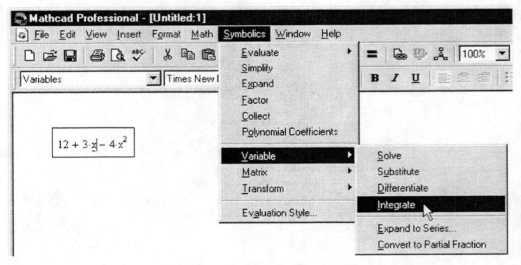

To perform the integration, use the Symbolics menu (Symbolics/Variable/Integrate) to obtain

$$12+3\cdot x-\ 4\cdot x^2$$

$$12\bullet x+\frac{3}{2}\bullet x^2-\frac{4}{3}\bullet x^3$$

The result (again, without the constant of integration) is placed below the original function. This approach is very handy, but is useful only for indefinite integrals with a single integration variable.

PRACTICE!

Use Mathcad's indefinite integral operator to evaluate these integrals (starting with the obvious):

a. $\int x \, dx.$

b. $\int (a + bx + cx^2) \, dx.$

c. $\int \int 2x^2 y \, dx \, dy.$

d. $\int \frac{1}{x} \, dx.$

e. $\int e^{-ax} \, dx.$

f. $\int \cos(2x) \, dx.$

6.7.2 Definite Integrals

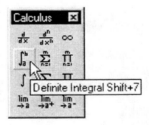

Mathcad evaluates definite integrals using the *definite integral operator* from the Calculus Toolbar. Definite integrals can be evaluated in a number of ways:

- symbolic evaluation with variable limits.
- symbolic evaluation with numeric limits.
- symbolic evaluation with mixed (variable and numeric) limits.
- numerical evaluation (requires numeric limits).

DEFINITE INTEGRALS: SYMBOLIC EVALUATION WITH VARIABLE LIMITS

The definite integral operator comes with four placeholders—the function and integration variable placeholders and two limit placeholders:

$$\int_{\blacksquare}^{\blacksquare} \blacksquare \, d\blacksquare$$

To evaluate the polynomial integrated from $x = A$ to $x = B$, simply include the limits in the appropriate placeholders:

$$\int_{A}^{B} (12 + 3 \bullet x - 4 \bullet x^2) \, dx$$

You instruct Mathcad to evaluate the integral either by using the symbolic evaluation symbol ($\rightarrow$) or by choosing Simplify from the Symbolics menu. In either case, the result is

$$\int_A^B \left(12 + 3 \bullet x - 4 \bullet x^2\right) dx \;\rightarrow\; 12 \bullet B - \frac{4}{3} \bullet B^3 + \frac{3}{2} \bullet B^2 - 12 \bullet A + \frac{4}{3} \bullet A^3 - \frac{3}{2} \bullet A^2$$

Definite Integrals: Symbolic Evaluation With Numeric Limits   To evaluate an integral with numeric limits, you can place the numbers in the limit placeholders, as, for example, in

$$\int_{-1}^2 \left(12 + 3 \bullet x - 4 \bullet x^2\right) dx \;\rightarrow\; \frac{57}{2}$$

Or you can assign values to variables before the integration and use the variables as limits, as in

$$A := -1 \qquad B := 2$$

$$\int_A^B \left(12 + 3 \bullet x - 4 \bullet x^2\right) dx \;\rightarrow\; \frac{57}{2}$$

Definite Integrals: Symbolic Evaluation With Mixed Limits   It is fairly common to have a numeric value for one limit and to want to integrate from that known value to an arbitrary (variable) limit. Mathcad handles this type of integration as well:

$$\int_{-1}^C \left(12 + 3 \bullet x - 4 \bullet x^2\right) dx \;\rightarrow\; 12 \bullet C - \frac{4}{3} \bullet C^3 + \frac{3}{2} \bullet C^2 + \frac{55}{6}$$

In the preceding example, the known limit was evaluated and generated the 55/6 in the result. The unknown limit was evaluated in terms of the variable C. The result can then be evaluated for any value of C.

[*Note:* In evaluating an integral from a known limit to a variable limit, it is common to use the integration variable as the variable limit as well. Thus, for the preceding example, we would have

$$\int_{-1}^x \left(12 + 3 \bullet x - 4 \bullet x^2\right) dx$$

Mathcad, however will not evaluate this expression. For Mathcad, the integration variable (the x in dx) is a dummy variable, but the limits are not. In Mathcad, you cannot use the same symbol to represent both a dummy variable and a limit variable in a single equation.]

MIXED LIMITS WITH MULTIPLE INTEGRATION VARIABLES

To obtain a formula for the volume of any cylinder, we would integrate the cylinder function over the variable r from 0 to some arbitrary radius R, over θ from 0 to 2π (for a completely round cylinder), and over 1 from 0 to an arbitrary length L. The result is the common expression for the volume of a cylinder:

$$\int_0^L \int_0^{2 \bullet \pi} \int_0^R r \, dr \, d\theta \, dl \;\rightarrow\; R^2 \bullet \pi \bullet L$$

Note the order of the integration symbols and the integration variables. Mathcad uses the limits on the inside integration symbol (0 to R) with the inside integration variable (dr), the limits on the middle integration operator (0 to 2π) with the middle integration variable ($d\theta$), and so forth.

**DEFINITE
INTEGRALS:
NUMERICAL
EVALUATION**

Numerical evaluation of an integral does not really fit in this chapter on symbolic math, but it is the final way that Mathcad can evaluate an integral. To request a numerical evaluation, use the equal sign instead of the $\rightarrow$ symbol:

$$\int_{-1}^{2} \left(12+3\bullet x-4\bullet x^2\right)dx = 28.5 \,\vert$$

Normally, you would see the result to 20 decimal places (by default), but this result is precise, at 28.5. Note that the result includes a units placeholder. Units can be used with numerical evaluation (and with the limits on symbolic integration as well).

PRACTICE!

Use Mathcad's definite integral operator to evaluate these expressions:

a. $\int_{0}^{4} x\, dx.$

b. $\int_{1}^{3} (ax + b)\, dx.$

c. $\int_{-3}^{0} \frac{1}{3}\, dx.$

d. $\int_{0}^{\pi}\int_{0}^{2\,\text{cm}} r\, dr\, d\theta.$

Find the area under the following curves in the range $x = 1$ and $x = 5$ (Part a has been completed as an example):

a. $3 + 1.5\,x - 0.25\,x^2$

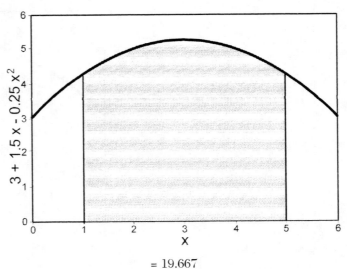

$= 19.667$

b. $0.2 + 1.7\,x^3$

c. $\sin\left[\dfrac{x}{2}\right]$

Find the area between the following curves in the range $x = 1$ and $x = 5$ (Part a has been completed as an example):

a. $3 + 1.5\,x - 0.25\,x^2$ and $0 + 1.5\,x - 0.25\,x^2$

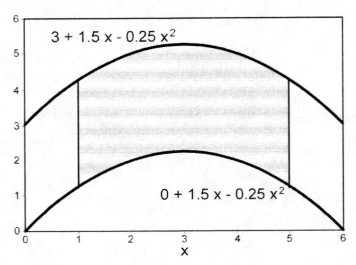

$$Area = \int_1^5 (3 + 1.5x - 0.25x^2) - (0 + 1.5x - 0.25x^2)\,dx$$

$$= \int_1^5 3\,dx$$

$$= 12$$

b. $3 + 1.5\,x - 0.25\,x^2$ and $0.1\,x^2$

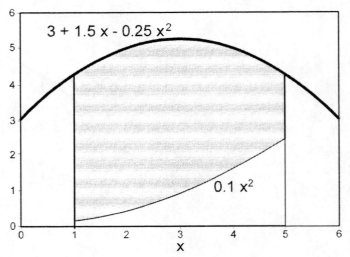

APPLICATIONS: ENERGY REQUIRED TO WARM A GAS

Warming up a gas is a pretty common thing to do, partly because we like to live in warm buildings and partly because we tend to burn things to warm those buildings. Combustion always warms up it products. It is common to need to know how much energy is required to warm a gas.

The amount of energy needed to warm a gas depends on the amount, heat capacity, and temperature change of the gas. Also, heat capacities of gases are strong functions of temperature, so the relationship between heat capacity and temperature must be taken into account. All of this is included in the equation

$$\Delta H = n \int_{T_1}^{T_2} C_p \, dT$$

where

δH is the change in enthalpy of the gas, which is equal to the amount of energy required to warm the gas if all of the energy added to the gas is used to warm it (i.e., if the energy is not used to make the gas move faster, etc.),

n is the number of moles of gas present (say, 3 moles),

C_p is the heat capacity of the gas at constant pressure,

T_1 is the initial temperature of the gas (say, 25°C), and

T_2 is the final temperature of the gas (say, 400°C).

Since heat capacities change with temperature, the relationship between heat capacity and temperature is often given as an equation. For example, for CO_2 the heat capacity is related to the temperature by the expression[1]

$$C_p = 36.11 + 4.233 \cdot 10^{-2}T - 2.887 \cdot 10^{-5}T^2$$

$$+7.464 \cdot 10^{-9}\, T^3 \ \text{(J/mole °C)},$$

and the equation is valid for temperatures between 0 and 1500°C.

We can use Mathcad to integrate this expression and determine the amount of energy required to warm 3 moles of CO^2 from 25 to 400°C:

$$n := 3$$

$$\Delta H := n \cdot \int_{25}^{400} (36.11 + 4.233 \cdot 10^{-2} \cdot T$$

$$-2.887 \cdot 10^{-5} \cdot T^2 + 7.464 \cdot 10^{-9} \cdot T^3) dT$$

$$\Delta H = 4.904 \cdot 10^4$$

The energy required is 49 kJ.

Note that this problem was worked without units for two reasons:

1. The units on the various terms in the heat capacity equation are complicated.
2. Mathcad doesn't have °C as a built-in unit, and the T_s in this heat capacity equation must be in °C.

---

[1] From *Elementary Principles of Chemical Processes* by R.M. Felder and R.W. Rousseau, 2nd ed, Wiley, New York (1986).

6.8 SYMBOLIC DIFFERENTIATION

You can evaluate derivatives with respect to one or more variables using the *Derivative* or *N*th *Derivative* buttons on the Calculus Toolbar. For a first derivative with respect to a single variable, you can also use Variable/Derivative from the Symbolics menu.

FIRST DERIVATIVE WITH RESPECT TO ONE VARIABLE

When you click on the Derivative button on the Calculus Toolbar, the derivative operator is placed on the worksheet:

$$\frac{d}{d\blacksquare}\blacksquare$$

The operator contains two placeholders—one for the function, the other for the differentiation variable. To take the derivative of the sample polynomial with respect to the variable x, the polynomial and the variable are inserted into their respective placeholders:

$$\frac{d}{dx}\left(12+3\bullet x-4\bullet x^2\right)$$

You tell Mathcad to evaluate the derivative either by using the $\rightarrow$ symbol, producing

$$\frac{d}{dx}\left(12+3\bullet x-4\bullet x^2\right) \rightarrow 3-8\bullet x$$

or by selecting the entire expression and then choosing Simplify from the Symbolics menu, resulting in

$$\frac{d}{dx}\left(12+3\bullet x-4\bullet x^2\right)$$

$$3-\;8\;\cdot x$$

Note that Mathcad does not have a "Derivative evaluated at" operator. To evaluate the result at a particular value of x, simply give x a value before performing the differentiation

$$x := -1$$

$$\frac{d}{dx}\left(12+3\bullet x-4\bullet x^2\right) \rightarrow 11$$

As an alternative to using the Derivative operator from the Calculus Toolbar, you can enter your function and select one variable (one of the *x*'s in the polynomial example):

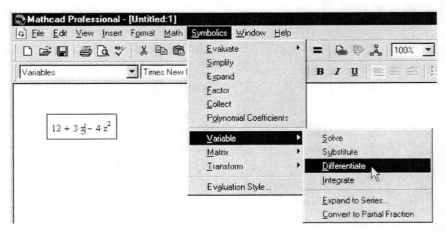

Then you differentiate the function with respect to the selected variable using Symbolics/Variable/Differentiate from the Symbolics menu. The result will be

```
12+3·x– 4 · x²
3– 8·x
```

This method works only for evaluating a first derivative with respect to a single variable.

HIGHER DERIVATIVES WITH RESPECT TO A SINGLE VARIABLE

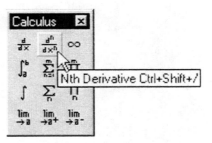

For higher derivatives, use the Nth Derivative operator from the Calculus Toolbox. This operator comes with four placeholders, but you can use only three:

When you add the power to the right placeholder in the denominator, the same power will appear in the numerator of the derivative operator. You cannot type directly into the placeholder in the numerator. In this example, we'll use a power of 2 to take the second derivative of the sample polynomial:

$$\frac{d^2}{dI^2}\blacksquare$$

The two remaining placeholders are for the function and the differentiation variable:e:

$$\frac{d^2}{dx^2}\left(12+3\bullet x-4\bullet x^2\right) \rightarrow -8$$

DIFFERENTIATION WITH RESPECT TO MULTIPLE VARIABLES

Use multiple derivative operators to evaluate derivatives with respect to multiple variables. For example, the indefinite integral of r with respect to r, θ, and 1 yields this result:

$$\int\int\int r\, dr\, d\theta\, dl \quad\rightarrow\quad \frac{1}{2}\bullet r^2\bullet\theta\bullet 1$$

If we take the result and differentiate it with respect to r, θ, and 1, we should get the original function back:

$$\frac{d}{dl}\frac{d}{d\theta}\frac{d}{dr}\left(\frac{1}{2}\bullet r^2\bullet\theta\bullet 1\right) \quad\rightarrow\quad r$$

The original function is simply r, all by itself.

As a more interesting example, consider the ideal-gas law, and take the derivative of pressure with respect to temperature and volume:

$$P = \frac{n \bullet R \bullet T}{V}$$

$$\frac{d}{dT} \frac{d}{dV} \left(\frac{n \bullet R \bullet T}{V} \right) \rightarrow -n \bullet \frac{R}{V^2}$$

PRACTICE!

Try using Mathcad to evaluate these derivatives:

a. $\dfrac{d}{dx} x^2.$

b. $\dfrac{d}{dx} (3x^2 + 4x).$

c. $\dfrac{d^2}{dx^2} x^3.$

d. $\dfrac{d}{dx} \dfrac{d}{dy} (3x^2 + 4xy + 2y^2).$

e. $\dfrac{d}{dx} \ln(ax^2).$

f. $\dfrac{d}{dx} \cos(2x).$

APPLICATION: ANALYZING STRESS-STRAIN DIAGRAMS

A fairly standard test for new materials is the tensile test. In essence, a sample of the material is very carefully prepared and then slowly pulled apart. The stress on the sample and the elongation of the sample are recorded throughout the test. We will consider data from a composite material in this example, but to allow for comparison, first consider a tensile test on a metal sample.

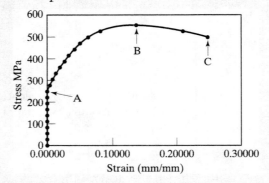

Note the units on strain in the foregoing diagram: mm/mm. This is millimeters of elongation divided by the original length of the sample. The test begins with no stress and no strain. As the pulling begins, the metal starts to stretch. From the origin of the graph to point A, the stretching is reversible: If the pulling pressure were released, the metal would return to its original size. Beyond point A, some of the stretching is irreversible. Point B is called the material's *ultimate stress*—the highest stress that the material can withstand without breaking. Beyond point B, the stress actually goes down as the sample pulls itself apart under the applied stress. At point C, the sample breaks.

The stress-strain curves for composite materials have a different shape, because of the way the materials respond to stress. There are many different composite materials with vastly different mechanical properties, so their stress-strain curves could be very different, but the curve shown in the preceding figure illustrates some interesting features.

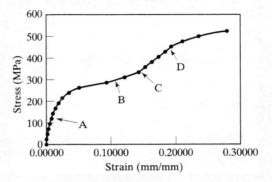

The big difference between this curve and the previous one is the presence of a second hump. Between the origin and point B, the curve looks a lot like an ordinary stress-strain curve, and then the second hump starts appearing at about point C. The explanation for this behavior is that the first hump represents mostly the matrix (surrounding the fibers) responding to the stress. The matrix then cracks and separates from the fibers, and the stress is transferred to the fibers between points B and C. From point C on, you are seeing the stress-strain response of the fibers.

There are a couple of analyses we can perform on these data:

a. Estimate Young's modulus for the matrix and the fibers.
b. Calculate the work done on the sample during the test.

Young's Modulus

Young's modulus is the proportionality factor relating stress and strain in the linear sections of the graph between the origin and point A and (sometimes visible) between points C and D. Because the material is a composite, neither of the values we will calculate truly represents Young's modulus for the pure materials, but they will help quantify how this composite material behaves under stress.

The linear region near the origin includes approximately the first four or five data points. Young's modulus for the matrix can be calculated from the change in stress and the measured change in strain:

$$Y := \frac{\text{Stress}_3 - \text{Stress}_0}{\text{Strain}_3 - \text{Strain}_0}$$

$$Y = 5.929 \cdot 10^4 \qquad \text{<<MPa}$$

Similarly, Young's modulus relating stress to strain in the region between C and D includes points 15–18:

$$Y_{\text{fiber}} := \frac{\text{Stress}_{18} - \text{Stress}_{15}}{\text{Strain}_{18} - \text{Strain}_{15}}$$

$$Y_{\text{fiber}} = 1.012 \cdot 10^4 \qquad \text{<<MPa}$$

Work

A little reshaping can turn a stress-strain diagram into a force-displacement diagram. The area under a force-displacement diagram is the work done on the sample.

Stress is the force per unit cross-sectional area of the sample. If the sample tested is $L = 10$ mm by $W = 10$ mm, the area and force on the sample can be computed as

```
A := L· W
F := Stress·A
```

To obtain a displacement, x. we need to multiply the strain by the original sample length (or height; the samples are usually vertical when tested). If $H = 10$ mm as well, then

```
x := Strain·H
```

We can now replot the stress-strain diagram as a force-displacement graph. The result will look like this:

The area under the graph is the work, but in order to use Mathcad's integration operator, we need a function relating force to displacement, not data points. In the last chapter, we saw how to fit a polynomial to data. That's what we need here. (*Note:* In the next chapter, integration methods using the data points themselves will be covered.)

Accordingly,

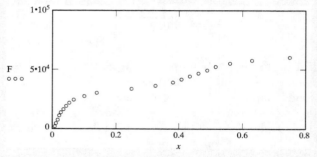

$$f(x) := \begin{bmatrix} x \\ x^2 \\ x^3 \\ x^4 \\ x^5 \end{bmatrix} \qquad b := \text{linfit}(x, F, f)$$

$$F_p := \overrightarrow{(b_0 \bullet x + b_1 \bullet x^2 + b_2 \bullet x^3 + b_3 \bullet x^4 + b_4 \bullet x^5)}$$

From the preceding graph, it looks like the fifth-order polynomial fits the data nicely. But F_p is a vector of values; we still need a *function*. Hence,

$$F_{func}(x) := b_0 \bullet x + b_1 \bullet x^2 + b_2 \bullet x^3 + b_3 \bullet x^4 + b_4 \bullet x^5$$

This function can be integrated using the definite integration operator from the Calculus Toolbox. As the graph shows, the upper limit on x is almost 0.8. The actual value can be found by using the max ( ) function on the x vector:

$$\text{Work} := \int_0^{max(x)} F_{func}(x)\, dx$$

$$\text{Work} = 3.069 \cdot 10_4$$

That's the work, but what are the units? F was determined from stress (MPa) and area (mm^2), and x came from strain (mm/mm) and length (mm). This work has units of MPa · (mm^3). We'll convert them:

```
Work := Work· MPa· mm³
Work = 30.695· N
```

(*Note:* The integration operator can handle units, but the linfit() function does not. That's why this problem was worked without units.)

SUMMARY

In this chapter, we looked at Mathcad's symbolic math capabilities—its ability to work directly with mathematical expressions, rather than numerical results. We saw that Mathcad's symbolic math features are housed in two areas and are used in slightly different ways. For example, you can solve for a variable in an equation from either the Symbolics menu or the Symbolic Keyword Toolbar. With the latter, there is a "live operator," so that if you make changes to the worksheet, the solve operation will be automatically recalculated, and you specify the variable you want to solve for as part of the operation. In order to solve for a variable using the Symbolics menu, you first select the variable of interest and then use Symbolics/Variable/Solve from the menu. The result is placed on the worksheet, but it is not a live operator, so the result will not be automatically recalculated if the worksheet changes. Both approaches are useful.

You also saw that Mathcad can replace (substitute) every occurrence of a variable with another mathematical expression and can factor common terms out of complex expressions. You can use symbolic math to find a common denominator using the simplify operation. Mathcad can manipulate expressions in a number of other ways as well.

Finally, you learned that Mathcad can do matrix math operations symbolically, as well as integrate and differentiate expressions.

KEY TERMS

Collecting term
definite integral operator
differentiation
Expanding
Factoring
indefinite integral operator
integration

integration limits
live symbolic operator
logarithmic curve
logistic curve
partial-fraction expansion
polynomial coefficients

power curve
Simplify menu command
Simplifying
substitute operation
Substituting
symbolic math

MATHCAD SUMMARY

OPERATIONS UNDER THE SYMBOLICS MENU:

Before using the Symbolics menu, you generally need to select the part of an expression you want to operate on. For example, you need to select a variable in an expression before using any of the Symbolics/Variable operations.

Symbolics/**Simplify**	Evaluates common math operations (e.g., square root) to try to simplify an expression.
Symbolics/**Expand**	Multiplies out powers and polynomials, expands numerators of fractions.
Symbolics/**Factor**	Reverses the expand operation: simplifies polynomials, pulls a common expression out of multiple terms.
Symbolics/**Collect**	Tries to rewrite a set of summed terms as a polynomial.
Symbolics/**Polynomial Coefficients**	If the selected expression can be written as a polynomial, returns the polynomial coefficients.
Symbolics/**Variable/Solve**	Solves an expression for the selected variable.
Symbolics/**Variable/Substitute**	Replaces each occurrence of the selected variable with the expression in the Windows clipboard.
Symbolics/**Variable/Differentiate**	Returns the first derivative of the expression with respect to the selected variable.
Symbolics/**Variable/Integrate**	Integrates the expression with respect to the selected variable—does not add a constant of integration.
Symbolics/**Variable/Convert to Partial Fractions**	Expands an expression into a sum of expressions with denominators containing only linear and quadratic terms and with no functions of the selected variable in the numerator.
Symbolics/**Matrix/Transpose**	Interchanges rows and columns in the matrix.
Symbolics/**Matrix/Invert**	Inverts the matrix using symbolic math operations, rather than decimal numbers—this preserves accuracy by avoiding round-off errors, but the resulting fractions can get unwieldy.
Symbolics/**Matrix/Determinant**	Calculates the determinant of a matrix using symbolic math operations.
Symbolics/**Evaluation Style ...**	Opens a dialog box that allows you to change the way the results of the calculations are presented.

OPERATIONS USING THE SYMBOLIC KEYWORD TOOLBOX:

With the Symbolic Keyword Toolbox, the symbolic evaluation operator $\rightarrow$ is used and any variables or expressions that must be specified in order to perform the operation are entered into placeholders as needed. You do not need to select a variable or a portion of the expression before performing the symbolic operation.

solve	Solves the expression for the specified variable.
simplify	Evaluates common math operations to try to simplify an expression.
susbtitute	Replaces each occurrence of the specified variable with the specified expression.
factor	Pulls the specified variable out of all terms in an expression.
expand	Evaluates powers and polynomials involving the specified variable; expands numerators of fractions involving the variable.
coeffs	Returns the polynomial coefficients, if there are any, for the specified variable.
collect	Tries to rewrite summed terms as a polynomial in the specified variable.

parfrac	Expands an expression into a sum of expressions, with denominators containing only linear and quadratic terms and with no functions of the selected variable in the numerator.
$M^T \rightarrow$	Transposes the matrix (interchanges rows and columns in the matrix).
$M^{-1} \rightarrow$	Inverts the matrix using symbolic math operations.
$|M| \rightarrow$	Calculates the determinant of a matrix using symbolic math operations.

OPERATIONS USING THE CALCULUS PALETTE:

Indefinite Integral	Integrates the expression in the function placeholder with respect to the variable in the integration variable placeholder. If the symbolic evaluation operator $\rightarrow$ is used after the integral, the integral is evaluated symbolically. Mathcad does not add a constant of integration. If an equal sign is used after the integral, the integral is evaluated numerically.
Definite Integral	Integrates the expression in the function placeholder with respect to the variable in the integration variable placeholder, using the specified limits. (The dummy integration variable cannot be used in a limit.) If the symbolic evaluation operator $\rightarrow$ is used after the integral, the integral is evaluated symbolically. If an equal sign is used after the integral, the integral is evaluated numerically.
Derivative	Takes the derivative of the variable in the function placeholder with respect to the variable in the differentiation variable placeholder. If the symbolic evaluation operator $\rightarrow$ is used, the derivative is evaluated symbolically. If an equal sign is used, the derivative is evaluated numerically. To evaluate the derivative at a particular value, assign the value to the differentiation variable before taking the derivative.
Nth Derivative	Takes second- and higher-order derivatives.

Problems

1. SOLVING FOR A VARIABLE IN AN EXPRESSION

   Use the equation

   $$A = 2 \cdot \pi \cdot r^2 + 2 \cdot \pi \cdot r \cdot L$$

   for the surface area of a cylinder. The equation is written using the symbolic equality, [CTRL–=].

   a. Use the solve operation on the Symbolic Keyword Toolbar to solve for the L in this equation.

   b. Use the expression returned by the solve operation to determine the cylinder length required to get 1 m^2 of surface area on a cylinder with a radius of 12 cm.

2. POLYNOMIAL EQUATIONS: COEFFICIENTS AND ROOTS

   The following equation clearly has three solutions (roots), at $x = 3$, $x = 1$, and $x = -2$:

   $$(x - 3) \cdot (x - 1) \cdot (x + 2) = 0$$

   a. Create a QuickPlot of $(x - 3) \cdot (x - 1) \cdot (x + 2)$ vs. x in the range from -3 to 3. Verify that the curve does cross the x-axis at $x = 3$, $x = 1$, and $x = -2$:

   b. Use the solve operation on x to have Mathcad find the roots:

   ```
   (x- 3)·(x- 1)·(x+2)  solve, x →
   ```

   c. Expand the function in x to see the expression written as a polynomial:

   ```
   (x- 3)·(x- 1)·(x+2)  expand, x →
   ```

   d. Obtain the polynomial coefficients as a vector using the *coeffs* operator from the Symbolic Math Toolbar:

```
(x- 3) · (x- 1) · (x+2)  coeffs, x →
```

3. **SYMBOLIC INTEGRATION**

Evaluate the following indefinite integrals symbolically:

a. $\int \sin(x)\ dx.$

b. $\int \ln(x)\ dx.$

c. $\int [\sin(x)^2 + \cos(x)]\ dx.$

d. $\int_{-3}^{0} \dfrac{x}{x+b}\ dx$

Note: In part c, notice how Mathcad indicates the sine-squared term: `sin(x)²`, not `sin²(x)`.

4. **DEFINITE INTEGRALS**

Evaluate the following definite integrals. Use either symbolic or numeric evaluations.

a. $\int_{0}^{\pi} \sin(\theta)\ d\theta.$

b. $\int_{0}^{2\pi} \sin(\theta)\ d\theta.$

c. $\int_{-3}^{0} \dfrac{x}{x-3}\ dx.$

d. $\int_{0}^{\infty} e^{\frac{-t}{4}}\ dt.$

Note: The numerical integrator cannot handle the infinite limit in part d; use symbolic integration. The infinity symbol is available on the Calculus Palette.

5. **INTEGRATING FOR THE AREA UNDER A CURVE**

Integrate $\int y\ dx$ to find the area under the curves represented by these functions:

a.	$y = -x^2 + 16$	between	$-2\ x$	4
b.	$y = e^{\frac{-t}{4}}$	between	$0\ t$	
c.	$y = e^{\frac{-t}{4}}$	between	$0\ t$	4

6. **INTEGRATING FOR THE AREA BETWEEN CURVES**

    Find the area between the curves represented by the functions

    $$x = -x^2 + 16$$

    and

    $$y = -x^2 + 9$$

    over the range $-3 \leq x \leq 3$

7. **AREA OF A SECTOR**

    The technical term for a pie-slice-shaped piece of a circle is a *sector*. The area of a sector can be found by integrating over r and θ :

    $$A = \int_{\theta=0}^{\alpha} \int_{r=0}^{R} r \, dr \, d\theta$$

    R = 2 cm

    a. Check the preceding equation by symbolically integrating over the entire circle ($\alpha = 2\pi$). Do you get the expected result, $A = \pi R^2$?
    b. Find the area of a 37° sector using Mathcad's numerical integration capability (i.e., use an equal sign rather than a symbolic evaluation operator ($\rightarrow$) to evaluate the integral.)

8. **DESIGNING AN IRRIGATION SYSTEM**

    An essential element of center-pivot irrigation systems is their ability to distribute water fairly evenly. Because the end of the pipe covers a lot more ground than the pipe near the center, water must be applied at a faster rate at the outside of the circle than near the center in order to apply the same number of gallons per square foot of ground.

    a. Use Mathcad's symbolic math capabilities to integrate the equation

    $$\text{Area}_{ring} = \int_{0}^{2\pi} \int_{R_i}^{R_0} r \, dr \, d\theta$$

    to obtain a formula for the area of a ring with inside radius R_i and outside radius R_o.

    b. At what rate must water be applied to provide one inch (depth) of water
        i. to the innermost ring: $R_i = 0, R_o = 20$ feet.
        ii. to the outermost ring: $R_i = 1300$ feet, $R_o = 1320$ feet.
    c. Write a Mathcad function that accepts the inside and outside radii and the desired water depth as inputs and returns the flow rate required to provide one inch of water. Use your function to determine the water flow rate for $R_i = 1000$ feet, $R_o = 1020$ feet. and depth = 2 inches.

9. **FINDING THE EQUATION FOR THE AREA OF AN ELLIPSE**

The equation of an ellipse centered at the origin is

$$\frac{x^2}{a^2} + \frac{y^2}{b^2} = 1$$

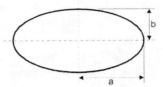

The area of the upper half of the ellipse can be determined by finding the area between the ellipse and the x – axis ($y = 0$).

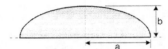

The total area of the ellipse is twice the area of the upper half.

a. Solve the equation of the ellipse for y. (You will obtain two solutions, since there are two y values on the ellipse at every x value.) Verify that the positive y values are returned by

$$y = \frac{b}{a} \cdot \sqrt{-(x^2) + a^2}$$

b. Substitute the expression for y from Part a in the integral for the area of an ellipse (twice the area of the upper half of the ellipse), and solve the following equation for the area of an ellipse symbolically:

$$2 \cdot \int_{-a}^{a} y \, dx \rightarrow$$

10. **WORK REQUIRED TO STRETCH A SPRING**

Hooke's law says that the force exerted against a spring as the spring is being stretched is proportional to the extended length. That is,

$$F = k\,x.$$

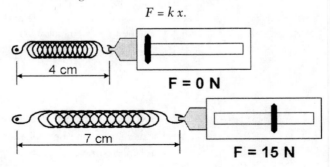

Work is defined as

$$W = \int F \, dx$$

From the accompanying figure, it can be seen that the length of the spring with no applied force is 4 cm. An applied force of 15 N extends the spring 3 cm to a total length of 7 cm. This information can be used to find the spring constant k. We write

$$15 \text{ N} = k \times 3 \text{ cm},$$

$$k = 5 \frac{\text{N}}{\text{cm}}$$

Calculate the work done on the spring as it was stretched from 4 to 7 cm (i.e., as the extended length went from 0 to 3 cm).

11. **WORK REQUIRED TO COMPRESS AN IDEAL GAS AT CONSTANT TEMPERATURE**
    One equation for work is

    $$W = \int P \, dV$$

    For an ideal gas, pressure and volume are related through the ideal gas law:

    $$PV = nRT$$

    a. Use Mathcad's ability to solve an expression for a variable to solve the ideal gas law for pressure P.
    b. Substitute the result for P from Part a into the work integral.
    c. Determine the work required to compress 10 moles of an ideal gas at 400 K from a volume of 300 liters to a volume of 30 liters. Express your result in kJ. (Assume that cooling is provided to maintain the temperature at 400 K throughout the compression.)
    d. Does the calculated work represent work done on the system (the 10 moles of gas) by the surroundings (the outside world) or by the system on the surroundings?

12. **ENERGY REQUIRED TO WARM A GAS**
    At what rate must energy be added to a stream of methane to warm it from 20°C to 240°C? Data are as follows:

Methane flow rate:	20,000 mole/min (these are gram moles);
Heat capacity equation:[*]	$Cp = 34.31 + 5.469 \cdot 10^{-2} T + 0.3661 \cdot 10^{-5} T^2$ $- 11.00 \cdot 109 \, T^3$ J/mole(C).

    [*]From *Elementary Principles of Chemical Processes* by R. M. Felder and R. W. Rousseau, 2nd ed., Wiley, New York (1986).

13. **YOUNG'S MODULUS**
    In the Mathcad Application analyzing stress-strain diagrams, values of Young's modulus for the matrix and the fiber were determined using algebra. An alternative approach would be to take the derivative of a function fit to the stress-strain data and evaluate the derivative in the linear regions of the stress-strain curve.

    Let

    $$f(x) := \begin{bmatrix} x \\ x^1 \\ x^3 \\ x^4 \\ x^5 \end{bmatrix} \quad b := \text{linfit (Strain, Stress, f)} \quad b = \begin{bmatrix} 5.951 \bullet 10^4 \\ -4.006 \bullet 10^6 \\ 1.195 \bullet 10^8 \\ -1.542 \bullet 10^9 \\ 7.184 \bullet 10^9 \end{bmatrix}$$

    be a fifth-order polynomial fit to the stress-strain curves.]

    Use Mathcad's derivative operator to differentiate the polynomial and then evaluate the derivative at strain values of 0.001 and 0.048 to find the values of Young's modulus for the matrix and the fibers, respectively.

14. CALCULATING WORK

The stress-strain data for the metal sample mentioned in the Application box on page 169 have been abridged and reproduced as follows:

STRAIN (MM/MM)	STRESS (MPA)
0.00000	0
0.00028	55
0.00055	110
0.00083	165
0.00110	221
0.00414	276
0.01324	331
0.02703	386
0.04193	441
0.06207	496
0.13793	552
0.20966	524
0.24828	496

a. Convert the following stress-strain diagram to a force-displacement graph (the sample size is 10 mm × 10 mm × 10 mm):

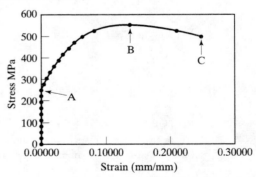

b. Fit a polynomial to the force-displacement data. (A fifth-order polynomial with no intercept works well.)

c. Integrate the polynomial to determine the work done on the sample during the tensile test.

7

Numerical Techniques

OBJECTIVES

- know how to use Mathcad's powerful iterative solver;
- know how to perform an integration on a data set, by — fitting the data set with a function and integrating the function, or by integrating, and using the data points directly;
- know how to perform differentiation on a data set, by — fitting the data set with a function and differentiating the function, or by differentiating, using the finite difference approximations on the data points.

7.1 ENGINEERING IN MEDICINE

Medical science has developed dramatically in the past generation, and with the increased understanding of the inner workings of the human body in health and disease comes the ability to apply that knowledge to try to improve the human condition. Engineers from every discipline can play a significant role in this enterprise. Many bodily processes are traditional areas of engineering study, but usually with a slight twist or complicating factor. For example, most engineers are familiar with fluid flows in tubes, but blood is a non-Newtonian fluid in pulsatile flow in nonrigid tubes. Each of these factors complicates the study of blood flow in the human body, but the engineer's knowledge of steady, Newtonian flow in rigid tubes provides a good foundation for the study of the more complex systems. Similar examples can be cited in other traditional fields of study, such as heat transfer (mechanisms for maintaining the body's temperature), mass transfer (carbon dioxide transfer from the blood in the lungs), reactor dynamics (controlled release of drugs into the body), mechanics (artificial limbs, improved athletic performance), and materials science (biologically inert materials for implants). In each of these areas engineers will work together, along with medical professionals, to expand our understanding of how our bodies work and to apply this knowledge to improve health care.

As only one example, designing an artificial limb requires a knowledge of anatomy and mechanics to design in the right motions, a knowledge of physiology and circuit theory to understand the electrical signals in the body, and a knowledge of control systems to use the signals to control the limb. Where the circuitry, the prosthesis, and the body come in contact, materials must be carefully chosen to meet mechanical, electrical, and biological constraints. This is definitely a field for team players, and the opportunities for engineers to make significant contributions in the field of medicine have never been greater.

7.2 ITERATIVE SOLUTIONS

Equations (or systems of equations) that cannot be solved directly occur often in engineering. For example, to determine the flow rate in a pipe with a given pressure drop, the friction loss must be known. But the friction loss depends on the flow rate. Thus, in order to calculate the friction loss, you must know the flow rate. But to calculate the flow rate, you must know the friction loss. To solve this very common problem, it is necessary to guess either the flow rate or the friction loss. If you guess the friction loss, you would calculate the flow rate and then calculate the friction loss at that flow rate. If the calculated friction loss equal the guessed friction loss, the problem is solved. If not, guess again.

Mathcad provides a better way to solve problems like this: the *iterative solver*. As a simple example, consider finding the value of x that satisfies the equation

$$x^3 + 12x - 21 = 0.$$

The x^3 suggests that there will be three solutions, but there could be duplicate roots or imaginary roots. In this example, two of the roots are imaginary. We'll try to find the one real root.

7.2.1 Using the Worksheet for Trial-and-Error Calculations

You can simply do trial-and-error calculations in the Mathcad workspace. For example, if we try $x = 0$, the expression $x^3 + 12x - 21$ yields -21. Since $-21 \neq 0$, the guessed value of x is incorrect. We might then try $x = 1$:

```
x := 1
x³+12·x−21 = −8
```

This result is closer to zero than the first attempt, so we're moving in the right direction, but the guessed x is still too small. Try $x = 2$:

```
x := 2
x³+12·x−21 = 11
```

The equation is still not satisfied, but this guess was too big. Try $x = 1.5$:

```
x := 1.5
x³+12·x−21 = 0.375
```

We're getting close, but $x = 1.5$ is a little high. With a few more tries, you'll find that a value of $x = 1.48$ comes very close to satisfying this equation.

Note: Iterative solutions always attempt to find values that "nearly" solve the equation. The process of choosing ever-closer guessed values could go on forever. To decide when the solution is "close enough" to stop the process, iterative methods test the calculated result against a preset tolerance. For Mathcad's iterative solver, the two sides of the equation are evaluated by using the computed value, and the difference between the two values is called the error. When the error falls below the preset tolerance, Mathcad stops iterating and presents the result. You can change the value of the tolerance from the default value of 0.001 to a larger number for less accurate solutions or (more likely) a smaller value for more accurate solutions. Very small tolerance values, such as 10^{-15}, may make it hard for Mathcad to find a solution because of computer round-off error.

7.2.2 Automating the Iterative Solution Process

Mathcad provides a better iterative solver than manual trial and error. Mathcad's approach uses an *iterative solve block*, since you can have Mathcad solve multiple equations simultaneously. The solve block is bounded by two keywords: given and find. The equations between these two words will be included in the iterative search for a solution. Before the given, you must provide an *initial guess* for each variable in the solve block. The iterative solve block for the preceding cubic example, with an initial guess of $x = 0$, would look like this:

$$x := 0$$

given

$$x^3 + 12 \cdot x - 21 = 0$$

$$x := \text{find}(x)$$

$$x = 1.4799$$

The equation between the given and find has been indented for readability. The line

$$x := \text{find}(x)$$

terminates the solve block and assigns the solution (returned by the `find()` function) to the variable x. Here the x variable was used to hold both the initial guess and the computed solution. This is common, but not necessary; you could assign the solution to any variable.

You can check the solution by using the computed value in the equation:

$$x := 1.4799$$

$$x^3 + 12 \cdot x - 21 = 0$$

You can adjust the displayed precision of any result by double-clicking on the displayed value and changing the number of displayed digits, but Mathcad will always drop trailing zeros. The zero on the right side of the equation is actually zero to at least three decimal places. (By default, Mathcad shows three decimal places.) The computed solution definitely satisfies the equation.

Keep in mind the following comments on using iterative solve blocks in Mathcad:

- Finding "a" solution does not imply that you have found "the" solution or all solutions. You should always try different initial guesses to check for other solutions. For the sample equation, Mathcad can solve for the three solutions symbolically. (Try it.) The results are pretty ugly, but the other two roots are imaginary: $-0.74 \pm 3.694i$

- Solve blocks do support units, but if you are solving for more than one variable, each iterated variable must have the same units. If the variables in your problem do not all have the same units (flow rate and friction loss, for example), you must solve the set of equations without any units on any variable.

- You must provide an initial guess for each iterated variable. (Use an imaginary initial guess to have Mathcad search for imaginary solutions.)

7.2.3 The root( ) Function: An Alternative to Using Solve Blocks

Mathcad provides a `root()` function that can be used to find a single solution to a single equation. The `root()` function does not require the use of a given/find solve block. The `root()` function is an iterative solver, so an initial guess is still required. The procedure is as follows:

define the function	$f(x) := x^3 + 12 \cdot x - 21$
provide a guess	$x := 0$
find a solution	$\text{Soln} := \text{root}(f(x), x)$
display the solution	$\text{Soln} = 1.48$

The root() function will find only one solution. For functions that have multiple solutions, you can provide other guesses (starting values) to search for other roots.

7.2.4 Finding All Roots of Polynomials

For polynomial functions, Mathcad provides a function that will find all of the roots at one time: the `polyroots()` function. To use the `polyroots()` function, the *polynomial coefficients* must be written as a column vector, starting with the constant. The polynomial we have been using as an example is

$$x^3 + 0\, x^2 + 12\, x - 21 = 0.$$

The $0\, x^2$ term was included in the polynomial as a reminder that the zero must be included in the coefficient vector v.

The coefficients of this polynomial would be written as the column vector

$$v := \begin{pmatrix} -21 \\ 12 \\ 0 \\ 1 \end{pmatrix}$$

The `polyroots()` function could then be used to find all solutions of this polynomial:

```
Soln := polyroots (v)
```

$$Soln = \begin{pmatrix} -0.74-3.694i \\ -0.74+3.694i \\ 1.48 \end{pmatrix}$$

The `polyroots()` function is a quick way to find all solutions, but only of polynomials

PROFESSIONAL SUCCESS

Use a QuickPlot to find good initial guesses.

1. Create an X-Y Plot (from the Graphics Toolbar or by pressing [Shift-2])
2. Enter your function on the *y*-axis.
3. Add a second curve to the plot (select your entire function and then press [comma]), and enter a zero in the *y*-axis placeholder for the second plot. This will draw a horizontal line across the graph at *y* = 0.
4. Enter the variable used in your function in the placeholder on the *x*-axis.
5. Adjust the limits on the *x*-axis as needed to see where your function crosses the *y* = 0 line.

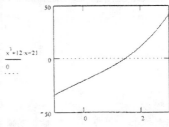

The locations where your function crosses the *y* = 0 line are the roots, or solutions, of the function. This function clearly has a root between 1 and 2, but Mathcad provides a way to get a more accurate value off the graph:

6. Click on the graph to select it.
7. Bring up the X-Y Trace dialog from the Format menu: Format / Graph / Trace... .

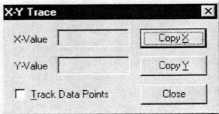

8. Position the X-Y Trace dialog so that the entire graph is visible.

9. Click on the spot where your function and the $y = 0$ curves cross.
10. Read the x-value at that location from the X-Y Trace dialog box.

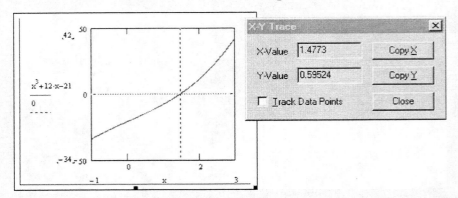

A guessed value of 1.4773 should be very close to the actual root, allowing the iterative solver to converge quickly.

PRACTICE!

Use Mathcad's iterative solver to find solutions for each of the expressions that follow. For each expression, how many solutions should there be? Use different initial guesses to search for multiple solutions.

    a. $(x - 3) \cdot (x - 4) = 0$
    b. $x^2 - 1 = 0$
    c. $x^3 - 2x^2 + 4x = 3$
    d. $e^{3x} - 4 = 0$
    e. $\sqrt{x^3} + 7x = 10$

APPLICATION: FRICTION LOSSES AND PRESSURE DROP IN PIPE FLOWS

Here's a typical pump-sizing problem:

> What size pump (HP) is required to move water at an average velocity of 3.0 ft/s through a 5,000-foot-long pipe with a 1-inch inside diameter? Assume that the viscosity of water is 0.01 poise at room temperature and the pump has an efficiency of 0.70.

Anytime you are designing a piping system, you will need to estimate the friction in the system, since friction can be responsible for much of the pressure drop from one end of the pipe to another. Because of this friction, you need a pump to move the fluid, and you must calculate how big the pump must be—so you have to estimate the friction losses ... to estimate the pressure drop ... to calculate the size of the pump.

There are many contributing factors to pipe friction: valves, bends in the pipe, rough pipe, a buildup of deposits in the pipes, etc. We will consider only the simplest situation: a clean, horizontal, smooth pipe with no valves or bends. For most flows in such a pipe, the Fanning friction factor f can be calculated using the von Karman equation,

$$\frac{1}{\sqrt{\dfrac{f}{2}}} = 2.5 \ln \left(N_{Re} \sqrt{\frac{f}{8}} \right) + 1.75.$$

Nomenclature

D	Inside pipe diameter.
V_{av}	Average velocity of the fluid in the pipe.
g	
ρ	Density of the fluid.
μ	Viscosity of the fluid.
L	Length of the pipe.
g_c	Gravitational constant: 32.174 ft $lb_m lb_f^{-1}$ s^{-2} in English units or 1 (no units) in SI.
η	Efficiency of the pump (no units).
P_P	Pump's power rating (HP or kW).
$\dot{m}$	Mass flow rate of fluid in the pipe.

The von Karman equation is valid for smooth pipes (e.g., PVC pipe, not steel pipe) and Reynolds numbers greater than 6,000. The Reynolds number is defined as

$$N_{Re} = \frac{D V_{avg} \rho}{\mu}$$

Once you know the friction factor, you can calculate the pressure drop in a horizontal pipe from

$$\Delta P = 4f \frac{L}{D} \frac{\rho \left(V_{avg} \right)^2}{2 g_c}$$

Once you have the pressure drop, you can determine the energy per unit mass required to overcome friction:

$$h_f = \frac{\Delta P}{\rho}.$$

And you can determine the pump power required:

$$\eta \, P_P = h_f \, \dot{m}$$

With Mathcad, the problem is solved like this:

Information From the Problem Statement:

INFORMATION FROM THE PROBLEM STATEMENT:

$V_{avg} := 3 \cdot \dfrac{ft}{sec}$ $L := 5000 \cdot ft$ $D := 1 \cdot in$

$\mu := 0.01 \cdot poise$ $\eta := 0.70$

Commonly Available Data:

COMMONLY AVAILABLE DATA:

$$\rho := 1000 \cdot \frac{kg}{m^3} \qquad \textit{Water density}$$

Definition of gc:

DEFINITION OF gc:

$$g_c := 1 \qquad \begin{array}{l}\textit{Define in SI, let}\\ \textit{Mathcad handle units}\end{array}$$

Calculate the Reynolds Number:

CALCULATE THE REYNOLDS NUMBER:

$$N_{Re} := \frac{D \cdot V_{avg} \cdot \rho}{\mu}$$

$$N_{Re} = 23226$$

Because $N_{Re} > 6,000$, von Karman can be used.

Solve for the Friction Factor:

SOLVE FOR THE FRICTION FACTOR:

$$f := 0.001 \qquad \begin{array}{l}\textit{Guessed starting value}\\ \textit{for the iterative}\\ \textit{solver}\end{array}$$

given

$$\frac{1}{\sqrt{\frac{f}{2}}} = 2.5 \cdot \ln\left(N_{Re} \cdot \sqrt{\frac{f}{8}}\right) + 1.75$$

$$f := \text{find}(f)$$

$$f = 0.0062 \qquad \textit{Calculated friction factor}$$

Solve for Pressure Drop:

SOLVE FOR PRESSURE DROP:

$$P := 4 \cdot f \cdot \frac{L}{D} \cdot \frac{\rho \cdot V_{avg}^2}{2 \cdot g_c} \qquad \Delta P = 6.158 \circ atm$$

$$\Delta P = 90.502 \circ psi$$

Solver for Energy Per Unit Mass Required to Overcome Friction:

SOLVE FOR ENERGY PER UNIT MASS REQUIRED TO OVERCOME FRICTION:

$$h_f := \frac{\Delta P}{\rho} \qquad h_f = 623.986 \cdot \frac{N \cdot m}{kg}$$

$$h_f = 208.756 \cdot \frac{ft \cdot lbf}{lb}$$

Solve For Mass Flow Rate:

SOLVE FOR MASS FLOW RATE:

$$A_{flow} := \pi \cdot \left(\frac{D}{2}\right)^2$$

$$m_{dot} := V_{avg} \cdot A_{flow} \cdot \rho$$

$$m_{dot} = 1.668 \cdot 10^3 \cdot \frac{kg}{hr}$$

$$m_{dot} = 3.677 \cdot 10^3 \cdot \frac{lb}{hr}$$

Solve for Required Pump Power:

SOLVE FOR REQUIRED PUMP POWER:

$$P_p := \frac{h_f \cdot m_{dot}}{\eta}$$

$$P_p = 0.413 \circ kW$$

$$P_p = 0.554 \circ hp$$

Surprised by the result? It doesn't take much of a pump just to overcome friction in a well-designed pipeline. (It takes a lot more energy to lift the water up a hill, but that wasn't considered here.) If the pipeline is not designed correctly, the friction losses can change dramatically.

7.3   NUMERICAL INTEGRATION

Numerical integration and differentiation of functions are very straightforward in Mathcad. But many times the relationship between the dependent and independent variables is known only through a set of data points. For example, earlier we used a data set representing a relationship between temperature and time. (That data set will be presented again shortly.) If you want to integrate the temperature data over time, you have two choices:

- Fit the data with an equation, and then integrate the equation.
- Use a numerical integration method on the data set itself.

Both approaches are common, and both will be described in this section.

7.3.1 Integration

INTEGRATING FUNCTIONS NUMERICALLY

If you have a function, such as the polynomial relating temperature and time that was obtained earlier, then integrating temperature over time from 0 to 9 minutes is easily performed using Mathcad's definite integral operator. Using the data arrays and the regression statements from before, we have

<table>
<tr><th></th><th>0</th></tr>
<tr><td>0</td><td>0</td></tr>
<tr><td>1</td><td>1</td></tr>
<tr><td>2</td><td>2</td></tr>
<tr><td>3</td><td>3</td></tr>
<tr><td>4</td><td>4</td></tr>
<tr><td>5</td><td>5</td></tr>
<tr><td>6</td><td>6</td></tr>
<tr><td>7</td><td>7</td></tr>
<tr><td>8</td><td>8</td></tr>
<tr><td>9</td><td>9</td></tr>
</table>

Temp =

<table>
<tr><th></th><th>0</th></tr>
<tr><td>0</td><td>298</td></tr>
<tr><td>1</td><td>299</td></tr>
<tr><td>2</td><td>301</td></tr>
<tr><td>3</td><td>304</td></tr>
<tr><td>4</td><td>306</td></tr>
<tr><td>5</td><td>309</td></tr>
<tr><td>6</td><td>312</td></tr>
<tr><td>7</td><td>316</td></tr>
<tr><td>8</td><td>319</td></tr>
<tr><td>9</td><td>322</td></tr>
</table>

Temp =

$$F(x) := \begin{bmatrix} 1 \\ x \\ x^2 \end{bmatrix}$$

b := linfit (Time, Temp, F)

$$b = \begin{bmatrix} 297.721 \\ 1.742 \\ 0.113 \end{bmatrix}$$

$$\int_0^9 \left(b_0 + b_1 \bullet t + b_2 \bullet t^2\right) dt = 2.777 \bullet 10^3$$

The symbol t was used instead of Time in the integration. The choice is irrelevant, because the integration variable is a dummy variable. Units were not used here. The integration operator does allow units on the limit values, but since linfit() does not support units, the problem is more easily solved without them.

PRACTICE!

Evaluate the following integrals, and check your results using the computational formulas shown to the right of each integral:

- Area under the curve y = 1.5x from x = 1 to x = 3 (a trapezoidal region):

$$\int_1^3 1.5\, x\, dx \qquad A_{\text{trap}} = \frac{1}{2}\left(y_{\text{left}} + y_{\text{right}}\right) \bullet \left(x_{\text{right}} - x_{\text{left}}\right).$$

- Volume of a sphere of radius 2 cm:

$$\int_0^{2\text{ cm}} 4\pi r^2\, dr \qquad V_{\text{sphere}} = \frac{4}{3}\pi R^3.$$

- Volume of a spherical shell with inside radius Ri = 1 cm and outside radius Ro = 2 cm:

$$\int_{1\text{ cm}}^{2\text{ cm}} 4\pi r^2\, dr \qquad V_{\text{shell}} = \frac{4}{3}\pi\left(R_o^3 - R_i^3\right).$$

APPLICATIONS: DETERMINING THE VOLUME OF LIQUID IN A CYLINDRICAL TANK

It is common to need to know how much product you have stored in a partially filled, horizontal, cylindrical tank—but the calculation is not trivial. We can use Mathcad's ability to integrate functions to solve this problem.

Some Fundamentals

- The integral $\int_a^b f(x)\,dx$ represents the area between the curve `f(x)` and the `x-axis`.
- If the `f` curve is above the `x-axis`, the calculated area will have a positive sign. A negative sign on the area implies that the curve lies below the `x-axis`.
- A circle of radius `r` and centered at the origin can be described by the function `x2+y2 = r2`.
- A horizontal line (representing the level of liquid in the tank) is described by the function `y = constant`. We will relate the constant to the depth of liquid in the tank later in this example.

Case 1: The Tank Is Less than Half Full

When the tank is less than half full, we can compute the volume by multiplying the cross-sectional area of the fluid (shown shaded in the circle at the left in the figure that follows) by the length of the tank, L. The trick is determining the cross-sectional area of the fluid.

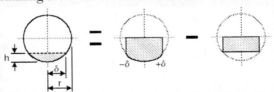

The shaded area in the center circle represents the area between the circle and the `x-axis`. Note that when the tank is less than half full, there is fluid between $-\delta$ and $+\delta$. We can integrate the formula for the circle between $-\delta$ and $+\delta$ to compute the shaded area in the center circle. Call this area A_1.

The shaded area in the rightmost circle represents the area between the function describing the level of the liquid and the x-axis. The integration limits are again $-\delta$ and $+\delta$. Call this area A_2. Subtracting A_2 from A_1 gives the desired cross-sectional area of the fluid in the tank. All that remains is to carry out these integrations, but first we need to know how δ depends on the level in the tank, h, and the tank radius r.

There is a right triangle involving the level of the liquid and the origin of the axis, shown at the right of the axis. Using the Pythagorean theorem, we can relate the lengths of the sides of the triangle:

$$(h - r)^2 + \delta^2 = r^2$$

Solving for δ yields the first required Mathcad function:

$$\delta(h, r) := \sqrt{r^2 - (r-h)^2}$$

The integral for the area A_1 is then written as a function of r and h as well:

$$A_1(h, r) = -\left[\int_{-\delta(h, r)}^{\delta(h, r)} \left(-\sqrt{r^2 - x^2}\right) dx \right]$$

Here, the function representing the circle was solved for y, and a negative sign was introduced to calculate the y values below the x-axis. (Since Mathcad's square root operator always returns the positive root, we need to change the sign to obtain the negative y values.) Hence, we have

$$y = -\sqrt{r^2 - x^2}$$

Also, the computed area is below the x-axis, so it will have a negative sign. A minus sign has been included in the function to cause it to return a positive area value.

The integral for A_2 is obtained by integrating the function representing the level of liquid in the tank. If the liquid depth is h, then the level is at a (negative) y value of $h-r$:

$$A_2(h, r) := -\left[\int_{-\delta(h, r)}^{\delta(h, r)} (h-r) \, dx \right]$$

Again, a minus sign was added to cause the function to return a positive area.

The cross-sectional area of fluid in the tank is then

$$A_{fluid}(h, r) := -\left[\int_{-\delta(h, r)}^{\delta(h, r)} \left(-\sqrt{r^2 - x^2}\right) dx \right.$$
$$\left. - \int_{-\delta(h, r)}^{\delta(h, r)} (h-r) \, dx \right]$$

or, simplifying slightly,

$$A_{fluid}(h, r) := -\int_{-\delta(h, r)}^{\delta(h, r)} \left[\left(-\sqrt{r^2 - x^2}\right) - (h-r)\right] dx$$

And the volume in the tank is simply the area times the length:

$$V_{fluid}(h, r, L) := L \bullet \left[-\left[\int_{-\delta(h, r)}^{\delta(h, r)} \left[\left(-\sqrt{r^2 - x^2}\right) - (h-r)\right] dx \right] \right]$$

Case 2: The Tank Is More than Half Full

When the tank is more than half full, the procedure is similar:

$$A_{fluid} = A_{total} - \int_{-\delta}^{\delta} f_{circle}(x)\,dx$$

$$+ \int_{-\delta}^{\delta} f_{level}(x)\,dx$$

The function relating δ to r and h is unchanged, and since the areas are above the x-axis, we don't have to worry about changing the signs. The result is the following function for the volume of the liquid in the tank:

$$V_{fluid}(h, r, L) := L \bullet \left[\pi \bullet r^2 - \int_{-\delta(h, r)}^{\delta(h, r)} \left[\left(\sqrt{r^2 - x^2}\right) - (h - r) \right] dx \right]$$

Creating a General Function for Either Case

Mathcad's if() function can be used to automatically select the appropriate formula:

$$V_{tank}(h, r, L) := L \bullet if \left[(h < r), \left[-\int_{-\delta(h, r)}^{\delta(h, r)} \left[\left(-\sqrt{r^2 - x^2}\right) - (h - r) \right] dx \right], \right.$$

$$\left. \left[\pi \bullet r^2 - \int_{-\delta(h, r)}^{\delta(h, r)} \left[\left(\sqrt{r^2 - x^2}\right) - (h - r) \right] dx \right] \right]$$

Here, if $h < r$, then the first formula is used; otherwise the second formula is used. Since both functions work for $h = r$ (a half-full tank), deciding which formula to use at that point is arbitrary.

7.3.2 Integrating Data Sets

Integration via Curve Fitting One approach to integrating a data set is to first fit an equation to the data and then integrate the equation. This was demonstrated in the previous example: A polynomial was fit to the temperature-time data, and then the polynomial was integrated using Mathcad's definite integral operator.

Integrating without Curve Fitting An alternative to curve fitting is to simply use the data values themselves to compute the integral. This is fairly straightforward if you recall that the integral represents the area between the curve and the x-axis when the data points are plotted. (See the following figure.)

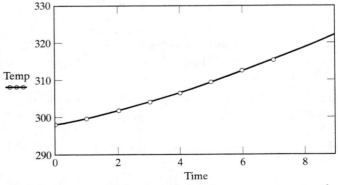

Any method that computes the area under the curve computes the value of the integral. A number of methods are commonly used. One of the simplest divides the area under the curve into a series of trapezoids. The area of each trapezoid is calculated from the data values, and the sum of the areas represents the result of the integration. Since there are 10 data points, there will be nine trapezoids to cover the entire time range. We will keep track of these nine regions by defining a range variable

$i \; := \; 0 \; .. \; 8$

Or we could define the range variable in more general terms as

$i \; := \; 0 \; .. \; (\mathtt{last(Time)} - 1)$

We then need a function that computes the area of the leftmost trapezoid:

$$A_0 \; := \; \frac{1}{2} \bullet (\mathtt{Temp_0} + \mathtt{Temp_1}) \bullet (\mathtt{Time_1} - \mathtt{Time_0}) \qquad A_0 \; = \; 298.7$$

We can now generalize this equation to obtain a function capable of calculating the area of any of the nine trapezoids:

$$A_i \; := \; \frac{1}{2} \bullet (\mathtt{Temp_i} + \mathtt{Temp_{i+1}}) \bullet (\mathtt{Time_{i+1}} - \mathtt{Time_i})$$

$$A = \begin{bmatrix} 298.7 \\ 300.424 \\ 302.643 \\ 305.164 \\ 307.916 \\ 310.862 \\ 313.974 \\ 317.235 \\ 320.629 \end{bmatrix}$$

Finally, we sum the area of all of these trapezoids to estimate the total area under the curve. This summation is carried out by using Mathcad's *range variable summation operator* from the Calculus Toolbar:

$$\sum_i A_i \; = \; 2.778 \bullet 10^3$$

The result compares well with that computed by using numerical integration of the polynomial in the preceding example. Again, this calculation was performed without using Mathcad's units capability, but units could have been used.

A TRAPEZOIDAL RULE FUNCTION

We can push this process one step further and write a function that will perform trapezoidal-rule integration on any data set:

$$\mathtt{trap(x, y)} \; := \; \sum_{i\,=\,0}^{\mathtt{length(x)-2}} \frac{y_i + y_{i+1}}{2} \bullet (x_{i+1} - x_i)$$

$$A_{\mathtt{total}} \; := \; \mathtt{trap(Time, \; Temp)}$$
$$A_{\mathtt{total}} \; = \; 2.778 \cdot 10^3$$

In the `trap()` function, the range variable is replaced by defined limits on the summation (Mathcad's standard *summation operator* is used), and the `length()` function is utilized to determine the size of the array, from which the number of trapezoids can be computed. The expressions

`length(x)-2`   used in the `trap()` function and
`last(x)-1`   used in the previous example

are equivalent as long as the array origin is set at zero, which is assumed in the trap() function, since the summation index, i, starts at zero.

PRACTICE!

Create a test data set, and then use the `trap()` function to integrate y = cos(x) from x = 0 to x = π / 2. Vary the number of points in the data set to see how the size of the trapezoids (over the same x range) affects the accuracy of the result. Then check your result using Mathcad's symbolic integrator. The following are the details of the procedure:

- Create the test data set:

$$N_{pts} := 20$$
$$I := 0 \ .. \ (N_{pts}-1)$$
$$x_i := \frac{\pi}{2} \cdot \frac{i}{N_{pts-1}}$$
$$y_i := \cos(x_i)$$

- Integrate by using the `trap()` function, and vary the number of points in the data set.

- Use symbolic integration to evaluate $\int_0^{x/2} \cos(x)\,dx$.

APPLICATIONS: CONTROLLED RELEASE OF DRUGS

When a patient takes a pill, there is a rapid rise in the concentration of the drug in the patient's bloodstream, which then decreases with time as the drug is removed from the bloodstream, often by the kidneys or the liver. Then the patient takes another pill. The result is a time-varying concentration of drug in the blood.

In some situations, there may be therapeutic benefits to maintaining a more constant (perhaps lower) drug concentration for prolonged periods of time. For example, a chemotherapy drug might be active only at concentrations greater than 2 mg/L. The pills for this drug might be designed to raise the concentration in the blood to 15 mg/L, to try to keep the concentration above 2 mg/L for as long as possible. If you could keep the concentration of a cancer-fighting drug from falling below 2 mg/L for a month or more, it might do a better job of killing the cancer cells. If you could also reduce the maximum concentration from 15 mg/L to perhaps 10 mg/L, the side effects of the drug might be reduced.

In this example, we will consider an implanted "drug reservoir" for chemotherapy. This drug reservoir is little more than a plastic bag containing a solution of the drug. The shape, materials of construction, and volume of the bag, as well as the concentration of the dissolved drug, can all be varied to change the drug release characteristics. This example considers only the volume and drug concentration in the reservoir.

For preliminary testing of the release characteristics, human subjects would not be used. Instead, the computer model used to generate the accompanying, graph assumes that the drug is being released into a body simulator (a 50-liter tank) with a slow (1 mL/min) feed of fresh water and removal of drug solution at the same rate. Three tests were simulated, with the drug reservoir volume and concentration adjusted to give a maximum drug concentration of 10 mg/L in the simulator. The results are shown in the graph (concentration in mg/L, time in hours).

The $conc_1$ curve was produced using a small reservoir containing a high drug concentration. $Conc_3$ used a larger reservoir with a much lower drug concentration. The curves show that, by varying the reservoir volume and concentration, the active period (concentration above 2 mg/liter) of the drug can be adjusted from approximately 800 hours (about 1 month) to almost 1,400 hours (nearly 2 months), without ever causing blood concentrations to exceed 10 mg/L.

While this simple drug delivery system is a long way from delivering a good, constant concentration of the chemotherapy drug, it does demonstrate that it is quite possible to change the way drugs are administered. By designing better drug delivery systems, we may be able to improve the performance of some drugs and the quality of life of patients.

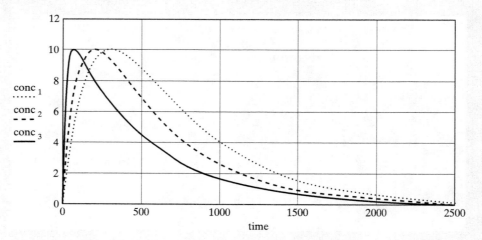

Total Drug Release

With the concentration vs. time data, and knowing the flow rate of fluid through the simulator, we can determine the total amount of drug that is released from the reservoir. Multiplying the time by the volumetric flow rate gives the volume that has passed through the simulator. The concentrations can then be plotted against volume (liters). This is shown in the following graph, where

$$Q := 60 \quad ml/hr$$

$$vol := \frac{time \cdot Q}{1000} \quad liters$$

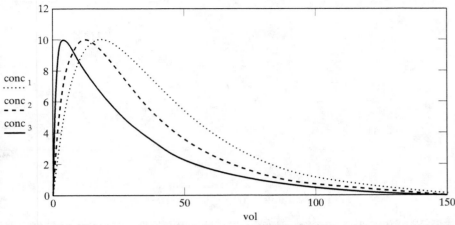

The area under each curve represents the amount of drug released from the associates reservoir in 2,500 hours. The `trap( )` function can be used to perform the integrations:

$$D_1 := \text{trap(vol, conc}_1)$$ $$D_1 = 343 \text{ mg}$$
$$D_2 := \text{trap(vol, conc}_2)$$ $$D_2 = 446 \text{ mg}$$
$$D_3 := \text{trap(vol, conc}_3)$$ $$D_3 = 546 \text{ mg}$$

SIMPSON'S-RULE INTEGRATION

Simpson's rule is a popular numerical integration technique that takes three data points, fits a curve through the points, and computes the area of the region below the curve. This operation is repeated for each set of three points in the data set. The common formula for Simpson's rule looks something like

$$A_{\text{total}} = \frac{h}{3} \sum_{\text{all regions}} \left(y_{i-1} + 4y_i + y_{i+1} \right)$$

where the unusual summation over "all regions" is necessary because an integration region using Simpson's method requires three data points. So, using Mathcad's default array indexing, we see that points 0, 1, and 2 make up the first integration region, points 2, 3, and 4 make up the second region, and so on. The number of integration regions is approximately half the number of data points. The distance between two adjacent points is h. The use of Simpson's rule comes with two restrictions:

- You must have an odd number of data points.
- The independent values (usually called x) must be uniformly spaced, with $h = \delta x$.

We will look at a way to get around these restrictions later, but first we try an example of applying Simpson's rule when the conditions are met. We create a data set containing seven values and strong curvature:

$$I := 0 \ .. \ 6$$
$$x_i := 1 + I$$
$$y_i := 1 + \cos(x_i)$$

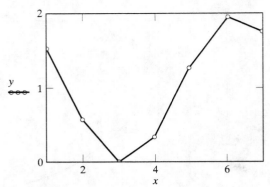

Then we calculate h (from any two x values, since h must be constant) and create a range variable j that will keep track of the index of the point at the center of each integration region:

INTEGRATION REGION, POINT NUMBERS		CENTRAL POINT
0, 1, 2		1
2, 3, 4		3
4, 5, 6		5

h := $x_1 - x_0$ h = 1
j := 1, 3 .. 5   j =

1
3
5

Next, we apply Simpson's rule to determine the area under the curve, again by using the range variable summation operator:

$$A_{Simpson} := \frac{h}{3} \cdot \sum_j \left(y_{j-1} + 4 \cdot y_j + y_{j+1} \right)$$

$A_{Simpson} := 5.814$

Now we can compare the results with trapezoidal-rule integration and exact integration of the cosine function:

$$A_{exact} := \int_1^7 \left(1 + \cos(x) \right) dx$$

Simpson's method came a lot closer to the exact result than trapezoidal integration did—it usually does. Because Simpson's rule connects data points with smooth curves rather than straight lines, it typically fits data better than the trapezoidal rule does. But Simpson's rule has those two restrictions that make it useless in many situations. Is there a way to get around these restrictions? Yes, there is: You can use a cubic spline to fit any data set with a smooth curve and then use cubic spline interpolation to compute a set of values that covers the same range as the original data, but has an odd number of data points and uniform point spacing. After that, you can use Simpson's rule on the interpolated data.

To test this approach, we will use the temperature-time data employed in the previous examples. These data consist of 10 uniformly spaced values. The uniform spacing is good, but 10 values won't work with Simpson's rule. [1]:

		0
Time =	0	0
	1	1
	2	2
	3	3
	4	4
	5	5
	6	6
	7	7
	8	8
	9	9

		0
Temp =	0	298
	1	299
	2	301
	3	304
	4	306
	5	309
	6	312
	7	316
	8	319
	9	322

```
vs := cspline(Time, Temp)
```

Then we can use the `interp()` function to find temperature values at 11 points over the same time interval, 0 to 9 minutes:

```
I := 0 .. 10        eleven values
```

$$t_i := \frac{9 \cdot i}{10}$$

		0
t =	0	0
	1	0.9
	2	1.8
	3	2.7
	4	3.6
	5	4.5
	6	5.4
	7	6.3
	8	7.2
	9	8.1
	10	9

```
Temp_interp_i := interp(vs, Time, Temp, t_i)
```

---

[1] Another common way to get around the odd-number-of-data-points restriction is to use Simpson's rule as far as possible and then, if there is an even number of points, finish the integration by using a trapezoid for the last two points.

$$\text{Temp}_{\text{interp}} =$$

	0
0	298
1	299.225
2	301.003
3	303.093
4	305.401
5	307.893
6	310.538
7	313.32
8	316.25
9	319.24
10	322.358

Now we use Simpson's rule on `t` and `Temp`$_{\text{interp}}$ instead of `Time` and `Temp`.

```
j := 1, 3 .. 9
h := t₁-t₀
```

$$A_{\text{Simpson}} := \frac{h}{3} \bullet \sum_{j} \left(\text{Temp}_{\text{interp}_{j-1}} + 4 \bullet \text{Temp}_{\text{interp}_j} + \text{Temp}_{\text{interp}_{j+1}} \right)$$

$$A_{\text{Simpson}} = 2.777 \cdot 10^3$$

The result compares well with that obtained from the trapezoidal integration, which is not surprising for this data set, since it does not show a lot of curvature. (There is not a lot of difference between connecting the points with lines or curves for the data set, so there is little difference between the results computed by the two methods.)

7.4 NUMERICAL DIFFERENTIATION

7.4.1 Evaluating Derivatives of Functions Numerically

If you have a function, such as

$$y = b_0 e^{b_1 t},$$

Mathcad can take the derivative. If you use the live symbolic operator ($\rightarrow$) to evaluate an expression symbolically, Mathcad will use its symbolic processor and give you another function:

$$\frac{d}{dt} \left(b_0 \bullet e^{b_1 \bullet t} \right) \rightarrow b_0 \bullet b_1 \bullet \exp(b_1 \bullet t)$$

Or if the values of b_0, b_1, and `t` are specified before evaluating the derivative, Mathcad's symbolic processor will calculate a numeric result:

```
b₀ := 3.4
b₁ := 0.12
t := 16
```

$$\frac{d}{dt} \left(b_0 \bullet e^{b_1 \bullet t} \right) \rightarrow 2.7829510554706259326$$

The extreme number of significant figures is a reminder that Mathcad solved for the value using the symbolic processor. The default number of digits displayed is 20.

On the other hand, if you use the "numerical evaluation" symbol (a plain equal sign, =), then Mathcad will use its numeric processor to calculate the value of the derivative:

$$b_0 := 3.4$$
$$b_1 := 0.12$$
$$t := 16$$

$$\frac{d}{dt}\left(b_0 \bullet e^{b_1 \bullet t}\right) = 2.783$$

If you use the numeric processor, you must specify the values of b_0, b_1, and t before Mathcad evaluates the derivative.

7.4.2 Derivatives from Experimental Data

If the relationship between your variables is represented by a set of values (a data set), rather than a mathematical expression, you have two choices for trying to determine the derivative at some specified point:

- Fit the data with a mathematical expression and then differentiate the expression at the specified value.
- Use numerical approximations for derivatives on the data points themselves.

USING A FITTING FUNCTION

The curve fitting process is summarized here:

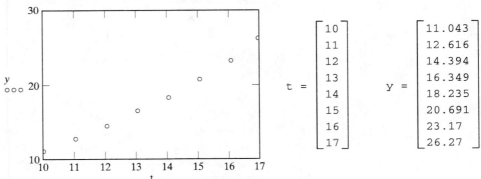

$$t = \begin{bmatrix} 10 \\ 11 \\ 12 \\ 13 \\ 14 \\ 15 \\ 16 \\ 17 \end{bmatrix} \qquad y = \begin{bmatrix} 11.043 \\ 12.616 \\ 14.394 \\ 16.349 \\ 18.235 \\ 20.691 \\ 23.17 \\ 26.27 \end{bmatrix}$$

The data are expected to fit the exponential model

$$y = b_0 e^{b_1 t},$$

which can be rewritten in linear form as

$$\ln(y) = \ln(b_0) + b_1 t.$$

We can then use linear regression and a bit of math to determine b_0 and b_1:

$$\text{in} := \text{intercept}\left(t, \overrightarrow{\ln(y)}\right) \qquad \text{in} = 1.187$$

$$\text{sl} := \text{slope}\left(t, \overrightarrow{\ln(y)}\right) \qquad \text{sl} = 0.123$$

$$b_0 := e_{\text{in}} \qquad\qquad b_0 = 3.276$$

$$b_1 := \text{sl} \qquad\qquad b_1 = 0.123$$

Once we have a mathematical expression, we can evaluate the derivative at $t = 16$ by using either the symbolic or numeric processor, as described earlier. The results of using the numeric processor are as follows:

$$b_0 := e_{in} \qquad\qquad b_0 = 3.276$$

$$b_1 := sl \qquad\qquad b_1 = 0.123$$

$$t := 16$$

$$\frac{d}{dt}\left(b_0 \bullet e^{b_1 t}\right) = 2.861$$

USING NUMERICAL APPROXIMATIONS FOR DERIVATIVES

The derivative physically represents the slope of a plot of the data at a specified point. You can approximate the derivative at any point by estimating the slope of the graph at that point. Just as there are several ways to estimate the slope, there are several ways to compute numerical approximations for derivatives. Since array index values are used in these calculations, here are the data (again), along with the array index values:

$$i = \begin{bmatrix} 0 \\ 1 \\ 2 \\ 3 \\ 4 \\ 5 \\ 6 \\ 7 \end{bmatrix} \qquad t = \begin{bmatrix} 10 \\ 11 \\ 12 \\ 13 \\ 14 \\ 15 \\ 16 \\ 17 \end{bmatrix} \qquad y = \begin{bmatrix} 11.043 \\ 12.616 \\ 14.394 \\ 16.349 \\ 18.235 \\ 20.691 \\ 23.17 \\ 26.27 \end{bmatrix}$$

One way to estimate the slope at point $i = 6$ (where $t = 16$) would be

$$\left.\frac{dy}{dt}\right|_{i=6} \approx \frac{y_7 - y_6}{t_7 - t_6}$$

If that equation is valid, then the following equation is equally valid (both are approximations):

$$\left.\frac{dy}{dt}\right|_{i=6} \approx \frac{y_6 - y_5}{t_6 - t_5}.$$

The first expression uses the point at $t = 16$ and the point to the right ($i = 7$ or $t = 17$) to estimate the slope and is called a *forward finite-difference approximation for the first derivative* at $i = 6$. The term *finite difference* is used because there is a finite distance between the t values used in the calculation. Finite-difference approximations are truly equal to the derivatives only in the limit as δt goes to zero.

The second expression uses the point at $t = 16$ and the point to the left ($t = 15$) to estimate the slope and is called a *backward finite-difference approximation for the first derivative* at $i = 6$. You can also write a *central finite-difference approximation for the first derivative* at $i = 6$:

$$\left.\frac{dy}{dt}\right|_{i=6} \approx \frac{y_7 - y_5}{t_7 - t_5}.$$

Central differences tend to give better estimates of the slope and are the most commonly used. Applying the preceding equation to calculate the derivative at point $i = 6$ ($t = 16$) in the data set, we find that it has a value of 2.79:

$$slope_{16} := \frac{y_7 - y_5}{t_7 - t_5}$$

$$slope_{16} = 2.79$$

There are also finite-difference approximations for higher order derivatives. For example, a *central finite-difference approximation for a second derivative* at $i = 6$ can be written (assuming uniform point spacing—i.e., δt constant) as

$$\left.\frac{d^2y}{dt^2}\right|_{i=6} \approx \frac{y_7 - 2y_6 + y_5}{(\Delta t)^2}$$

PRACTICE!

Use central and forward difference approximations to estimate dy/dx at $x = 1$. Try both the clean and noisy data sets.

$$x := \begin{bmatrix} 0.0 \\ 0.5 \\ 1.0 \\ 1.5 \\ 2.0 \\ 2.5 \\ 3.0 \end{bmatrix} \quad y_{clean} := \begin{bmatrix} 0.00 \\ 0.48 \\ 0.84 \\ 1.00 \\ 0.91 \\ 0.60 \\ 0.14 \end{bmatrix} \quad y_{noisy} := \begin{bmatrix} 0.24 \\ 0.60 \\ 0.69 \\ 1.17 \\ 0.91 \\ 0.36 \\ 0.18 \end{bmatrix}$$

A polynomial can be fit to the noisy data as follows:

$$f(x) := \begin{bmatrix} x \\ x^2 \\ x^3 \end{bmatrix} \quad b := linfit(x, y_{noisy}, f) \quad b = \begin{bmatrix} 1.434 \\ -0.588 \\ 0.041 \end{bmatrix}$$

Try using the differentiation operator on the Calculus Toolbox to evaluate

$$\frac{d}{dx}(1.434x - 0.588x^2 + 0.041x^3)$$

at $x = 1$.

(*Note*: The derivative values you calculate in this "Practice!" box will vary widely. Calculating derivatives from noisy data is highly prone to errors, and you should try to avoid doing that if possible. If you must take derivatives from experimental data, try to get good, clean data sets.)

SUMMARY

In this chapter, you learned to use several standard numerical methods in Mathcad, including an iterative solve block and numerical integration and differentiation. The numerical in tegration techniques involved using Mathcad's integration operators (from the Calculus Toolbox) when you were working with a function, and numerical techniques like trapezoidal- or Simpson's-rule integration when you were working with a data set. Similarly, Mathcad' differentiation operators apply when you need to take the derivative of a function, and finite difference methods were discussed for evaluating derivatives when you have a data set.

KEY TERMS

finite difference	iterative solve block	Numerical integration
initial guess	iterative solver	polynomial coefficients

MATHCAD SUMMARY *Iterative Solutions:*

`Given`	The keyword that begins an iterative solve block. Remember to specify an initial guessed value before using this keyword.
`Find()`	The keyword that closes an iterative solve block and the function that performs the iteration and returns the solution. Remember to assign the value returned by `find( )` to a variable.
root(f(x, y), x)	The `root()` function uses an iterative solver to find a single root of a function of one or more variables. Before using the `root()` function, the function to be solved must be defined and an initial guess for the iteration variable must be set. The `root()` function takes two arguments: the function to be solved, `f(x,y)`, and the iteration variable x.
polyroots(v)	The `polyroots()` function returns all roots of a polynomial. The coefficients of the polynomial are sent to the `polyroots()` function as a column vector, with the constant in the polynomial as the first element of the vector.

Integration:

of a function	Use Mathcad's integration operators from the Calculus Toolbox.
of a data set	Trapezoidal and Simpson's rules can be used to approximate the integral, or you can fit a function to the data and then integrate the function.

Differentiation:

of a function	Use Mathcad's differentiation operators from the Calculus Toolbar.
of a data set	Finite differences can be used to estimate the values of the derivative, or you can fit a function to the data and then differentiate the function.

Problems

1. FINDING SOLUTIONS WITH THE root( ) FUNCTION
    Use the `root()` function to find the solution(s) of the following equations:

    a. $x - 3 = 0$ (admittedly, this one is kind of obvious)

    b. $x^2 - 3 = 0$

    c. $x^2 - 4x + 3 = 0$

2. FINDING INTERSECTIONS
    Use the `root()` function to find the intersection(s) of the listed curves. (Part has been completed as an example):

    a. $y = x2 - 3$ and $y = x + 4$

    The intersections are at the locations where the y values are equal, so start by eliminating y from the equations:

    $$x^2 - 3 = x + 4.$$

    The get all terms on one side of the equation, so that the equation is set equal to zero.

    $$x^2 - x - 7 = 0.$$

Create a QuickPlot to find good initial guesses for x, then use the root( ) function to find more precise x values at each intersection.

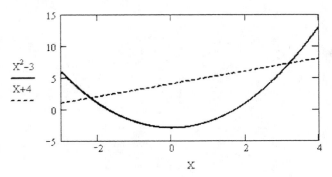

```
guess:   x := -2
         root(x² - x - 7, x)  = -2.193

         x := 3
         root(x² - x - 7, x)  = -3.193
```

b. $y = x^2 - 3$ and $y = -(x^2) + 4$

c. $y = x2 - 3$ and $y = e^{-x}$

3.   **FINDING THE ZEROES OF BESSEL FUNCTIONS**

Bessel functions are commonly used when solving differential equations in cylindrical coordinates. Two Bessel functions, J_0 and J_1, are shown in the following graph. [2]

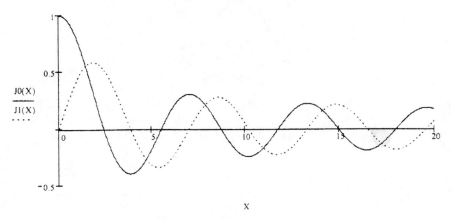

These Bessel functions are available as built-in functions in Mathcad and are called J0 ( ) and J1 ( ). Use the root ( ) function with different initial guesses to find the roots of J0(x) and J1(x) in the range 0 < x < 20.

[*Note:* The J0( ) function has a zero in its name, not an "oh."]

[2] More precisely, these are Bessel functions of the first kind, of order zero and one, respectively.

4. **FINDING POLYNOMIAL ROOTS**

Use the `polyroots()` function to find all roots for the following polynomial expressions.

  a. $x - 3 = 0$ (admittedly, not much of a polynomial

  b. $x^2 - 3 = 0$

  c. $x^2 - 4x + 3 = 0$

  d. $x^3 - 3x^2 + 4x - 12 = 0$

5. **FINDING INTERSECTIONS OF POLYNOMIALS**

Use the `polyroots()` function to find all intersections of the following polynomials. (Part a has been completed as an example):

  a. $y = x^2 - 3$ and $y = x + 4$
  Eliminate y from the equations.

$$x^2 - 3 = x + 4$$

  The get all terms on one side of the equation:

$$x^2 - x - 7 = 0.$$

  Create a column vector containing the coefficients of the polynomial (with the constant on top). Then use the `polyroots()` function to find each intersection:

$$v := \begin{pmatrix} -7 \\ -1 \\ 1 \end{pmatrix}$$

$$polyroots(v) = \begin{pmatrix} -2.193 \\ 3.193 \end{pmatrix}$$

  b. $y = x^2 - 3$ and $y = -(x^2) + 4$
  c. $y = x^2 - 3$ and $y = 2x^3 - 3x^2 + 4x - 12$
  $y = 2x^3 - 3x^2 + 4x - 12$ and $y = -(x^2) + 4$

6. **ITERATIVE SOLUTIONS**

Use a solve block (given/find) to find the roots of these equations (you may want to use a QuickPlot to find out how many roots to expect):

  a. $(x - 5) \cdot (x + 7) = 0$
  b. $x^{0.2} = \ln(x)$
  c. $\tan(x) = 2.4x^2$ search for roots in the range $-2 < x < 2$

7. **FRICTION LOSSES AND PRESSURE DROP IN PIPE FLOWS**

In a Mathcad Application section, the friction loss in a well-designed pipeline was determined. What if the pipeline is not well designed? That's the subject of this problem.

When you are moving water in a pipeline, the flow velocity is typically around 3 ft/s—the value that was used in the sample problem. This is a commonly used velocity that allows you to move a reasonable amount of water quickly and without too much friction loss. What happens to the friction loss and the required pump power when you try to move water through the same pipeline at a velocity of 15 ft/s?

8. **REAL GAS VOLUMES**

The Soave-Redlich-Kwong (SRK) equation of state is a commonly used equation that relates the temperature, pressure, and volume of a gas under conditions when the behavior of the gas cannot be considered ideal (e.g., moderate temperature and high pressure). The equation is

$$P = \frac{RT}{(\hat{V} - b)} - \frac{\alpha a}{\hat{V}(\hat{V} + b)},$$

where α, a, and b are parameters specific to the gas, R is the ideal gas constant, P is the absolute pressure, T is absolute temperature, and

$$\hat{V} = \frac{V}{n}$$

is the molar volume (volume per mole of gas).

For common gases, the parameters α, a, and b can be readily determined from available data. Then, if you know the molar volume of the gas, the SRK equation is easy to solve for either pressure or temperature. However, if you know the temperature and pressure and need to find the molar volume, an iterative solution is required.

Determine the molar volume of ammonia at 300°C and 1,200 kPa by

a. using the ideal gas equation.
b. using the SRK equation and an iterative solve block.

For ammonia at these conditions;

$$\alpha = 0.7007;$$

$$a = 430.9 \text{ kPa} \cdot \text{L}^2/\text{mole}^2;$$

$$b = 0.0259 \text{ L/mole}.$$

9. **REQUIRED SIZE FOR A WATER RETENTION BASIN**

In urban areas, as fields are turned into streets and parking lots, water runoff from sudden storms can become a serious problem. To prevent flooding, retention basins are often built to hold excess water temporarily during storms. In arid regions these basins are dry most of the time, so designers sometimes try to build in alternative uses. A proposed design is a half-pipe for skateboarders that can hold 100,000 cubic feet of water during a storm. The radius of the half-cylinder needs to be scaled to fit the skateboarders, and a radius of 8 feet is proposed.

a. What is the required length of the basin to hold the 100,000 ft³ of storm water? (There may be several short sections of half-pipes to provide the required total volume.)
b. If the basin is filled with water to a depth of 4 feet after a storm, what volume of water is held in the basin?

10. WORK REQUIRED TO STRETCH A SPRING

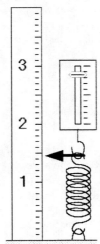

The device shown in the accompanying figure can be used to determine the work required to extend a spring. This device consists of a spring, a spring balance, and a ruler. Before stretching the spring, its length is measured and found to be 1.3 cm. The spring is then stretched 0.4 cm at a time, and the force indicated on the spring balance is recorded. The resulting data set is shown in the following table:

Measurement (Cm)	Unextended Length (Cm)	Extended Length (Cm)	Force(N)
1.3	1.3	0.0	0.00
1.7	1.3	0.4	0.88
2.1	1.3	0.8	1.76
2.5	1.3	1.2	2.64
2.9	1.3	1.6	3.52
3.3	1.3	2.0	4.40
4.1	1.3	2.8	6.16
4.5	1.3	3.2	7.04
4.9	1.3	3.6	7.92

Work can be computed as

$$W = \int F \, dx \, ,$$

where x is the extended length of the spring.

a. Calculate the work required to stretch the spring from an extended length of 0 cm to 3.6 cm. Watch the signs on the forces in this problem. Force is a vector quantity, so there is an associated direction.

b. Is the force being used to stretch the spring in the same direction as the movement of the spring or in the opposite direction?

11. WORK REQUIRED TO EXPAND A GAS

In problems 7.10 and 7.11 work was calculated as

$$W = \int F\,dx.$$

But force divided by area is pressure, and length times area is volume, so work can also be found as

$$W = \int P\,dV.$$

This form is handier for dealing with gas systems like that shown in the accompanying figure. As the piston is lifted, the pressure in the sealed chamber will fall. By monitoring the change in position on the ruler and knowing the cross-sectional area of the chamber, we can calculate the chamber volume at each pressure. Care must be taken to allow the system to equilibrate at room temperature before taking the readings. The pressure and volume after equilibrium are listed in the accompanying table.

VOLUME (ML)	PRESSURE (ATM)
1.3	4.50
1.7	3.44
2.1	2.79
2.5	2.34
2.9	2.02
3.3	1.77
3.7	1.58
4.1	1.43
4.5	1.30
4.9	1.19

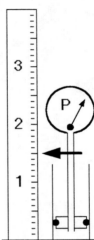

a. Calculate the work required to expand the gas from a volume of 0.3 mL to 3.9 mL.

b. Is this work being done by the gas on the surroundings or by the surroundings on the gas?

12. CALCULATING SPRING CONSTANTS

The extension of a linear spring is described by Hooke's law,

$$F = k\,x,$$

where x is the extended length of the spring (i.e., the total length of the stretched spring minus the length of the spring before stretching) and k is the spring constant. The spring constant quantifies the "stiffness" of the spring. Hooke's law can also be written in differential form as

$$\frac{dF}{dx} = k.$$

For a linear spring, dF/dx is a constant, the spring constant. For a nonlinear spring, dF/dx will not be constant, but taking this derivative at various spring extensions can help you see how the spring characteristics change as the spring is pulled. Use the data from Problems 7.10 and 7.11 to compute

a. the spring constant for the linear spring (Problem 7.10).

b. the derivative dF/dx as a function of x for the nonlinear spring (Problem 7.11). Use a central difference approximation for the derivative whenever possible, and create a plot of dF/dx vs. x.

13. THERMAL CONDUCTIVITY

Thermal conductivity is a property related to a material's ability to transfer energy by conduction. Good conductors, like copper and aluminum, have large thermal conductivity values. Insulating materials should have low thermal conductivities to minimize heat transfer.

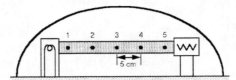

The preceding figure illustrates a device that could be used to measure thermal conductivity. A rod of the material to be tested is placed between a resistance heater (on the right) and a cooling coil (on the left). Five (numbered) thermocouples have been inserted into the rod at 5-cm intervals. The entire apparatus is placed in a bell jar, and the air around the rod is pumped out to reduce heat losses.

To run the experiment, a known amount of power is sent to the heater, and the system is allowed to reach steady state. Once the temperatures are steady, the power level and temperatures are recorded. A data sheet might look like the following:

ROD DIAMETER:	2 CM
TC SPACING:	5 CM
POWER:	100 WATTS

TC #	TEMP. (K)
1	348
2	387
3	425
4	464
5	503

The thermal conductivity can be determined from Fourier's law,

$$\frac{q}{A} = -k\frac{dT}{dx},$$

where q is the power being applied to the heater and A is the cross-sectional area of the rod. (*Note:* The term q/A is called the *energy flux* and is a vector quantity—that is, it has a direction as well as a magnitude. As drawn, with the energy source on the right, the energy will be flowing in the -x direction, so the flux in this problem is negative.)

a. Use finite-difference approximations to estimate dT/dx at several locations along the rod, and then calculate the thermal conductivity of the material.

b. Thermal conductivity is a function of temperature. Do your dT/dx values indicate that the thermal conductivity of the material changes appreciably between 348 and 503 K?

14. CALCULATING WORK

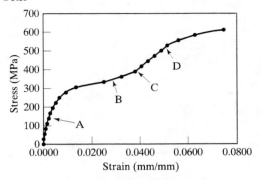

In the previous chapter, there was a note in the "Application: Analyzing Stress-Strain Diagrams" box to the effect that an alternative method of integrating a force-displacement graph is available to calculate work. The alternative method is numerical integration using a function such as trap(). The stress-strain data (shown in the accompanying graph) for a composite material have been converted to force-displacement data, abridged, and tabulated as follows:

F (N)	x (MM)
0	0.000
5500	0.009
8300	0.014
13800	0.023
16500	0.033
22100	0.051
24800	0.066
30300	0.137
33100	0.248
38600	0.380
41400	0.407
46900	0.461
49600	0.488
55200	0.561
57900	0.628
60700	0.749

Calculate the work done on the sample.

8

Engineering Graphics

OBJECTIVES
- Describe visual thinking
- Differentiate perspective, isometric, and orthographic projections
- Understand the basis CAD
- Understand the relationship between design and CAD

OVERVIEW

Engineering designs start as images in the mind's eye of an engineer. Engineering graphics has evolved to communicate and record these ideas on paper both two- and three-dimensionally. In the past few decades, the computer has made it possible to automate the creation of engineering graphics. Today engineering design and engineering graphics are inextricably connected. Engineering design is communicated visually using engineering graphics.

8.1   THE IMPORTANCE OF ENGINEERING GRAPHICS

"Visualizing" a picture or image in your mind is a familiar experience. The image can be visualized at many different levels of abstraction. Think about light and you might see the image of a light bulb in your "mind's eye." Alternatively, you might think about light versus dark. Or you might visualize a flashlight or table lamp. Such visual thinking is necessary in engineering and science. Albert Einstein said that he rarely thought in words. Instead, he laboriously translated his visual images into verbal and mathematical terms.

Visual thinking is a foundation of engineering. Walter P. Chrysler, founder of the automobile company, recounted his experience as an apprentice machinist where he built a model locomotive that existed "within my mind so real, so complete, that it seemed to have three dimensions there." Yet, the complexity of today's technology rarely permits a single person to build a device from his own visual image. The images must be conveyed to other engineers and designers. In addition, those images must be constructed in such a way that they are in a readily recognizable, consistent, and readable format. This assures that the visual ideas are clearly and unambiguously conveyed to others. *Engineering graphics* is a highly stylized way of presenting images of parts or assemblies.

A major portion of engineering information is recorded and transmitted using engineering graphics. In fact, 92 percent of the design process is graphically based. Written and verbal communications along with mathematics account for the remaining eight percent. To demonstrate the effectiveness of engineering graphics compared to a written description try to visualize an ice scraper based on this word description:

> An ice scraper is generally in the shape of a $140 \times 80 \times 10$ mm rectangular prism. One end is beveled from zero thickness to the maximum thickness in a length of 40 mm to form a sharp edge. The opposite end is semicircular. A 20 mm diameter hole is positioned so the center of the hole is 40 mm from the semicircular end and 40 mm from either side of the scraper.

It is evident immediately that the shape of the ice scraper is much more easily visualized from the graphical representation shown in Figure 8.1 than from the word description. Humans grasp information much more quickly when that information is presented in a graphical or visual form rather than as a word description.

Engineering drawings, whether done using a pencil and paper or a computer, start with a blank page or screen. The engineer's mind's eye image must be transferred to the paper or computer screen. The creative nature of this activity is similar to that of an artist. Perhaps the greatest example of this is Leonardo da Vinci, who had exceptional engi-

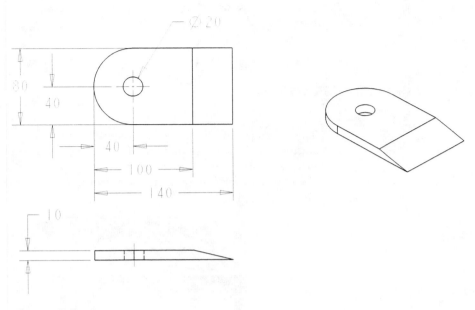

Figure 8.1

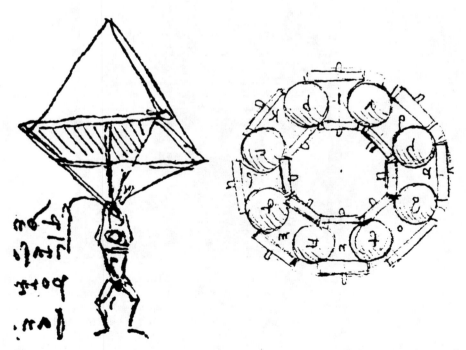

Figure 8.2 The creative genius of da Vinci is evident in these sketches of a parachute and a ball bearing, both devised hundreds of years before they were re-invented. (Parachute used with permission of the Biblioteca-Pinacoteca Ambrosiana, Milan, Italy. Property of the Ambrosian Library. All rights reserved. Reproduction is forbidden. [*The Inventions of Leonardo da Vinci*, Charles Gibbs-Smith, Phaidon Press, Oxford, 1978, p. 24.] Ball bearing used with permission of EMB-Service for Publishers, Lucerne, Switzerland. [*The Unknown Leonardo*, edited by Ladislao Reti, McGraw-Hill, 1974, p. 286])

neering creativity devising items such as parachutes and ball bearings, shown in **FIGURE 8.2**, hundreds of years before they were re-invented. He also had exceptional artistic talent, creating some of the most famous pictures ever painted such as *Mona Lisa* and *The Last Supper*.

8.2   ENGINEERING GRAPHICS

The first authentic record of engineering graphics dates back to 2130 BC, based on a statue now in the Museum of the Louvre, Paris. The statue depicts an engineer and governor of a small city-state in an area later known as Babylon. At the base of the statue are measuring scales and scribing instruments along with a plan of a fortress engraved on a stone tablet.

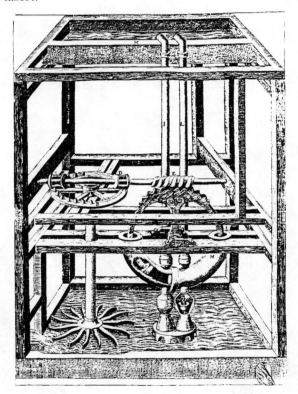

Figure 8.3 An example of pictorial perspective by Agostino Ramelli in 1588. (Used with permission of the Syndics of Cambridge University Library. [*The Various and Ingenious Machines of Agostino Ramelli (1588)*, translated by Martha Teach Gnudi, Johns Hopkins University Press, 1976. p. 83.])

Except for the use of pen and paper rather than stone tablets, it was not until printed books appeared around 1450 that techniques of graphics advanced. Around the same time, *pictorial perspective* drawing was invented by artist Paolo Uccello. This type of drawing presents an object much like it would look to the human eye or in a photograph, as shown in Figure 8.3. The essential characteristic of a perspective drawing is that parallel lines converge at a point in the distance like parallel railroad tracks seem to converge in the distance. Copper-plate engravings permitted the production of finely detailed technical drawings using pictorial perspective in large numbers. The pictorial perspective drawings were crucial to the advancement of technology through the Renaissance and until the beginning of the Industrial Revolution. But these drawings could not convey adequately details of the construction of an object. One solution to this problem was the use of the *exploded view* developed in the 15th century and perfected by Leonardo da Vinci. The exploded view of an assembly of individual parts shows the parts spread out along a common axis, as shown for the hoist in Figure 8.4. The exploded view reveals details of the individual parts along with showing the order in which they are assembled.

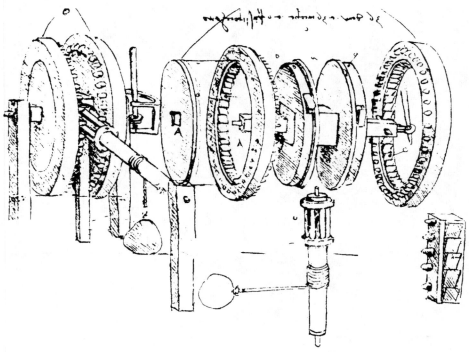

Figure 8.4 Assembled and exploded view of a hoist by Leonardo da Vinci, circa 1500. (Used with permission of the Biblioteca-Pinacoteca Ambrosiana, Milan, Italy. Property of the Ambrosian Library. All rights reserved. Reproduction is forbidden. [*The Inventions of Leonardo da Vinci*, Charles Gibbs-Smith, Phaidon Press, Oxford, 1978, p. 64.])

The Industrial Revolution brought with it the need to tie more closely the concept of a design with the final manufactured product using technical drawing. The perspective drawing of a simple object in Figure 8.5a shows pictorially what the object looks like. However, it is difficult to represent accurately dimensions and other details in a perspective drawing. *Orthographic projections*, developed in 1528 by German artist Albrecht Dürer, accomplish this quite well. An orthographic projection typically shows three views of an object. Each view shows a different side of the object (say the front, top, and side). An example of an orthographic projection is shown in Figure 8.5b. Orthographic projections are typically easy to draw, and the lengths and angles in orthographic projections have little distortion. As a result, orthographic drawings can convey more information than a perspective drawing. But their interpretation takes more effort than a pictorial perspective, as is evident from Figure 8.5. French philosopher and mathematician René Descartes laid the foundation for the mathematical principles of projections by connecting geometry to algebra in the 17th century. Much later Gaspard Monge, a French mathematician, "invented" the mathematical principles of projection known as *descriptive geometry*. These principles form the basis of engineering graphics today. But because these principles were thought to be of such strategic importance, they remained military secrets until 1795. By the 19th century, orthographic projections were used almost universally in mechanical drawing, and they are still the basis for engineering drawings today.

The *isometric view* is used more often today than the pictorial perspective view. Historically, it was used for centuries by engravers. Then in the early 19th century, William Farish, an English mathematician, formalized the isometric view and introduced it to engineers. The isometric view simplifies the pictorial perspective. In an isometric view, parallel lines remain parallel rather than converging to a point in the distance, as shown in Figure 8.5c. Keeping parallel lines parallel distorts the appearance of the object slightly. But the distortion in an isometric view is negligible for objects of limited depth. For situations in which the depth of the object is large, such as an architectural view down a long hallway, the pictorial perspective is preferable. The advantage of the isometric view, though, is that it is much easier to draw than a pictorial perspective view.

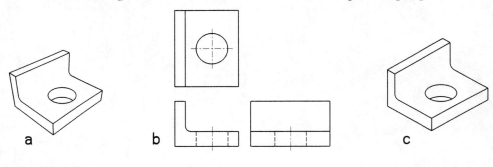

a   b   c

Figure 8.5

8.3   CAD

The introduction of the computer revolutionized engineering graphics. Pioneers in computer-aided engineering graphics envisioned the computer as a tool to replace paper and pencil drafting with a system that is more automated, efficient, and accurate. The first demonstration of a computer-based drafting tool was a system called SKETCHPAD developed at the Massachusetts Institute of Technology in 1963 by Ivan Sutherland. The system used a monochrome monitor with a light pen for input from the user. The following year IBM commercialized computer-aided drafting.

During the 1970s, computer-aided drafting blossomed as the technology changed from scientific endeavor to an economically indispensable industrial tool for design. Commands for geometry generators to create commonly occurring shapes were added. Functions were added to control the viewing of the drawing geometry. Modifiers such as rotate, delete, and mirror were implemented. Commands could be accessed by typing on the keyboard or by using a mouse. Perhaps most importantly, three-dimensional modeling techniques became a key part of engineering graphics software.

By the 1980s, computer-aided drafting became fully developed in the marketplace as a standard tool in industry. In addition, the current technology of solids modeling came about. Solids models represent objects in the virtual environment of the computer just as they exist in reality, having a volume as well as surfaces and edges. The introduction of Pro/ENGINEER® in 1988 and SolidWorks® in the 1990s revolutionized computer-aided design and drafting. Today solids modeling remains the state-of-the-art technology.

What we have been referring to as computer-aided drafting is usually termed *CAD*, an acronym for Computer Aided Design, Computer Aided Drafting, or Computer Aided Design and Drafting. Originally the term Computer Aided Design included any technique that uses computers in the design process including drafting, stress analysis, and motion analysis. But over the last 35 years CAD has come to refer more specifically to Computer Aided Design and Drafting. Computer Aided Engineering (CAE) is used to refer to the broader range of computer-related design tools.

8.4   DESIGN AND CAD

Inextricably connected with engineering graphics is the *design process* in which an engineering or design team faces a particular engineering problem and devises a solution to that problem. Often the design team includes persons responsible for engineering, product design, production system design, manufacturing, marketing, and sales. The idea is to simultaneously develop the product and the manufacturing process for the product. This is known as *concurrent engineering* or *integrated product and process design*. Key to the success of concurrent engineering is communication of information. Engineering graphics is one of the primary methods used by concurrent engineering teams to record and transfer information during the design process.

The process of bringing a product to market is shown in Figure 8.6. The process begins with the identification of a market, or user need. After this, the design process is the key to bridging the gap between a user need and the manufacture and sales of a product. The design process can be broken down into three parts as indicated in Figure 8.6. The first part is the *specification* of the problem. The *design specification* is a list of requirements that the final product must meet, including size, performance, weight, and so on. The second part of the design process is called *ideation* or conceptual design. In this phase, the design team devises as many ideas for solutions to the design problem as possible and then narrows them down to the best one based on the specification. In many cases, a designer or engineer will quickly sketch ideas to explore or communicate the design concept to the rest of the design team. These freehand sketches form the basis for the details of the design that are laid down in the third phase of the design process. It is in this last phase of the *design process*, known as *detail design*, that CAD is crucial. The conceptual ideas for the product that were seen in a designer's mind's eye or are on paper as rough sketches must then be translated into the visual language of engineering graphics. In this way, the ideas can be understood clearly and accurately by the design team and other designers, engineers, fabricators, suppliers, and machinists. It is in this phase of the design that the nitty gritty details have to be worked out. Should the device be 30 mm long or should it be 35 mm long? How will one part fit with another? What size hole should be used? What material should be used? What manufacturing process will be used to make the part? The number of individual decisions that need to be made can be very large, even for a relatively simple part. Once the engineering drawings have been created, the product can be manufactured and eventually sold.

The use of CAD has had a great impact on the design process. For example, a part may be modified several times to meet the design specification or to mate with another part. Before the advent of CAD, these modifications were very tedious, time-consuming, and prone to error. However, CAD has made it possible to make these changes relatively easily and quickly. The connectivity of computers using local area networks then

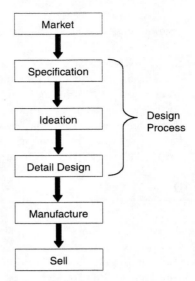

Figure 8.6

makes the revised electronic drawings available to a team of engineers at an instant. This is crucial as engineering systems become more complex and operational requirements become more stringent. For example, a modern jet aircraft has several million individual parts that must all fit together and perform safely for several decades.

Although CAD had a great impact on making the design process speedier and more accurate, the capabilities of the first few generations of CAD were still limited. Early CAD systems only provided a means of automating the drafting process to create orthographic engineering drawings. The designer or engineer would simply generate a line on the computer screen rather than drawing the line on paper. Current computer graphics software such as "paint" or "draw" programs for personal computers work this way. As CAD became more sophisticated, it helped automate the drafting process based on the "intelligence" of the software. CAD software lacking such intelligence required an engineer to draw a pair of parallel lines an exact distance apart by specifying coordinates of the endpoints of the lines. More advanced generations of CAD software permitted an engineer to draw approximately parallel lines using a mouse. Then the engineer would specify a particular distance between the lines and that the lines should be parallel. The CAD software then automatically placed these lines the specified distance apart and made them parallel. However, the major problem with the early generations of CAD software was that the designer or engineer was simply creating two-dimensional orthographic views of a three-dimensional part using a computer instead of a pencil and paper. From these two-dimensional views, the engineer still needed to reconstruct the mind's eye view of the three-dimensional image in the same way as if the drawings were created by hand.

The current generation of CAD software has had a very profound effect on the design process, because it is now possible to create a virtual prototype of a part or assembly on a computer. For example, the solids model of a pizza cutter is shown in Figure 8.7. Rather than translating a three-dimensional image from the mind's eye to a two-dimensional orthographic projection of the object, current CAD software starts with generating a three-dimensional virtual model of the object directly on the computer. This virtual model can be rotated so that it can be viewed from different angles. Several parts can be virtually assembled on the computer to make sure that they fit together. The assembled parts can be viewed as an assembly or in an exploded view. All of this is done in a virtual environment on the computer before the two-dimensional orthographic engineering drawings are even produced. It is still usually necessary to produce the orthographic engineering drawings. But these drawings only to serve as a standard means of engineering graphics communication, rather than as a tedious, time-consuming task necessary to proceed with the design process.

Figure 8.7

What Happened to Pencil and Paper Drawings?

CAD drawings have already replaced pencil and paper drawings. Through the 1970s and even into the 1980s many engineering and design facilities consisted of rows and rows of drafting tables with a designer or engineer hunched over a drawing on each table. Engineering colleges and universities required a full-year course in "engineering drafting" or "graphics communication" for all engineering students. Many of these students purchased a set of drawing instruments along with their first semester textbooks. They spent endless hours practicing lettering and drawing perfect circles.

Now nearly all of the drafting tables and drafting courses have been replaced by CAD. One can still find a drafting table here and there, but it is not for creating engineering drawings. Most often it is used for displaying a large CAD drawing to designers and engineers. They can make notes on the drawing or freehand sketch modifications on the drawing. The pencil is still an ideal means for generating ideas and quickly conveying those ideas to others. But eventually, all of the pencil markings are used as the basis for modifying the CAD drawing.

In some companies with traditional products that have not changed for decades (like a spoon or a chair), pencil and paper drawings are gradually being converted into electronic form. In some cases, the original drawing is simply scanned to create an electronic version. The scanned drawing cannot be modified, but the electronic version takes much less storage space than a hard copy. In other cases, the original pencil and paper drawings are being systematically converted to CAD drawings, so that they can be modified if necessary. In any case, though, the pencil and paper drawing is now just a part of the history of engineering.

KEY TERMS

CAD	Engineering graphics	Orthographic projections
descriptive geometry	exploded view	pictorial perspective
design process	ideation	specification
detail design	isometric view	

Problems

1. Research and report on an important historical figure in engineering graphics such as Leonardo da Vinci, Albrecht Dürer, Gaspard Monge, René Descartes, William Farish, M. C. Escher, Frank Lloyd Wright, Ivan Sutherland, or Paolo Uccello.

2. Using the World Wide Web, search for computer-aided design web sites. Report on the variety of software available for CAD and its capabilities.

3. Trace the early development of CAD and report on your findings. A particularly useful starting point is an article by S. H. Clauser in the November 1981 issue of *Mechanical Engineering*.

4. Computer hardware and user interface development has had a profound effect on the evolution of CAD software. Research and report on the impact of the light pen, the graphics tablet, the direct view storage tube, raster graphics technology, the work-station computer, the personal computer, or the mouse on the capability and evolution of CAD. (Many textbooks on engineering graphics discuss these items.)

5. Outline the design process and indicate how the three steps in the design process would relate to:

   a. the design of a suspension system for a mountain bike.
   b. the design of an infant car seat.
   c. the design of headphones for a portable cassette player.
   d. the design of a squirrel-proof bird feeder
   e. the design of a car-mounted bicycle carrier.
   f. the design of children's playground equipment.

9

Projections Used in Engineering Graphics

SECTIONS

- 9.1 Projections
- 9.2 3-D Projections
- 9.3 Multiview Projections
- 9.4 Working Drawings
- Key Terms

OBJECTIVES

- Understand the spatial relation between 3-D projections and multiview projections
- Be able to differentiate isometric, trimetric, perspective, and oblique 3-D projections
- Understand how multiview projections are related to the views of the sides of an object
- Know the proper placement of orthographic views
- Know the difference between third-angle and first-angle orthographic projections
- Be able to differentiate the various kinds of working drawings

OVERVIEW

Engineering graphics is a highly stylized scheme to represent three-dimensional objects on a two-dimensional paper or computer screen. This can be accomplished by representing all three dimensions of an object in a single image or by presenting a collection of views of different sides of the object. Working drawings are the practical result of using engineering graphics to represent objects.

9.1   PROJECTIONS

The goal in engineering graphics, whether it is freehand sketching or CAD, is to represent a physical object or the mind's eye image of an object so that the image can be conveyed to other persons. Objects can be shown as *3-D projections* or *multiview projections*. Figure 9.1 shows the handle of a pizza cutter shown in both ways. The 3-D projection clearly suggests the three-dimensional character of the handle, even though it is displayed on a two-dimensional medium (the page). 3-D projections are useful in that they provide an image that is similar to the image in the designer's mind's eye. But 3-D projections are often weak in providing adequate details of the object, and there is often some distortion of the object. For instance, a circular hole at the right end of the handle becomes an ellipse in an isometric 3-D projection.

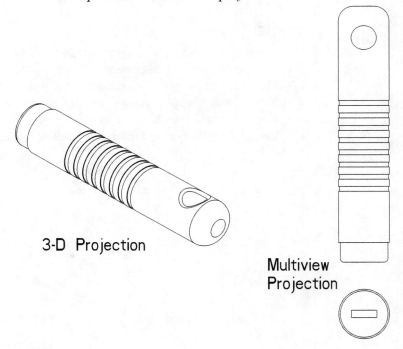

3-D Projection

Multiview Projection

Figure 9.1

Multiview projections are used to overcome the weaknesses of 3-D projections. Multiview projections are a collection of flat 2-D drawings of the different sides of an object. For instance, the side and bottom end of the pizza cutter handle are shown in the multi-view projection in Figure 9.1. Because there are two views, it is quite easy to depict details of the object. In addition, taken together, multiview projections provide a more accurate representation of the object than the 3-D projection—a circular hole appears as a circle in a multiview projection. On the other hand, multiview projections require substantial interpretation, and the overall shape of an object is often not obvious upon first glance. Consequently, the combination of the overall image provided by 3-D projections and details provided by multiview projections yield a representation of an object that is best. The shape of the object is immediately evident from the 3-D projection, and the detail needed for an accurate description of the object is available from the multiview projection.

9.2   3-D PROJECTIONS

Three different types of 3-D projections are available in most CAD software: isometric, trimetric, and perspective. These three views of a cube are shown in Figure 9.2. In all three cases, these 3-D projections represent all three dimensions of the cube in a single planar image. Although it is clear in all three cases that the object is a cube, each type of 3-D projection has its advantages and disadvantages.

The *isometric* projection has a standard orientation that makes it the typical projection used in CAD. In an isometric projection, the width and depth dimensions are sketched at 30° above horizontal as shown in Figure 9.2. This results in the three angles at the upper front corner of the cube being equal to 120°. The three sides of the cube are also equal, leading to the term iso (equal) -metric (measure). Isometric drawings work quite well for objects of limited depth. However, an isometric drawing distorts the object when the depth is significant. In this case, a pictorial perspective drawing is better.

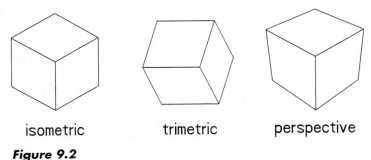

isometric   trimetric   perspective

Figure 9.2

In general, the *trimetric projection* offers more flexibility in orienting the object in space. The width and depth dimensions are at arbitrary angles to the horizontal, and the three angles at the upper front corner of the cube are unequal. This makes the three sides of the cube each have a different length as measured in the plane of the drawing; hence the name tri-metric. In most CAD software, the trimetric projection fixes one side along a horizontal line and tips the cube forward as shown in Figure 9.2. A *dimetric* projection sets two sides of the cube, usually those of the front face, equal.

A pictorial perspective, or simply *perspective*, projection is drawn so that parallel lines converge in the distance as shown in Figure 9.2, unlike isometric or trimetric projections where parallel lines remain parallel. A *perspective projection* is quite useful in providing a realistic image of an object when the object spans a long distance, such as the view of a bridge or aircraft from one end. Generally, small manufactured objects are adequately represented by isometric or trimetric views.

Two types of pictorial sketches are used frequently in *freehand sketching*: isometric and oblique. The isometric projection was discussed with respect to 3-D CAD projections. The isometric projection is often used in freehand sketching because it is relatively easy to create a realistic sketch of an object. But the *oblique projection* is usually even easier to sketch. The oblique projection places the principal face of the object parallel to the plane of the paper with the axes in the plane of the paper perpendicular to one another. The axis into the paper is at an arbitrary angle with respect to the horizontal. Figure 9.3 compares an isometric projection and an oblique projection of a cube with a hole in it. The advantage of the oblique projection is that details in the front face of the object retain their true shape. For instance, the circle on the front face is circular in the oblique projection, while it is elliptical in the isometric projection. This feature often makes oblique freehand sketching somewhat easier than isometric sketching.

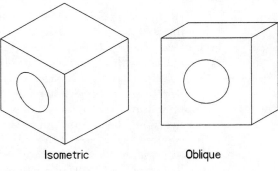

Isometric   Oblique

Figure 9.3

9.3   MULTIVIEW PROJECTIONS

The standard means of *multiview projection* in engineering graphics is what we have referred to earlier as the *orthographic projection*. Although 3-D projections provide a readily identifiable visual image of an object, multiview projections are ideal for showing the details of an object. Dimensions can be shown easily and most features remain undistorted in multiview projections.

An orthographic projection is most easily thought of as a collection of views of different sides of an object—front, top, side, and so forth. For instance, two orthographic projections could be used for a coffee mug. The front view would show the sidewall of the mug along with the loop forming the handle. The top view would show what one would see looking down into the mug—a circular rim of the mug, the bottom of the inside of the mug, and the top of the handle that sticks out of the side of the mug. Dimensions of the mug could easily be added to the projections of each side of the mug to create an engineering drawing.

One useful way of looking at multiview projections is to imagine a glass box surrounding the object as shown in Figure 9.4. The image of each side of the object can be projected onto the wall of the glass box. Now an observer on the outside of the box can see each side of the object as projected on each of the six walls of the box. Solid lines show the edges evident in the projection, and dashed lines show lines that are hidden by the object. Now imagine unfolding the glass box as if each of the edges of the glass box were a hinge, so that the front view is in the middle. Now the unfolded glass box represents all six sides of the object in a single plane as shown in Figure 9.5. In unfolding the

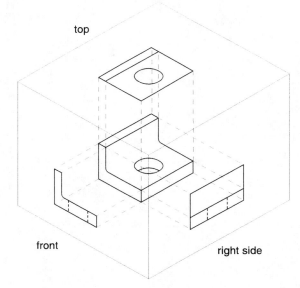

Figure 9.4

glass box, the top view is positioned above the front view, the bottom view is below the front view, the right-side view is to the right of the front view, and so on. The dimensions of the object remain the same in all views. For example, the horizontal dimension (width of the object) in the front view is identical in that same dimension in the top view and bottom view. The views also remain aligned so that the bottom edge in the front view is even with the bottom edge in the right side, left side, and rear views. Likewise, the top edges remain aligned. Finally, the same edges in adjacent views are closest together. For instance, the same edge of the object is at the left-side of the front view and the right side of the left side view. This edge in the front view is closest to the same edge in the left-side view.

In many cases, three views are needed to represent an object accurately, although in some cases (like a coffee mug) only two views are necessary, and in other cases more than three views are needed to show complex features of the object. It is helpful to select the side of the object that is most descriptive of the object as the front view. Sometimes this may place an object so that what is normally thought of as the front of the object is not shown in the front view of the multiview projection. For example, what is usually described as being the side of a car should be chosen as the front view, because this view is probably most descriptive and easily recognizable as a car. A view of the front of a car (grille, bumper, and windshield) is not as descriptive or as obvious as the side of the car. Furthermore, the object should be properly oriented in the front view. For instance, a car should be shown with its wheels downward in their normal operating position for the front view. The other views that are shown in addition to the front view should be views that best represent features of the object. Normally the minimum number of views necessary to accurately represent the object is used. The standard practice is to use the front, top, and right-side views. But the choice of which views to use depends on the object and which details need to be shown most clearly.

A complication that arises in multiview projections is that two different standards are used for the placement of projections. In North America (and to some extent, in Great Britain) the unfolding of the glass box approach places the top view above the front view, the right-side view to the right of the front view, and so on. This placement of

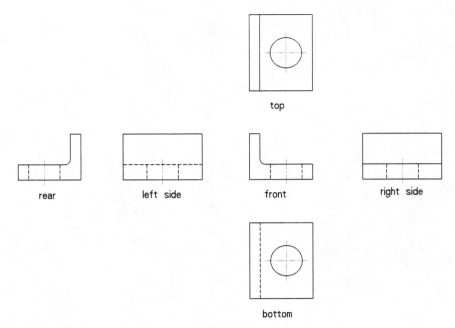

top

rear   left side   front   right side

bottom

Figure 9.5

views is called *third-angle projection*. But in most of the rest of the world an alternative approach for the placement of views is used. In this case the placement of views is what would result if the object were laid on the paper with its front side up for the front view and then rolled on one edge for the other views. For instance, if the object were rolled to the right so that it rests on its right side, then the left side would be facing up. So the left-side view is placed to the right of the front view. Likewise, if the object were lying on the paper with the front view up and then rolled toward the bottom of the paper, it would be resting on its bottom side, so that the top side faces upward. Thus, the top view is placed below the front view. This placement of views, known as the *first-angle projection*, simply reverses the location of the top and bottom views and the location of the left-side and right-side views with respect to the front view compared to the third-angle projection. The views themselves remain the same in both projections.

Although, the difference between the two projections is only in the placement of the views, great potential for confusion and manufacturing errors can result in engineering drawings that are used globally. To avoid misunderstanding, international projection symbols, shown in Figure 9.6, have been developed to distinguish between third-angle and first-angle projections on drawings. The symbol shows two views of a truncated cone. In the first-angle projection symbol, the truncated end of the cone (two concentric circles) is placed on the base side of the cone, as it would be in a first-angle projection. In the third-angle projection symbol, the truncated end of the cone is placed on the truncated side of the cone, as it would be in a third-angle projection. Usually these symbols appear in or near the title block of the drawing when the possibility of confusion is anticipated. Most CAD software automatically uses the third-angle projection for engineering drawings.

A problem that frequently occurs in orthographic projections is that one of the faces of the object is at an angle to the orthographic planes that form the imaginary glass box. An example is the object shown in Figure 9.7. The circular hole with a keyway (rectangular cutout) that is perpendicular to the angled face appears in both the top

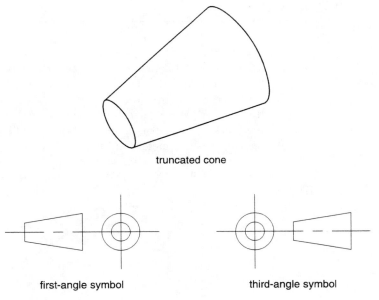

truncated cone

first-angle symbol   third-angle symbol

Figure 9.6

view and the right-side view. However, it is distorted in both of these views, because it is on an angled plane of the object. An auxiliary view is used to avoid this distortion. In this case, a view of the object is drawn so that the angled face is parallel to the auxiliary view plane. The view is based on the viewer looking at the object along a line of sight that is perpendicular to the angled face. When viewed in this direction, the circular hole in the auxiliary view appears as a circle without any distortion. As suggested by the dash-dot lines in Figure 9.7, the auxiliary view is projected from the front view in the same way as the top and right-side views are projected. Thus, its position with respect to the front view depends on the orientation of the angled face. It is normal practice not to project hidden lines or other features that are not directly related to the angled surface.

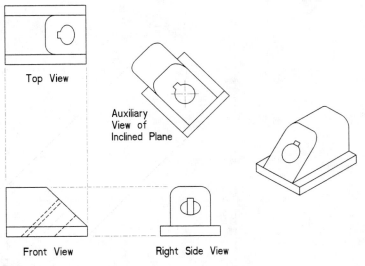

Top View

Auxiliary
View of
Inclined Plane

Front View   Right Side View

Figure 9.7

9.4 WORKING DRAWINGS

Several types of *working drawings* are produced during the design process. Initially *freehand sketches* are used in the ideation phase of the design process. These are usually hand-drawn pictorial sketches of a concept that provide little detail, but enough visual information to convey the concept to other members of the design team. An example is the isometric sketch of a sheet metal piece that holds the blade of a pizza cutter, shown in Figure 9.8. The general shape of the object is clear, although details such as the thickness of the sheet metal and the radius of the bends in the sheet metal are not included. These conceptual sketches eventually evolve to final detailed drawings that define enough detail and information to support production.

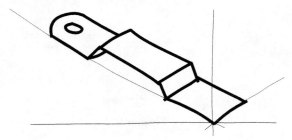

Figure 9.8

Detail drawings document the detailed design of individual components using orthographic views. The detail drawing is the final representation of a design that is specific enough so that all of the information necessary for the manufacture of the part is provided. As a result, it is imperative that it includes the necessary views, dimensions, and specifications required for manufacturing the part. Figure 9.9 shows an example of

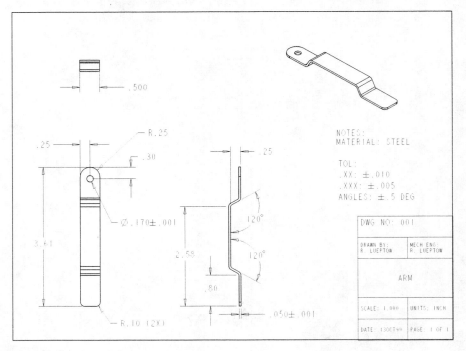

Figure 9.9

a detail drawing of the part of the pizza cutter that was sketched in Figure 9.8. The detail drawing includes fully dimensioned orthographic views, notation of the material that the part is to be made from, information on the acceptable tolerances for the dimensions, and a title block that records important information about the drawing. Often an isometric view is included in the detail drawing to further clarify the shape of the part. Detail drawings provide sufficient detail so that the part can be manufactured based on the drawing alone.

Assembly drawings show how the components of a design fit together. Dimensions and other details are usually omitted in assembly drawings to enhance clarity. Several styles of assembly drawings are commonly used. Sometimes the assembly drawing is just an isometric view of the fully assembled device. But an exploded isometric view is often helpful to show the individual parts are assembled, as shown in Figure 9.10 for a pizza cutter. In some cases, a sectioned assembly, or cut-away view, shows how complicated devices are assembled. A cutting plane passes through the assembly and part of the device is removed to show the interior of the assembly. Numbers or letters can be assigned to individual parts of the assembly on the drawing and keyed to a parts list.

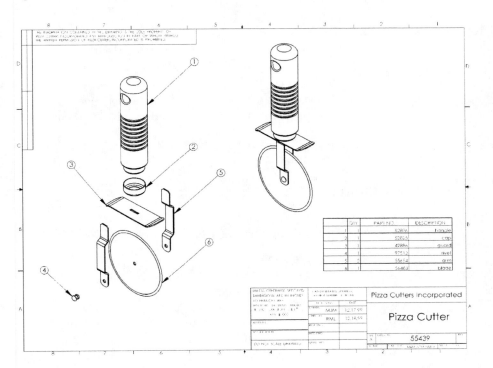

Figure 9.10

Finally a *parts list*, or *bill of materials*, must be included with a set of working drawings. The parts list includes the part name, identification number, material, number required in the assembly, and other information (such as catalog number for standard parts such as threaded fasteners). An example is shown in Figure 9.11 for a pizza cutter. The parts list is used to ensure that all parts are ordered or manufactured and brought to the central assembly point.

	QTY.	PART NO.	DESCRIPTION
1	1	52806	handle
2	1	52825	cap
3	1	42886	guard
4	1	97512	rivet
5	2	55654	arm
6	1	56483	blade

Figure 9.11

Taken together, the detail drawings of each individual part, the assembly drawing, and the bill of materials provide a complete set of working drawings for the manufacture of a part.

KEY TERMS

3-D projections

Assembly drawings

bill of materials

Detail drawings

first-angle projection

freehand sketching

multiview projection

multiview projections

oblique projection

orthographic projection

perspective projection

third-angle projection

trimetric projection

working drawings

Problems

1. Describe or sketch the front view that should be used in an orthographic projection of:

   a. a stapler.

   b. a television set.

   c. a cooking pot.

   d. a hammer.

   e. a pencil.

   f. a bicycle.

   g. an evergreen tree.

   h. a paper clip.

   i. a coffee mug.

   j. a padlock.

2. Identify the views shown in Figure 9.12 as isometric, trimetric, or perspective.

Figure 9.12

3. For the drawings shown in Figure 9.13, determine whether the multiview projection is first-angle or third-angle.

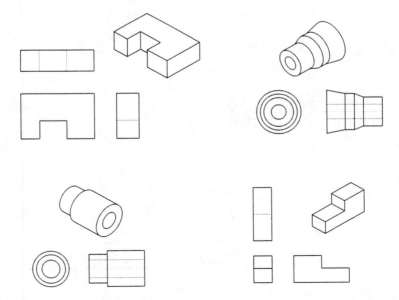

Figure 9.13

4.   Develop a bill of materials for:

   a.   a pencil.
   b.   a squirt gun.
   c.   a click-type ball point pen.
   d.   a videocassette (take an old one apart).
   e.   an audio cassette (take an old one apart).
   f.   a disposable camera (ask a local photo developer for a used one to take apart).
   g.   eyeglasses.
   h.   a household cleaner pump bottle.
   i.   a claw-type staple remover.
   j.   an adhesive tape dispenser.
   k.   a bicycle caliper brake.
   l.   a floppy disk (take an old one apart).
   m.   a utility knife.
   n.   a Vise-Grip wrench.

10

Freehand Sketching

SECTIONS

- 10.1 Why Freehand Sketches?
- 10.2 Freehand Sketching Fundamentals
- 10.3 Basic Freehand Sketching
- 10.4 Advanced Freehand Sketching
- Key Terms

OBJECTIVES

- Explain why freehand sketching is important in design
- Freehand sketch lines and circles
- Sketch an oblique 3-D projection
- Sketch an isometric 3-D projection
- Sketch an orthographic multiview projection

OVERVIEW

In this chapter you will learn useful techniques for freehand sketching to create both two-dimensional orthographic sketches and three-dimensional pictorial sketches. You will learn how to quickly make rough sketches to convey a concept and how to make more refined sketches of objects that are more complex.

10.1 WHY FREEHAND SKETCHES?

An integral part of the creative design process is *ideation*, the generation of concepts or ideas to solve a design problem. Often freehand sketching can be used to explore and communicate mental concepts that come about in the mind's eye. The process of sketching can solidify and fill out rough concepts. Furthermore, sketching captures the ideas in a permanent form that can be used to communicate the concept to others. In this way, sketches often act as stepping stones to refine and detail the original concept or generate new ideas. Many great design ideas are first sketched on the back of an envelope or in a lab notebook, such as the freehand sketch of one of helicopter inventor Igor Sikorsky's designs, (Figure 10.1).

While computers are the workhorses for engineering graphics, initially generating ideas on a computer screen is very rare. A more common scenario is sketching an idea on paper and subsequently refining the concept on paper using more rough sketches. This often occurs simply because all that is needed for a freehand sketch is a pencil and a paper. Freehand sketching *quickly* translates the image of the concept in the mind's eye to paper. Engineers often communicate via rough freehand sketches to refine and improve the design. Sketches are much more useful than detailed CAD drawings early in the design process, because they are informal, quickly and easily changed, and less restrictive. It is only after clarifying the design concept by iterating through several freehand sketches that it is possible to draw the object using computer graphics. In fact, often an engineer will sit down to create a CAD drawing of an object using a freehand sketch as a guide.

This chapter focuses on the rudimentary elements of freehand technical sketching, because in many ways freehand sketching is the first step in CAD.

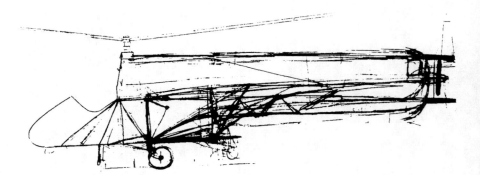

Figure 10.1 Helicopter inventor Igor Sikorsky's sketch of an early helicopter prototype demonstrates the visual impact of freehand sketching. (Used with permission of the Sikorsky Aircraft Corporation, Stratford, CT. ["Straight Up," by Curt Wohleber, *American Heritage of Invention and Technology*, Winter, 1993, pp. 26-39.])

10.2 FREEHAND SKETCHING FUNDAMENTALS

Freehand sketching requires few tools: just a pencil and paper. It may be tempting to use straight-edged triangles or rulers for drawing straight lines and a compass to draw circles. But these instruments often slow down the process and distract from the purpose of sketching, which is to create a quick, rough graphical representation of the image in the mind's eye. Generally sketching has three steps, although the steps are usually subconscious. First, the sketch is planned by visualizing it in the mind including the size of the sketch on the paper, the orientation of the object, and the amount of detail to be included in the sketch. Second, the sketch is outlined using very light lines to establish the orientation, proportion, and major features of the sketch. Finally, sharpening and darkening object lines and adding details develops the sketch.

All sketches are made up of a series of arcs and lines, so the ability to draw circles and straight lines is necessary. A straight line is sketched in the following way. First, sketch the endpoints of the line as dots or small crosses. Then place your pencil on the starting endpoint. Keeping your eyes on the terminal point, use a smooth continuous stroke to draw the line between the points as shown in Figure 10.2. Nearly horizontal or vertical lines are frequently easier to draw than inclined lines, so it may be helpful to shift the paper to draw the line horizontally or vertically. For long lines, it may be helpful to mark two or three points along the line and use the procedure between consecutive points or to make two or three shorter passes lightly with the pencil before a final darker line.

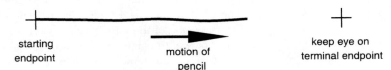

starting endpoint	motion of pencil	keep eye on terminal endpoint

Figure 10.2

A circle can be sketched using the following steps, illustrated in Figure 10.3. First, draw light horizontal and vertical lines crossing at the center of the circle. Second, lightly mark the radius of the circle on each line. Finally, connect the radius marks with a curved line to form a circle. Another technique is to lightly draw a square box the same size as the circle diameter as shown in Figure 10.3. Then lightly draw diagonals of the box and centerlines between midpoints of the sides of the box. The diagonals and centerlines should intersect at the center of the circle. Mark the radius on these lines, and sketch the circle within the box. It is sometimes helpful to mark the radius on the edge of a scrap paper and mark the radius at as many points as desired in addition to the marks on the centerlines and diagonals. Arcs are sketched in much the same way as circles, except that only a portion of the circle is sketched. It is generally easier to sketch an arc with your hand and pencil on the concave side of the arc.

10.3 BASIC FREEHAND SKETCHING

Many times, particularly during the conceptual stage of design, it is necessary to immediately communicate a graphical image to others. It has been said that some of the best design engineers are the ones who can sketch an idea clearly in a minute or so. The goal of the sketch in this case is not to show the details of the part, but to provide another person with a clear concept of the idea. For example, a design engineer may need to show a sketch to a manufacturing engineer to get input on the manufacturability of a

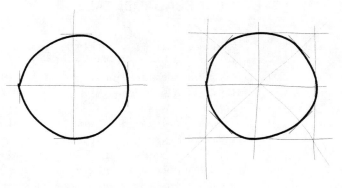

Figure 10.3

part. If the concept is at an early phase, CAD drawings would not have been created yet. So the design engineer needs to use a freehand sketch of the part.

The sketch of Sikorsky's helicopter in Figure 10.1 exemplifies the power of free-hand sketching. A brief glance at this sketch provides immediate insight to the concept that is being shown. One does not need to study the sketch to know what is being sketched, even if the viewer has never seen the concept before. These quick ideation sketches are not difficult to draw and require no artistic talent, just some practice.

Two types of pictorial sketches are used frequently in freehand sketching: oblique and isometric. The *oblique projection* places the principal face of the object parallel to the plane of the paper. The *isometric projection* tilts the part so that no surface of the part is in the plane of the paper. The advantage of the oblique projection is that details in the front face of the object retain their true shape. This often makes oblique freehand sketching easier than isometric sketching, where no plane is parallel to the paper. The disadvantage of the oblique projection is that it does not appear as "photorealistic" as an isometric projection. In other words, an isometric projection is similar to what a photograph of the object would look like.

10.3.1 Oblique Sketching

Often freehand sketching begins with light thin lines called *construction lines* that define enclosing boxes for the shape that is being sketched. Construction lines are used in several ways. First, the construction lines become the path for the final straight lines of the sketch. Second, the intersection of construction lines specify the length of the final lines. Third, points marked by the intersection of construction lines guide the sketching of circles and arcs. And finally, construction lines guide the proportions of the sketch. This last item is of crucial importance if the sketch is to clearly represent the object. For example, if an object is twice as wide as it is high, the proportions in the sketch must reflect this. Proper proportions of the boxes defined by the construction lines will result in proper proportions of the sketch.

An oblique freehand sketch is easy, since it begins with a two-dimensional representation of the face of the object. Figure 10.4 shows the steps in quickly sketching a part with a circular hole.

Step 1: Horizontal and vertical construction lines are lightly drawn to outline the basic shape of the main face of the part. This is known as *blocking-in* the sketch. If you are using a pencil or felt-tip marker, press lightly when drawing the construction lines to produce a thin or light line. If you are using a ball-point pen, draw a single, light line.

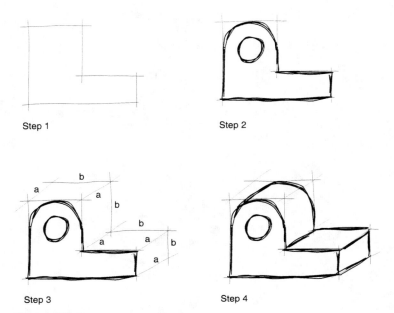

Figure 10.4

Step 2: Sketch in the face of the part using the construction lines as a guide. How you sketch the outline of the part depends on the type of pen or pencil that you are using. The idea is to thicken the lines of the part compared to the construction lines. If you are using a pencil or a felt-tip marker, pressing hard for the outline of the part will result in heavy or dark lines. If you are using a ball-point pen, the line width does not depend much on how hard you press. In this case, the outline of the part is sketched with a back and forth motion of the pen to thicken the lines of the part compared to the construction lines as shown in Figure 10.4. The straight lines are usually sketched first, followed by the arcs. The circle for the hole in the part is added last to complete the face of the part.

Step 3: Sketch *receding construction lines* (lines into the plane of the paper labeled *a*) at a convenient angle. All of the receding lines must be parallel to each other and are usually at an angle of 30° to 45°. The receding lines end at the appropriate depth for the object. Then vertical and horizontal lines at the back plane of the part are added (lines labeled *b*). This blocks in the three-dimensional box enclosing the object.

Step 4: Sketch in and darken the lines outlining the part. Again it is usually easiest to sketch in the straight lines first, then the arcs, and finally any details. Because the construction lines are light compared to the outline of the part, they are not erased.

The final sketch, while rough and lacking detail, clearly shows the design intent for the part.

10.3.2 Isometric Sketching

Isometric freehand sketches are somewhat more difficult to master than oblique sketches because no face is in the plane of the paper in an isometric view. The steps to construct a simple freehand isometric sketch are shown in Figure 10.5.

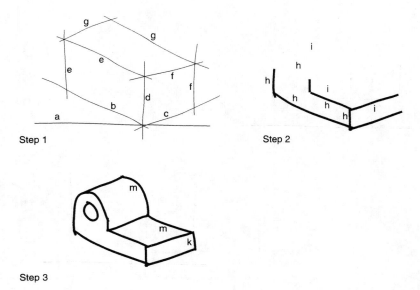

Figure 10.5

Step 1: Sketch a light horizontal line (*a*). From this line draw two intersecting lines at an angle of approximately 30° to the horizontal (*b* and *c*). Then draw a vertical line (*d*) through the intersection of the previous three lines. The three lines labeled *b*, *c*, and *d* form the isometric axes of the sketch. Next sketch the box to block in the front face of the part (*e*). These lines should be parallel to axes *b* and *d*. Similarly, sketch the lines to block in the right face (*f*) making sure that the lines are parallel to axes *c* and *d*. Finish this step by sketching lines parallel to the axes to complete the box that encloses the part (*g*).

Step 2: The outline for the front face is added by sketching in lines and curves (*h*). Then outline the front face using heavy lines. In this case, a single heavy line such as might be produced from pressing hard on a pencil or felt-tip marker is used. Next, lines are sketched to indicate the depth of the features of the front view (*i*). These lines should be parallel to axis *c*. They can be darkened after they are drawn lightly.

Step 3: Finally, a line is added to complete the back corner of the part (*k*). Lines and arcs are added to complete the back face of the part (*m*). Then the hole detail is added. Circular holes appear as ellipses in isometric views, as discussed in the next section.

The choice of whether to use an oblique projection or an isometric projection is often arbitrary. Because the oblique projection is easier to sketch, it is sometimes preferred. On the other hand, an isometric projection provides a more photorealistic image of the object.

10.4 ADVANCED FREEHAND SKETCHING

The sketching methods described in the previous section were focused on sketches in which the face of the object is in a single plane. Freehand sketching is somewhat more difficult when the face of the object is not in a single plane. The difficulty here is accurately depicting the depth of the object. Oblique and isometric projections are still useful, though somewhat more complicated than those in the previous section. In addition, orthographic projections are also valuable.

10.4.1 Freehand Oblique Sketching

An example of the steps leading to an oblique freehand sketch of a complicated object are shown in Figure 10.6. Because the face of the base of the object and the face of the upper portion of the object are in different planes, it is necessary to begin with a box that encloses the entire object before sketching either face. Some of the construction lines are removed after they are used in this example. This was done here to make the sketch more clear. However, this is not necessary in practice, if the construction lines are drawn as light lines.

Step 1: To begin, construction lines to form a box that encloses the object are drawn to block-in the sketch. Notice that the front and back faces of the box are rectangular with horizontal and vertical sides. The receding construction lines are parallel and at an angle of 30° to 45° to horizontal. The easiest way to draw this box is to first draw the front rectangle (*a*). Then draw an identical second rectangle above and to the right of the first rectangle (*b*). Finally connect the corners with receding construction lines (*c*).

Step 2: Now the front face of the base of the object can be sketched in the front rectangle. The lines are appropriately darkened.

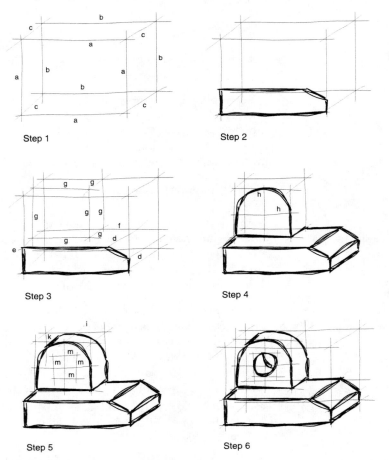

Figure 10.6

Step 3: Certain features of the front face of the base extend backward along or parallel to the receding construction lines. For example, the lines (*d*) forming the chamfer (angled cut on the right side of the base) can be sketched parallel to receding lines. Likewise the receding line for the upper left corner of the base can be sketched (*e*). Then the base can be finished with a horizontal line on the back face (*f*). Now it is possible to block in the upper rounded portion of the object to create a box (*g*) that encloses the upper protrusion within the larger box that encloses the entire object.

Step 4: The front face of the upper portion of the object can be sketched in this box. Then receding lines corresponding to the chamfer and the left edge of the base can be darkened. In addition, the lines forming the back face can be sketched. Note that the line forming the back edge of the chamfer is parallel to the line forming the front edge of the chamfer. Construction lines (*h*) on the front face of the upper portion are drawn to center of the circle for the hole.

Step 5: A receding construction line (*i*) extending from the peak of the front face to the plane of the back face is sketched to aid in aligning the curved outline of the back of the upper portion. The back face is identical to the front face except that it is shifted upward and to the right. This results in the left side of the back face being hidden. A darkened receding line (*k*) finishes the left side of the upper portion of the object. Finally, four construction lines (*m*) are sketched to block in the circle for the hole.

Step 6: Now the hole can be sketched in and darkened. The back edge of the hole is also added to complete the sketch. The construction lines may be erased, but usually the construction lines are retained if they are made properly as light lines.

Oblique sketching is often aided by the use of graph paper with a light, square grid. The process is identical to that shown in Figure 10.6, but it is easier to keep the proportions correct by counting the number of boxes in the grid to correspond to the approximate dimensions of the part. Graph paper further improves the sketch by helping keep lines straight as well as more accurately horizontal or vertical.

10.4.2 Isometric Sketching

Isometric freehand sketches of more complex objects start with an isometric box to block in the sketch. Then faces are sketched and additional features are blocked in. Finally details are added. The steps to construct an isometric sketch are shown in Figure 10.7 Some of the construction lines are removed after they are used, to make the sketch more clear in this figure. Normally, removing construction lines is not necessary.

Step 1: To begin, sketch a light horizontal line (*a*). From this line draw two intersecting lines at an angle of approximately 30° to the horizontal (*b* and *c*) and a vertical line (*d*) through the intersection of the previous three lines to form the isometric axes of the sketch. Finish blocking in by sketching lines (*e*) to complete the box so that it will completely enclose the object. Unlike the oblique sketch, it is often better not to sketch hidden construction lines when blocking in.

Step 2: Block in the front face of the part (*f*) so that the construction line is parallel to the isometric axis. Similarly, sketch the line to block in the right face (*g*).

Step 3: Sketch the left face and the right face and darken the lines. This completes the faces that are in the front planes of the box. Now sketch in three lines (*h*) parallel to the isometric axis (*c*). The left line (*h*) is the top edge of the base. The middle line (h) finishes the chamfer. The right line (h) is used to aid in sketching a construction line for the back edge of the base (i), which is sketched next.

Step 4: Now the face of the chamfer can be darkened and the angled line at the back edge of the chamfer can be added. This completes the angled face of the chamfer. Next the protrusion above the base can be blocked in with seven lines (k).

Step 5: The front face of the upper protrusion is sketched first using light lines. Construction lines (m) are added to help identify the location of the endpoints of the arc of the front and back faces of the protrusion. The rounded rear face (n) is sketched lightly to be identical to the front face, except that part of it is not visible. The line at the top left edge of protrusion (o) is added. Then all lines forming the upper portion of the object are darkened In addition, the line forming the top edge of the base on the back side is darkened.

Step 6: The details related to the hole are added next. Circles in isometric projections are difficult to draw because they appear as ellipses with their major axes at an angle to horizontal. The center of the hole is where two lines (m) intersect on the front face of the upper portion of the object. The lines (p) forming the parallelogram to enclose the ellipse for the hole are added. Each side of the parallelogram should be parallel to one of the isometric axes. The sides should be equal in length to one another.

Step 7: To help in sketching the ellipse, construction lines forming the diagonals of the parallelogram (r) are added.

Step 8: Now the ellipse that represents the circular hole can be sketched. A few simple points help in sketching ellipses more easily. The major axis and minor axis of the ellipse are perpendicular to one another. The major and minor axes also coincide with the diagonals of the parallelogram enclosing the ellipse (r). The ellipse touches the parallelogram at the midpoints of the sides of the parallelogram. Start drawing the hole by sketching short elliptical arcs between the midpoints of the parallelogram on either side of the minor axis. Finish the hole by sketching sharply curved elliptical arcs between the midpoints of the parallelogram on either side of the major axis of the hole. Finally, darken and make heavy the lines outlining the hole and any remaining edges of the part.

Isometric sketching is made substantially easier by the use of isometric grid paper. This paper has a grid of lines at horizontal and 30° to horizontal (corresponding to lines b, c, and d in Figure 10.7). The procedure for using isometric grid paper is the same as that described above, but using the isometric grid paper keeps proportions of the part consistent. One simply counts grid boxes to approximate the dimensions of the object. The grid paper also aids in sketching straight lines parallel to the isometric axes.

10.4.3 Orthographic Sketching

In some cases it is necessary to sketch orthographic projection views rather than oblique or isometric pictorial views. Because orthographic views are two-dimensional representations, they are not as difficult to sketch as pictorial views. But there are several techniques that make freehand sketching of orthographic views easier and more efficient. The process for sketching three orthographic views of the object in the previous two figures is shown in Figure 10.8.

Step 1: Begin by blocking in the front, top, and side views of the object using the overall width, height, and depth. The construction lines extend between views to

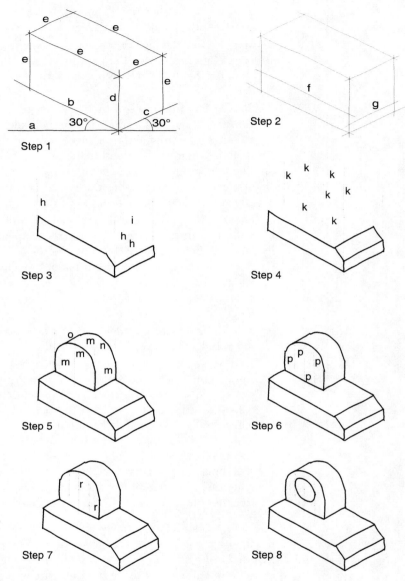

Figure 10.7

properly align the views and maintain the same dimension in different views. For instance, line (*a*) represents the bottom edge and line (*b*) represents the top edge in both the front view and the right-side view. The distance between lines (*a*) and (*b*) is the height dimension in both views. The space between the views should be large enough so that the drawing does not look crowded and should be the same between all views.

Step 2: In the second step the upper protrusion is blocked in. Note that line (*c*) extends across the top and front views, to assure that the width of the protrusion is consistent in both views. Likewise, line (*d*) extends across the front and right-side views.

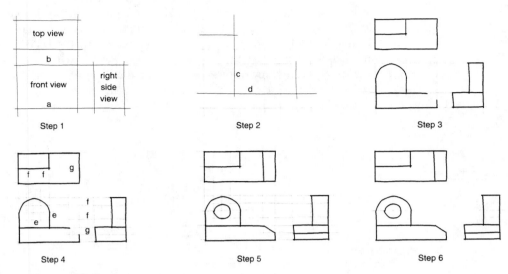

Figure 10.8

Step 3: The outline of the object is darkened to clearly show the shape of the object in all three views. Care must be taken in darkening lines. For instance, the right corner of the front view should not be darkened, because the detail of the chamfer has not yet been added.

Step 4: Construction lines for the holes and other details are added next. The center of the hole is positioned with construction lines (*e*). Then construction lines that block in the hole (*f*) are drawn. These construction lines extend between views to project the hole to the top view and to the right-side view. Construction lines extending between views (*g*) are also added for the chamfer.

Step 5: Now the hole and chamfer are sketched and darkened to show the completed object.

Step 6: Finally, centerlines (long-dash, short-dash) that indicate the center of the hole are added. Hidden lines (dashed lines) that indicate lines hidden behind a surface are also added. Construction lines may be erased as was done in this figure, but this is not usually necessary.

The quality of the sketch can often be improved by using square grid graph paper to keep proportions and act as a guide for horizontal and vertical lines. Some engineers prefer to use a straight-edge to produce a nicer sketch, but this is usually not necessary with practice and sufficient care in sketching.

Will Freehand Sketching Ever Become Obsolete?

CAD has almost totally eliminated pencil and paper drawings. But what about pencil and paper freehand sketching? Although many computers and palm-tops offer sketching programs, it is unlikely that freehand sketching will disappear soon. Just as it is easier to do a calculation in your head or on a piece of scratch paper rather than finding a calculator and punching in the numbers, it is easier to sketch an image on a piece of paper (or a napkin!) than to find a computer, log in, and start the appropriate "paint" program. Pencil and paper freehand sketches are quick, efficient, easily modified, and easily conveyed to others. And all that is needed is a pencil and a scrap of paper.

Even if the pencil and paper are totally replaced by palm-top computers some day, freehand sketching skills will still be useful. Instead of using a pencil on a piece of paper, we will use a stylus on a touch screen. The only difference is the medium. The freehand sketching techniques themselves are unlikely to change much. Perhaps one could imagine sketching software that assists in generating oblique or isometric sketches as they are drawn at some time in the future.

KEY TERMS

blocking-in	ideation	receding construction lines
construction lines		

Problems

For all of the problems, the items shown in Figure 10.9, Figure 10.10, and Figure 10.11 are 2 inches wide, 1.5 inches high, and 1 inch deep. The holes in Figure 10.9b, Figure 10.9c, Figure 10.9d, Figure 10.10c, and Figure 10.10d are through holes. The hole in Figure 10.10b is through the front face only.

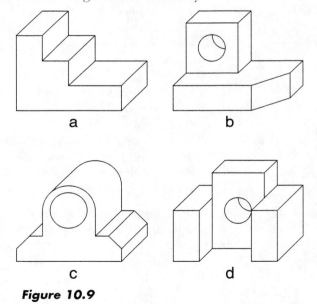

Figure 10.9

1. Create freehand oblique sketches of the objects in Figure 10.9. (The objects are shown as oblique projections, so you must simply recreate the drawing by freehand sketching.)

2. Create freehand oblique sketches of the objects in Figure 10.10. (The objects are shown as isometric projections.)

3. Create freehand oblique sketches of the objects in Figure 10.11. (The objects are shown as orthographic projections.)

4. Create freehand isometric sketches of the objects in Figure 10.10. (The objects are shown as isometric projections, so you must simply recreate the drawing by freehand sketching.)

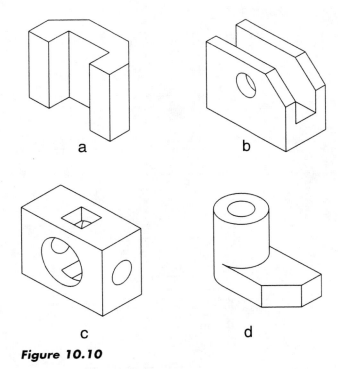

a   b

c   d

Figure 10.10

5. Create freehand isometric sketches of the objects in Figure 10.9. (The objects are shown as oblique projections.)

6. Create freehand isometric sketches of the objects in Figure 10.11. (The objects are shown as orthographic projections.)

7. Create freehand orthographic sketches of the objects in Figure 10.11. (The objects are shown as orthographic projections, so you must simply recreate the drawing by freehand sketching.)

8. Create freehand orthographic sketches of the objects in Figure 10.9. (The objects are shown as oblique projections.)

9. Create freehand orthographic sketches of the objects in Figure 10.10. (The objects are shown as isometric projections.)

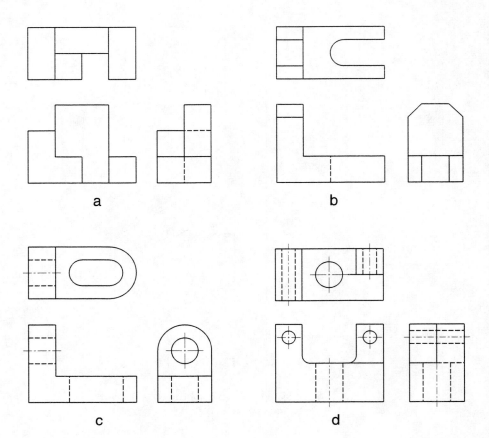

a

b

c

d

Figure 10.11

11

Computer Aided Design and Drafting

OBJECTIVES

- Differentiate 2-D, 2 1/2-D, and 3-D models
- Differentiate wireframe, surface, and solids models
- Explain how a cross-section is extruded or revolved to create a solids model
- Explain the analogy between creating a solids model of a part and machining the part
- Explain feature-based modeling
- Explain constraint-based modeling
- Explain history-based modeling

OVERVIEW

Several different models for representing a part's geometry have been used in CAD, including 2-D models and 3-D wireframe and surface models. However, solids modeling is the current state-of-the-art in CAD. Solids modeling has the inherent advantage of more accurately representing the "design intent" of the part that modeled.

11.1 CAD MODELS

A CAD *model* is a computer representation of an object or part. It can be thought of as a "virtual" part in that it exists only as a computer image. The model is an engineering document of record. It contains all of the design information including geometry, dimensions, tolerances, materials, and manufacturing information. A CAD model replaces the paper blueprints and engineering drawings of just a few decades ago.

The simplest model used in CAD is a *2-D model*. This model is essentially the computer graphics equivalent to an orthographic projection created using a pencil and paper as shown in Figure 11.1. A 2-D model represents a three-dimensional object with several views, each showing the view of one side of the object projected onto a plane. On the computer, a 2-D model appears as lines and curves on a flat surface, and it is up to the engineer or designer to interpret several views to create a mind's eye image of the three-dimensional object. The CAD software electronically stores the 2-D model as several views but does not inherently "know" that the views can be connected to one another to form a three-dimensional object.

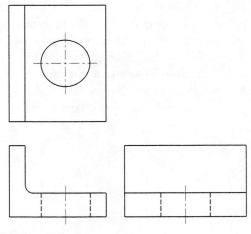

Figure 11.1

A *2 1/2-D model* has a third dimension that is recognized by the CAD software, but the third dimension is simply an extrusion of a two-dimensional shape. In this case, the CAD software electronically stores the cross-section shape of the object and the depth that it is *extruded*, or stretched, in the third dimension. Thus, the only objects that can be represented using a 2 1/2-D model model are those that have a constant cross-section. For instance, the simple shape shown in Figure 11.2 is the 2 1/2-D model of the object shown using a 2-D model in Figure 11.1 without the hole. The object, including the hole, cannot be represented as a 2 1/2-D model because the hole results in a change in the cross-section. A 2 1/2-D model could be used to represent a shape such as an I-beam or C-channel.

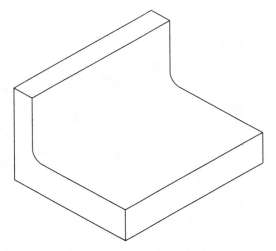

Figure 11.2

A *3-D model* is the most general model used in CAD software. In this case, the CAD software electronically stores the entire three-dimensional shape of the object. Most simply, one can think of the software storing the three-dimensional coordinates of various points on the object and then defining how these points are connected. Of course, a two-dimensional drawing representing the orthographic views of the object can be automatically created from the 3-D model. The current generation of CAD software is based on 3-D models.

The simplest 3-D model is a *wireframe model*. Figure 11.3 shows a wireframe representation of the object that we have been considering. In a wireframe model, only edges of the object are represented. Thus, the CAD software needs to store the locations of the vertices (intersections of lines) and which vertices are to be connected to each other by lines. A circle or curved section can be represented by a series of closely spaced vertices with linear edges connecting them or as an arc defined by a center, radius, and end points. Before more powerful computers were available, the low storage requirements of a wireframe model made it quite popular. The problem inherent in a wireframe representation is quite clear in Figure 11.3—it is difficult to interpret the drawing because all of the edges are visible. In fact, there are many situations where a wireframe representation cannot be unambiguously interpreted because it is not clear which lines would remain hidden if the surfaces of the part were filled in. This problem can be solved using various methods to remove "hidden lines" from the wireframe. This is tricky because the CAD software has to first determine how the edges of the wireframe form a surface and then determine if that surface hides any lines. Figure 11.3 shows the object with the hidden lines shown as dashed lines to indicate that they are behind a surface. 3-D models other than wireframes are able to deal with hidden lines more effectively and offer other advantages.

A 3-D *surface model* defines the object in terms of surfaces such as plates (flat) and shells (curved) in addition to edges. This makes it easy to determine whether a line or surface is hidden, because the surfaces are defined. Using a surface model also permits the construction of smoothly curved surfaces, such as a circular hole, rather than using many line segments to form a curved line as with some wireframe models. It is also possible to "fair" or smooth one surface into another surface to provide a sculpted

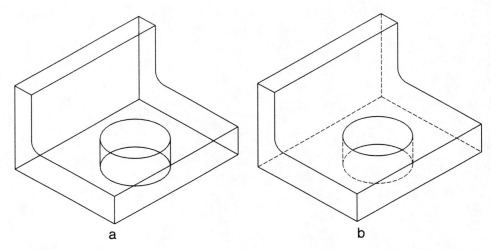

Figure 11.3

shape. Figure 11.4 shows the simple object with hidden lines removed altogether. Although a surface model can be displayed to look like a wireframe, either with or without hidden lines, it can also be displayed by assigning different degrees of shading to the surfaces. A virtual light source is assumed to be near the object to provide a three-dimensional lighting effect as shown in Figure 11.4. This is known as *shading* or *rendering*. Although a variety of shading techniques are available, all depend on determining how much light from a virtual light source strikes each portion of the virtual object. The use of shading provides a very realistic image of the object, which permits a much more vivid communication of the nature of the object. However, the problem that remains with a surface model is that the interior of the object remains undefined. The surface model just represents the shell of the object.

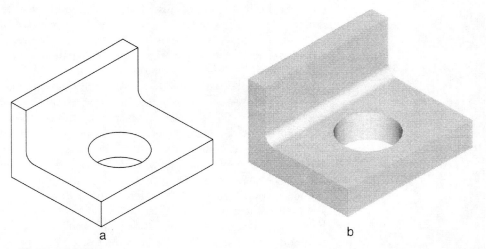

Figure 11.4

11.2   CAD AND SOLIDS MODELING

Solids modeling, the current state-of-the-art in CAD, is the most sophisticated method of representing an object. Unlike wireframe or surface models, a solids model represents an object in the virtual environment just as it exists in reality, having volume as well as surfaces and edges. In this way, the interior of the object is represented in the model as well as the outer surfaces.

The first attempt at solids modeling was a technique known as *constructive solid geometry* or *primitive modeling*, which is based on the combination of geometric primitives such as right rectangular prisms (blocks), right triangular prisms (wedges), spheres, cones, and cylinders. Each primitive could be scaled to the desired size, translated to the desired position, and rotated to the desired orientation. Then one primitive could be added to or subtracted from other primitives to make up a complex object. It is easy to see how two blocks plus a negative cylinder (hole), as shown in Figure 11.5, could represent an object similar to the one shown in Figure 11.4. (The rounded surface, or fillet, at the corner between the horizontal and vertical surfaces has been omitted.) The problem with constructive solid geometry was that the mental process of creating a solid model based on geometric primitives was much more abstract than the mental processes required for designing real world objects.

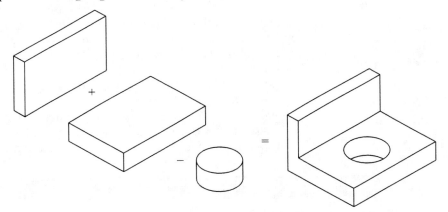

Figure 11.5

Constraint-based solids modeling overcomes the weakness of constructive solid geometry modeling by making the modeling process more intuitive. Instead of piecing together geometric primitives, the constraint-based modeling process begins with the creation of a 2-D sketch of the profile for the cross-section of the part. Here, "sketch" is the operative word. The sketch of the cross-section begins much like the freehand sketch of the face of an object in an oblique view. The only difference is that CAD software draws straight lines and perfect arcs. The initial sketch need not be particularly accurate; it need only reflect the basic geometry of the part's cross-sectional shape. Details of the cross-section are added later. The next step is to constrain the 2-D sketch by adding enough dimensions and parameters to completely define the shape and size of the 2-D profile. The name *constraint-based modeling* arises because the shape of the initial 2-D sketch is "constrained" by adding dimensions to the sketch. Finally, a three-dimensional object is created by *revolving* or extruding the 2-D sketched profile. Figure 11.6 shows the result of revolving a simple L-shaped cross-section by 270° about an axis and extruding the same L-shaped cross-section along an axis. In either case, these solid bodies form the basic geometric solid shapes of the part. Other features can be subsequently added to modify the basic solid shape.

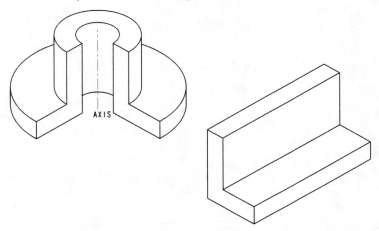

Figure 11.6

Once the solids model is generated, all of the surfaces are automatically defined, so it is possible to shade it in the same way as a surface model is shaded. It is also easy to generate 2-D orthographic views of the object. This is a major advancement from other modeling schemes. With solids modeling, the two-dimensional drawings are produced as views of the three-dimensional virtual model of the object. In traditional CAD, the three-dimensional model is derived from the two-dimensional drawings. One might look at solids modeling as the sculpting of a virtual solid volume of material. Because the volume of the object is properly represented in a solids model, it is possible to slice through the object and show a view of the object that displays the interior detail. Once several solid objects have been created, they can be assembled in a virtual environment to make sure that they fit together and to visualize the assembled product.

PROFESSIONAL SUCCESS

How Solids Models are Used

Solids models are useful for purposes other than visualization. The solids model contains a complete mathematical representation of the object, inside and out. This mathematical representation is converted easily into specialized computer code that can be used for stress analysis, heat transfer analysis, fluid flow analysis, and computer-aided manufacturing.

Finite Element Analysis (FEA) is a method to subdivide the object under study into many small, simply shaped elements. The simple geometry of the finite elements allows the relatively simple application of the appropriate equations for the stress and deformation of the elements or for the heat transfer between elements. By properly relating nearby elements to one another, all of these equations for each element can be solved simultaneously. The final result is the stress, deformation (strain), or temperature throughout the object for a given applied load or thermal condition. The stress, deformation, or temperature is often displayed as a color map on the solid model, visually displaying the regions of high stress or temperature. From these results, the engineer can redesign the object to avoid stress concentrations, large deformations, or undesirable temperatures. Likewise, the fluid flow through or around an object can be calculated by applying similar FEA techniques using the equations of fluid flow to the regions bounded by the object. These analysis tools have greatly improved and enhanced the design of many products.

Solids models can also be used in the manufacturing process. Software is available to automatically generate machine tool paths to machine the object based on the solids model. Then the software simulates the removal of material from an initial block of material on the computer. This allows the engineer to optimize the machining operation. These tool paths can be downloaded onto Computer Numerical Control (CNC) machine tools. The CNC machine tool automatically removes the desired surfaces from a block of material with high precision, allowing many identical parts to be machined automatically based directly on the solids model. Alternatively, the solids model can be downloaded onto a rapid prototyping machine. This machine automatically drives lasers that solidify liquid plastic resin, drives a robotic system to dispense a fine bead of molten plastic, or drives a laser that cuts layers of paper. In all three cases, layers are built up to become a physical model of the computer solids model, often within just a few hours. These manufacturing tools have made it possible to obtain parts from CAD models in several hours instead of several weeks.

11.3 THE NATURE OF SOLIDS MODELING

Solids modeling grew steadily in the 1980s, but it was not until Pro/ENGINEER® was introduced in 1988 and SolidWorks® was introduced in the 1990s that solids modeling delivered on its promised gains in productivity. These gains result from four characteristics of the software: feature-based, constraint-based, and parametric, associative modeling.

Feature-based modeling attempts to make the modeling process more efficient by creating and modifying geometric *features* of a solid model in a way that represents how geometries are created using common manufacturing processes. Features in a part have a direct analogy to geometries that can be manufactured or machined. A *base feature* is a solid model that is roughly the size and shape of the part that is to be modeled. The base feature is the 3-D solid created by revolving or extruding a cross-section, such as those shown in Figure 11.6. It can be thought of as the initial work block. All subsequent features reference the base feature either directly or indirectly. Additional features shape or refine the base feature. Examples of additional features include holes or cuts in the initial work block.

The analogy between feature-based modeling and common manufacturing processes is demonstrated in Figure 11.7 for making a handle for a pizza cutter. Beginning at the top of the figure we follow the steps that an engineer would use to create a solid model, or virtual part, on the left and the steps that a machinist would take to create the same physical part in a machine shop on the right. The engineer using solids modeling software begins by creating a two-dimensional profile, or *cross-section*, of a part, in this case a circle (shown in isometric projection). The analogous step by a machinist is to choose a circular bar stock of material with the correct diameter. Next the engineer *extrudes*, or stretches, the circular cross-section along the axis perpendicular to the plane of the circle to create a three-dimensional base feature (a cylinder in this case). The equivalent action by a machinist is to cut off a length of bar stock to create an initial work block. Now the engineer adds features by cutting away material on the left end to reduce the diameter and by rounding the right end of the cylinder. The machinist performs similar operations on a lathe to remove material from the cylinder. Next the engineer creates a circular cut to form a hole through the cylinder on the right end. The machinist drills a hole in the right end of the cylinder. Finally, the engineer creates a pattern of groove cuts around the handle. Likewise the machinist cuts a series of grooves using a lathe. In similar fashion a geometric shape could be added to the base feature in the solids model, analogous to a machinist welding a piece of metal to the work block. Feature-based techniques give the engineer the ability to easily create and modify common manufactured features. As a result, planning the manufacture of a part is facilitated by the correspondence between the features and the processes required to make them.

Constraint-based modeling permits the engineer or designer to incorporate "intelligence" into the design. Often this is referred to as *design intent*. Unlike traditional CAD software, the initial sketch of a two-dimensional profile in constraint-based solids modeling does not need to be created with a great deal of accuracy. It just needs to represent the basic geometry of the cross-section. The exact size and shape of the profile is defined through assigning enough parameters to fully "constrain" it. Some of this happens automatically. For example, if two nearly parallel edges are within some preset tolerance range of parallel (say 5 degrees), then the edges are automatically constrained to be parallel. As the part is resized, these edges will always remain parallel no matter what other changes are made. Likewise, if a hole is constrained to be at a certain distance from an edge, it will automatically remain at that distance from the edge, even if the edge is moved. This differs from traditional CAD where both the hole and the edge would each be fixed at a particular coordinate location. If the edge were moved, the hole location would need to be respecified so that the hole will remain the same distance from the edge. The advantage of constraint-based modeling is that the design intent of the engineer remains intact as the part is modified.

Another aspect of constraint-based modeling is that the model is *parametric*. This means that parameters of the model may be modified to change the geometry of the model. A dimension is a simple example of a parameter. When a dimension is changed, the geometry of the part is updated. Thus, the *parameter drives the geometry*. This is in contrast to other modeling systems in which the geometry is changed, say by stretching a part, and the dimension updates itself to reflect the stretched part. An additional feature of parametric modeling is that parameters can reference other parameters through relations or equations. For example, the position of the hole in Figure 11.4 could be specified with numerical values, say 40 mm from the right side of the part. Or the position of the hole could be specified parametrically, so that the center of the hole is located at a position that is one-half of the total length of the part. If the total length was specified as 80 mm, then the hole would be 40 mm from either side. However, if the length was changed to 100 mm, then the hole would automatically be positioned at half of this distance, or 50 mm from either side. Thus, no matter what the length of the part is, the hole stays in the middle of its length. The power of this approach is that when one dimension is modified, all linked dimensions are updated according to specified mathematical relations, instead of having to update all related dimensions individually.

The last aspect of constraint-based modeling is that the order in which parts are created is critical. This is known as *history-based modeling*. For example, a hole should not be created before a solid volume of material in which the hole occurs has been modeled. If the solid volume is deleted, then the hole should be deleted with it. This is known as a *parent-child relation*. The child (hole) cannot exist without the parent (solid volume) existing first. Parent-child relations are critical to maintaining design intent in a part. Most solids modeling software recognizes that if you delete a feature with a hole in it, you do not want the hole to remain floating around without being attached to a feature. Consequently, careful thought and planning of the base feature and initial additional features can have a significant effect on the ease of adding subsequent features and making modifications.

The *associative* character of solids modeling software causes modifications in one object to "ripple through" all associated objects. For instance, suppose that you change

Engineer		Machinist
Draw Cross-Section		Select Bar Stock
Extrude the Cross-Section to Create the Base Feature		Cut Off Bar Stock
Create Cut on Left End and Round on Right End		Turn on a Lathe to Reduce Diameter on Left End and Round Right End
Create a Circular Cut to Form a Hole		Drill Hole
Create Groove Cuts		Cut Grooves on a Lathe

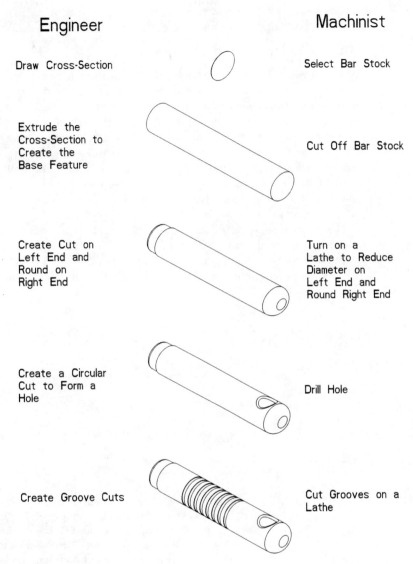

Figure 11.7

the diameter of a hole on the engineering drawing that was created based on your original solid model. The diameter of the hole will be automatically changed in the solid model of the part, too. In addition, the diameter of the hole will be updated on any assembly that includes that part. Similarly, changing the dimension in the part model will automatically result in updated values of that dimension in the drawing or assembly incorporating the part. This aspect of solids modeling software makes the modification of parts much easier and less prone to error.

As a result of being feature-based, constraint-based, and associative, solids modeling captures "*design intent*," not just the design. This comes about because solids modeling software incorporates engineering knowledge into the solid model with features, constraints, and relationships that preserve the intended geometrical relationships in the model.

PROFESSIONAL SUCCESS

Has CAD Impacted Design?

CAD has not only automated and provided a more accurate means of creating engineering drawings, it has created a new paradigm for design. Parts can be modeled, visualized, revised, and improved on the computer screen before any engineering drawings have even been created. Parts that have been modeled can be assembled in the virtual environment of the computer. The relative motion of moving parts can be animated on the computer. The stresses in the parts can be assessed computationally and the part redesigned to minimize stress concentrations. The flow of fluids through the part or around the part can be modeled computationally. The machine tool path or mold-filling flow to fabricate the part can be modeled on the computer. The part model can be downloaded to a rapid prototyping system that can create a physical model of the part in a few hours with virtually no human intervention.

Although some of the analyses described above are outside of the capability of the CAD software itself, the ability to produce a CAD model makes these analyses possible. Without the ability to create a complex solid geometry computationally using CAD, much of the engineering analysis that is used to design, improve, and evaluate a new design would be much more difficult.

KEY TERMS

associative	Feature-based modeling	parent-child relation
base feature	features	Solids modeling
Constraint-based solids modeling	history-based modeling	surface model
design intent	parametric	wireframe model
extruded		

Problems

1. The wireframe model shown in Figure 11.8 is a small cube centered within a large cube. The nearest corners of the two cubes are connected. For instance, the lower left front corners of both cubes are connected with a line. This wireframe model is ambiguous; that is, it could represent several different solid bodies. Freehand sketch or trace the figure. Then use dashed lines to indicate hidden lines to show two different solids model configurations that are possible for this wireframe model.

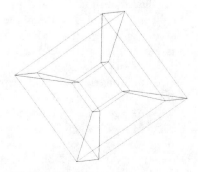

Figure 11.8

2. Using a technique similar to that shown in Figure 11.5, freehand sketch the geometric primitives that could be added or subtracted to form the objects shown in Figure 11.9. (The hole in Figure 11.9 is only through the face shown, not the back face. The holes in Figures 4.9c and 4.9d are through holes.)

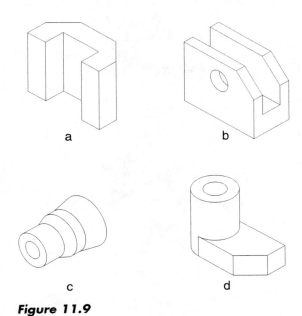

Figure 11.9

3. Sketch the cross-section that should be revolved to create the objects shown in Figure 11.10. Include the axis about which the cross-section is revolved in the sketch.

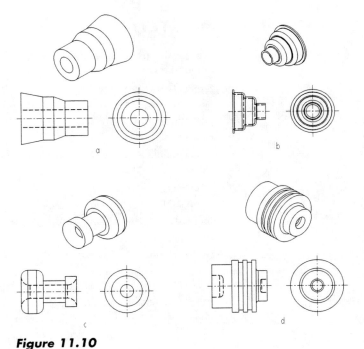

Figure 11.10

4. Sketch at least two cross-sections that could be extruded to form a base feature for the objects shown in Figure 11.11. Use cross-sections that can be extruded into a base feature from which material is only removed, not added. Make sure that the cross-sections that you propose minimize the number of additional features necessary to modify the base feature. (The hole in Figure 11.11 is only through the face shown, not the back face. The holes in Figure 11.11 are through holes.)

5. Consider the following objects. Sketch what the base feature would look like. List what features would be added to model the object. The type of base feature to be used (extrude, revolve, or both) is noted.

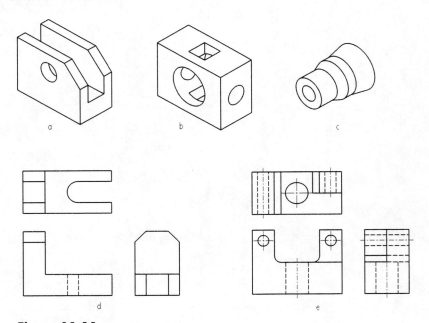

Figure 11.11

a. hexagonal cross-section wooden pencil that is sharpened to a point (do not include eraser)—extrude.

b. plastic 35 mm film container and cap—extrude and revolve.

c. nail—extrude and revolve.

d. push pin—revolve.

e. baseball bat—revolve.

f. broom handle—revolve and extrude.

g. ceiling fan blade--extrude.

h. cinder block—extrude.

i. compact disk—revolve and extrude.

j. single staple (before being deformed)—extrude.

k. automobile tire—revolve.

l. gear—extrude.

m. round toothpick—revolve.

6. Describe parametric modeling and give an example of a family of parts where parametric modeling would be useful.

7. Describe constraint-based modeling and explain how it relates to design intent.

12

Standard Practice for Engineering Drawings

OBJECTIVES

- Explain why drawing standards are used
- Choose the proper sheet layout
- Read and understand the scale of a drawing
- Differntiate different linetypes used in engineering drawing
- Properly place dimensions on a drawing
- Ready and understand section and detail views on a drawing
- Read and understand screw thread designations on a drawing
- Read an assembly drawing

OVERVIEW

Drawing standards and conventions are used to clarify engineering drawings and simplify their creation. For example, standard sizes for drawings are used, and standard types and weights of lines designate different items on a drawing. The proper placement of dimensions on drawings is helpful in making the drawing more readable. In addition, internal or small details of the part can be displayed using special views. Screw threads are difficult to draw, so standard representations are used for screw threads.

12.1 INTRODUCTION TO DRAWING STANDARDS

Not only is the accurate and clear depiction of details of a part necessary in an engineering drawing, but it is also necessary that the drawing conforms to commonly accepted standards, or conventions. There are two reasons for the existence of standards and conventions. First, using standard symbols and projections ensures clear interpretation of the drawing by the viewer. An example of the problem of differing presentations is the use of the third-angle orthographic projection in North America and the first-angle orthographic projection elsewhere in the world. (Recall that the top and bottom views and the right and left views are reversed in third-angle and first-angle projections.) This can bring about confusion if, for example, a U. S. engineer tries to interpret a German drawing. If a single standard existed in the world, there would be no confusion. A second reason for using conventions is to simplify the task of creating engineering drawings. For example, the symbol $\tilde{A}$ associated with a dimension indicates that the dimension is a diameter of a circular feature. Without this convention, it would be more difficult to unambiguously represent diameter dimensions on a drawing.

Most CAD programs automatically use a standardized presentation of drawings, usually based on standards from the American National Standards Institute (ANSI) in the United States and the International Standards Organization (ISO) in the rest of the world. Even with the use of CAD software to assure standard presentation in drawings, it is up to the engineer to implement drawing standards in some cases. An example is in the placement of dimensions in a drawing. The user controls where dimensions appear on the drawing. Even in cases where the CAD software automatically implements drawing standards, it is still necessary to understand what the conventions mean so they are properly interpreted.

12.2 SHEET LAYOUTS

Engineering drawings are created on standard size sheets that are designated by the code indicated in Table 12-1. The ISO drawing sizes are just slightly smaller than ANSI sizes. Engineering drawings are almost always done in "landscape" orientation so that the long side of the drawing is horizontal. The choice of drawing size depends upon the complexity of the object depicted in the drawing. The drawing should be sized so that the projections of the part, dimensions, and notes all fall within the borders of the drawing with adequate spacing so that the drawing is not cluttered. The drawing should be large enough so that all details are readily evident and readable. As a result, regardless of the physical size of the part, simple parts are usually drawn on smaller sheets because it is not necessary to show much detail. Complex parts are usually drawn on larger sheets to readily show adequate detail. When using CAD software, it is necessary to consider the printed drawing size in addition to the drawing size on the computer screen. On the computer screen, it is possible to Zoom In or Zoom Out to read detail, but this cannot be done for a printed drawing. Consequently, the sheet size should be chosen carefully.

TABLE 12-1   Standard Sheet Sizes

ANSI	ISO
A—8.50′ × 11.00′	A4—210 mm × 297 mm
B—11.00′ × 17.00′	A3—297 mm × 420 mm
C—17.00′ × 22.00′	A2—420 mm × 594 mm
D—22.00′ × 34.00′	A1—594 mm ″ × 841 mm
E—34.00′ × 44.00′	A0—841 mm × 1189 mm

The *title block* on a drawing records important information about the working drawing. Normally the title block of a drawing is in the lower right corner of the drawing. ANSI standard title blocks can be used, but often individual companies use their own standard title block. The title block, such as the one shown in Figure 12.1, is used primarily for drawing control within a company. The title block includes information regarding the part depicted in the drawing, such as its name and part number; the person who created the drawing; persons who checked or approved the drawing; dates the drawing was created, revised, checked, and approved; the drawing number; and the name of the company. This information allows the company to track the drawing within the company if questions arise about the design.

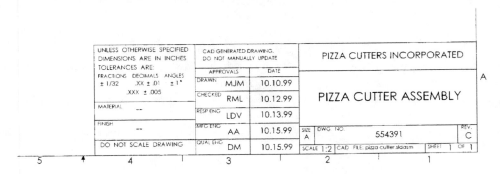

Figure 12.1

Other information can appear in the title block to provide details about the manufacture of the part, such as the material for the part, the general tolerances, the surface finish specifications, and general instructions about manufacturing the part (such as "remove all burrs"). Many times, though, this information is shown as notes on the drawing rather than in the title block.

Finally the title block provides information about the drawing itself, such as the units used in dimensioning (typically inches or millimeters) and the scale of the drawing. The *scale* of the drawing indicates the ratio of the size on the drawing to the size of the actual object. It can be thought of as the degree to which the object is enlarged or shrunk in the drawing. Scales on drawings are denoted in several ways. For instance, consider an object that is represented in the drawing as half of its actual size. Then the drawing is created such that 1 inch on the drawing represents 2 inches on the physical object. This can be reported in the Scale box in the title block as HALF SCALE, HALF SIZE, 1 = 2, 1:2, or 1/2" &= 1". In the numerical representations, the left number is the length on the drawing and the right number is the length of the actual object. A part that is drawn twice as large as its physical size would be denoted as DOUBLE, 2× (denoting "2 times"), 2 = 1, or 2:1. In some cases, such as architectural drawings, the scale can be quite large. For instance 1/4" = 1' corresponds to a scale of 1:48, where " denotes inches and ' denotes feet. Common scales used in engineering drawing are 1 = 1, 1 = 2, 1 = 4, 1 = 8, and 1 = 10 for English units and 1:1, 1:2, 1:5, 1:10, 1:20, 1:50, and 1:100 for metric units. A 1:1 scale is often specified as FULL SCALE or FULL SIZE.

12.3 LINES

The types of lines used in engineering drawing are standardized. Different linetypes have different meanings and a knowledge of linetypes makes interpreting drawings easier. The linetypes vary in thickness and in the length and number of dashes in dashed lines. Most CAD software automatically produces linetypes that correspond correctly to the application. Figure 12.2 shows some of the more commonly used linetypes, each of which is described below:

Visible lines (thick, solid lines) represent the outline of the object that can be seen in the current view.

Hidden lines (thin, dashed lines) represent features that are hidden behind surfaces in the current view.

Centerlines or *symmetry lines* (thin, long-dash/short-dash lines) mark axes of rotationally symmetric parts or features.

Dimension lines (thin lines with arrowheads at each end) indicate sizes in the drawing.

Extension lines or *witness lines* (thin lines) extend from the object to the dimension line to indicate which feature is associated with the dimension.

Leader lines (thin, solid lines terminated with arrowheads) are used to indicate a feature with which a dimension or note is associated.

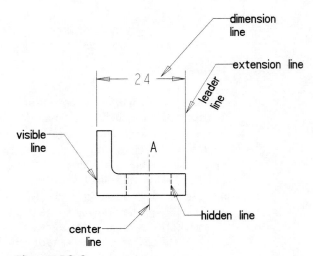

Figure 12.2

Other linetypes are used for break lines (lines with zigzags) that show where an object is "broken" in the drawing to save drawing space or reveal interior features and *cutting plane lines* (thick lines with double short dashes and perpendicular arrows at each end) that show the location of cutting planes for section views.

The arrowheads for dimension lines, leader lines, and other types of lines may be filled or not filled. Most CAD software uses unfilled arrowheads as a default, although many engineering graphics textbooks prefer filled arrowheads.

It is common in technical drawings that two lines in a particular view coincide. When this happens, a convention called the *precedence of lines* dictates which line is shown. Visible lines have precedence over hidden lines, which have precedence over centerlines, which have precedence over extension lines.

Conventions also exist for the intersection of lines in a drawing. For instance, an extension line is always drawn so that there is a slight, visible gap between its end and the outline of the object as shown in Figure 12.2. Similarly, perpendicular centerlines that cross are drawn so that the short dashes of each line intersect to form a small cross. Fortunately, most CAD software takes care of all of the details related to linetypes automatically. The engineer or designer need only know how to properly interpret the various linetypes.

12.4 DIMENSION PLACEMENT AND CONVENTIONS

Engineering drawings are usually drawn to scale, but it is still necessary to specify numerical dimensions for convenience and to ensure accuracy. In general, sufficient dimensions must be provided to define precisely the geometry of the part, but redundant dimensions should be avoided. Furthermore, dimensions on the drawing should reflect the way the part is made or the critical dimensions of the part. For example, consider the three drawings of a plate with two holes shown in Figure 12.3. The left drawing is over-dimensioned, having one redundant dimension. It is clear that given the distances from the left edge to the left hole, the distance from the right edge to the right hole, and the overall width of the plate, the distance between the holes has to be 6-mm. Thus, the 6-mm dimension could be omitted, suggesting that the distance between each hole and the nearest edge of the plate is most important. But suppose that the distance between the holes is critical. This might be necessary if the holes in the plate are supposed to align with another part. Then the dimensions on the middle drawing would clearly show that the distance between the holes is most important by omitting the dimension from the right hole to the right edge. The right drawing indicates that the distance from the left edge to each hole, not the distance between the holes, is critical. The engineer or designer must consider the optimal way to display dimensions to clearly show which dimensions are most important.

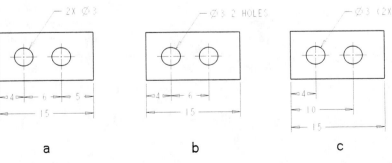

a   b   c

Figure 12.3

It is natural for a person reading the drawings to look for the dimensions of a feature in the view where the feature occurs in its most characteristic shape and where it is visible (as opposed to hidden). This is known as *contour dimensioning*. For example, the location and size of a hole should be dimensioned in the view where the hole appears as a circle. Likewise, it is best to show the overall dimensions of the object in a view that is most descriptive of the object. If possible both the horizontal and vertical location of a feature should be dimensioned in the same view. The upper part of Figure 12.4 shows an object properly dimensioned in millimeters to show the relation of the dimensions to the features in the most obvious manner. In the lower part of Figure 12.4, the dimensioning has several problems. The overall dimensions of the L-shaped profile are shown on the view where it is not clear that the object is L-shaped. The diameter of the hole is shown in a view where the hole is shown only as a pair of parallel hidden lines, not as a circle. And the vertical location of the hole is shown in one view, while the horizontal location is shown in another view.

The conventions for millimeter and inch dimensioning are different. For millimeter dimensioning, dimensions less than 1 mm have a zero preceding the decimal point, and integer dimensions may or may not include a decimal point and following zeros. Thus, legitimate millimeter dimensions are 0.8, 6, 8.00, and 1.5. Inch dimensions do not include a zero before the decimal point for values less than 1 inch. Zeros to the right of the decimal point are usually included. Legitimate inch dimensions are .800, 6.00, 8.00, and 1.500. For both millimeter and inch dimensions, the number of digits to the right of the decimal point may be used to indicate the tolerance (acceptable variation). It is standard practice to omit the units for dimensions. However, it is wise to note the units in the title block or as a note on the drawing.

Circles and arcs are dimensioned using special symbols and rules. A radius is denoted using a leader line with an arrow pointing at the arc as shown in Figure 12.4. Sometimes a small cross is placed at the center of the radius. The position of the center should be dimensioned unless the radius is for a rounded edge, in which case the arc is positioned by virtue of being tangent at its ends to the sides forming the corner that is rounded, as shown in Figure 12.4. The dimension for a radius begins with a capital letter R to indicate radius. Full circles are dimensioned using the diameter with a leader line having an arrow pointing at the circle, as shown in Figure 12.4. If space permits, the leader line extends across a diameter of the circle with arrows at each end of the diameter. The dimension for a diameter begins with the Greek letter phi (ø) to indicate diameter. The location of the center of the circle must also be dimensioned. Sometimes maintaining clarity makes it necessary to dimension several concentric circles from a side view, where the circle does not appear as a circle, thus violating the rule to dimension a feature in its most characteristic shape.

Angles are dimensioned as decimals or in degrees and minutes (60 minutes is one degree), so that 32.5° and 32°30' are equivalent, where ' indicates minutes. The dimension line for an angle is drawn as an arc with its center at the apex of the angle. When lines are drawn at right angles, a 90° angle is implied.

Multiple features that are identical need not be individually dimensioned. For example, the diameter of the two 3-mm holes in Figure 12.3 could be dimensioned with a leader line to one hole with the dimension 2 × ø3. The 2 × indicates "two times." Alternative dimensions are ø 3 (2×), ø 3 2 PLACES, or ø 3 2 HOLES.

There are several other "rules" for dimensioning:

- Dimension lines should be outside of the outline of a part whenever possible.
- Dimension lines should not cross one another.

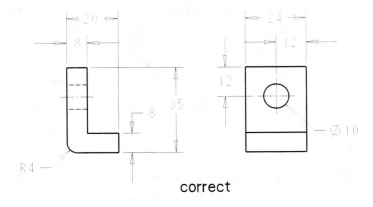

correct

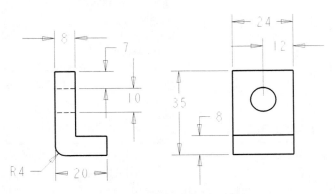

poorly dimensioned

Figure 12.4

- Dimensions should be indicated on a view that shows the true length of the feature. This is particularly important when dimensioning features on a surface that is at an angle to the plane of the orthographic view.

- Each feature should be dimensioned only once. Do not duplicate the same dimension in different views.

- Dimension lines should be aligned and grouped when possible to promote clarity and uniform appearance. See for example the placement of the horizontal dimensions in Figure 12.3.

- The numerical dimension and arrows should be placed between the extension lines where space permits. If there is space only for the dimension, but not the arrows, place the arrows outside of the extension lines. When the space is too small for either the arrows or the numerical value, place both outside of the extension lines. See Figure 12.4 for examples.

- Place the dimension no closer than about 10 mm (3/8 inch) from the object's outline.

- Dimensions should be placed in clear spaces, as close as possible to the feature they describe.

- When dimensions are nested (such as the horizontal dimensions in Figure 12.3) the smallest dimensions should be closest to the object.
- Avoid crowding dimensions. Leave at least 6 mm (1/4 inch) between parallel dimension lines.
- Extension lines may cross visible lines of the object.
- Dimensions that apply to two adjacent views should be placed between the views, unless clarity is enhanced by placing them elsewhere. The dimension should be attached to only one view. Extension lines should not connect two views.
- Dimension lines and extension lines should not cross, if possible. Extension lines may cross other extension lines.
- A centerline may be extended to serve as an extension line, in which case it is still drawn as a centerline.
- Centerlines should not extend from view to view.
- Leader lines are usually sloped at about 30°, 45°, or 60° and are never horizontal or vertical.
- Numerical values for dimensions should be centered between arrowheads, except in a stack of dimensions (like Figure 12.3).
- When a rough, noncritical dimension (such as a round) is indicated on a drawing, add the note **TYP** to the dimension to indicate that the dimension is "typical" or approximate.

12.5 SECTION AND DETAIL VIEWS

The cutaway view of a device appeared first in various forms in the 15th and 16th centuries to show details of parts hidden by other elements. These cutaway views have evolved to *section views* in which interior features that cannot be effectively displayed by hidden lines are exposed by slicing through a section of the object. To create a section view, a cutting plane is passed through the part and the portion of the part on one side of the cutting plane is imagined to be removed. In a section view, all visible edges and contours behind the cutting plane are shown. Hidden lines are usually omitted. The portion of the object that is sliced through is designated with angled crosshatch lines known as section-lining.

Key to the interpretation of a section view is the clear representation of where the cutting plane is and from which direction it is viewed. This is accomplished using a *cutting plane line* (long dash - short dash - short dash - long dash with perpendicular arrows at each end). The cutting plane line shows where the cutting plane passes through the object. The arrows on either end of the cutting plane line show the direction of the line of sight for the section view. An example of a block with a hole that has a large diameter partway into it and a smaller diameter through it is shown in Figure 12.5. In this case, the object is sectioned along a plane parallel to the right and left edges of the front view and through the center of the hole, as indicated by the position of cutting plane line A-A. The arrows indicate that the section view will be shown as if we are looking in the direction of the arrows. Thus, the section view shown to the right of the front view (as if unfolding the glass box) shows what the viewer would see if the portion of the object to the right of the cutting plane line was removed. The viewer sees the two diameters of the hole with the material that has been "cut" shown as cross-hatched. This view is designated Section A-A to correspond to the cutting plane line A-A. This type of section in which a single plane goes completely through an object is known as a *full section*.

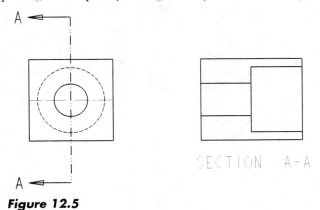

Figure 12.5

A slightly more complicated example of a full section is shown in Figure 12.6. The whole object is shown in the upper left portion of the figure, and the sectioned object is shown with a portion removed just below it. The right side of the figure shows a top view of the object with the cutting plane displayed. Imagine that the material on the side of the cutting plane in the direction the arrows are pointing is retained, and the material behind the arrows is removed. Then the projection of the retained portion appears as **SECTION B-B** when viewed in the direction of the arrows.

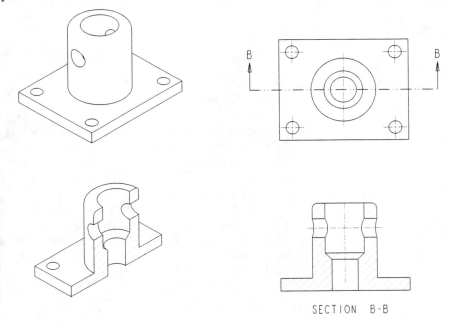

Figure 12.6

Much more sophisticated section views can be created for complicated parts. In all cases, though, the clear definition of the cutting plane line and the direction of the line of sight for the view are critical. For example, Figure 12.7 shows a *half section* of the same part. The cutting plane extends halfway through the object to show the interior of one half of the object and the exterior of the other half. This type of section is ideal for symmetrical parts in which it is desired to show internal and external features in a single view. An *offset section* like that shown in Figure 12.8 is used to show internal details that are not in the same plane. The cutting plane for offset sections is bent at 90° angles to pass through important features. Note that the change of plane that occurs at the 90° bends is not represented with lines on the section view. When only a portion of the object needs to be sectioned to show a particular internal detail, a *broken-out section* like that shown in Figure 12.9 can be used. A break line separates the sectioned portion from the unsectioned portion, but no cutting plane line is drawn.

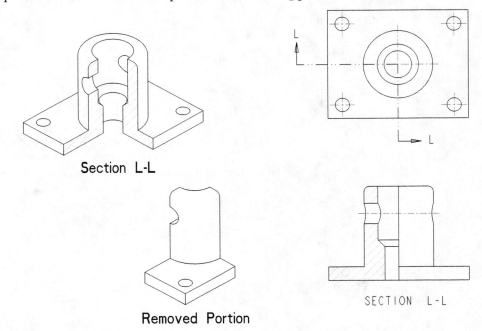

Section L-L

Removed Portion

SECTION L-L

Figure 12.7

In some cases it is necessary to clarify details of the part that may not be readily evident in the views normally shown in the drawing. For instance, a particular detail may be so small that it cannot be shown clearly on the same scale as the remainder of the part. This is done using an auxiliary *detail view* consisting of a small portion of the object magnified to make clear the small feature. An example is shown in Figure 12.10. In this case the small rivet holding the blade onto the arms of the pizza cutter is too small to see in the orthographic views. The region of interest near the rivet is circled in the left-most projection of the pizza cutter, and a note directs the reader to a magnified detail view in the upper right part of the drawing. The cross section of the rivet is clearly visible in this detail view.

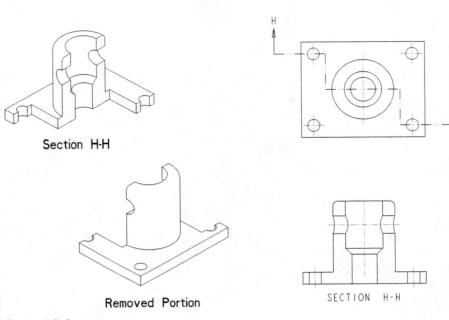

Section H-H

Removed Portion

SECTION H-H

Figure 12.8

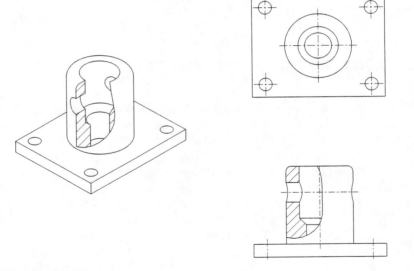

Figure 12.9

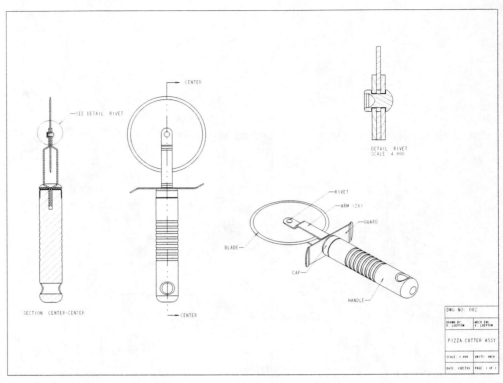

Figure 12.10

12.6 FASTENERS AND SCREW THREADS

Fasteners include a broad range of items such as bolts, nuts, screws, and rivets used to "fasten" parts together. In most cases, fasteners are standard parts purchased from an outside vendor, so detail drawings of fasteners are rarely necessary. Nevertheless, threaded holes and threaded shafts must be represented on a drawing.

The geometry of screw threads is too complicated to draw exactly in an engineering drawing and screw threads are standard, so either of two simple conventions is used to indicate screw threads, as shown in Figure 12.11. The *schematic representation* is used when a realistic representation of the side view of a screw thread is desired. For an external thread, the lines that extend across the entire diameter represent the *crest*, or peak, of the thread, while the shorter lines in between represent the *root*, or valley, of the thread. The distance between crests or between roots is called the *pitch*. On a drawing, the crests and roots are shown perpendicular to the axis of the threaded section rather than helical as they actually appear on the physical thread. In the end view, threads are depicted with concentric circles. The outer circle is the largest diameter of the screw thread, known as the *major diameter*, and the inner circle is the smallest diameter of the screw thread, or *minor diameter*. In the end view of the external thread, both diameters are shown as solid circles. In the *simplified representation* of external screw threads, the threads are omitted altogether. The major diameter is represented as a solid line in the side view, and the minor diameter is represented with a dashed line.

The end view of an internal thread is shown as two concentric circles representing the major and minor diameter, but the major diameter is a hidden line. For a side view

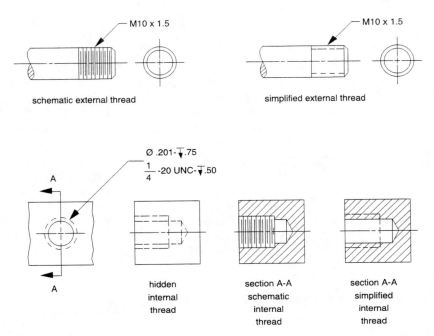

M10 x 1.5

schematic external thread

M10 x 1.5

simplified external thread

Ø .201-↧.75

$\frac{1}{4}$-20 UNC-↧.50

A

A

hidden
internal
thread

section A-A
schematic
internal
thread

section A-A
simplified
internal
thread

Figure 12.11

of a hidden internal screw thread, the major and minor diameters are both shown as hidden lines for both schematic and simplified screw thread representations. In a cross-section, internal threads can be shown in either the schematic or the simplified representation, as shown. For a hole that does not go completely through the part, called a *blind hole*, the lines in the side view representing the minor diameter continue deeper than the thread and come to a point. This represents the hole that is drilled prior to tapping, or cutting threads in the hole. The hole needs to be longer than the threaded section to permit the tool that is used to cut the threads, or tap, to penetrate deeply enough to fully cut the threads in the portion of the hole to be tapped.

Screw threads are specified in terms of the nominal (major) diameter, the pitch, and the thread series. For instance, the designations 1/4-20 UNC or .25-20 UNC or 1/4-20 NC all indicate a major diameter of .25 inches, a pitch of 20 threads per inch, and the United Course series. The diameter of the hole drilled before tapping an internal thread is specified in a wide variety of machinist and engineering handbooks. In this case the proper hole to be drilled has a diameter of .2010 inches, which corresponds to a number 7 drill. To make an internal thread of this size, a machinist would first drill a hole using a number 7 drill bit and then cut the threads using a 1/4-20 tap. For screw threads with a nominal diameter less than .25 inches, a number designation is used to specify the nominal diameter. For example, the designation 10-32 UNF indicates a nominal diameter of .1900 inches, 32 threads per inch, and the United Fine series. The pitch is equal to 1 divided by the number of threads per inch.

Metric threads are specified in a slightly different way. A designation M10 × 1.5 indicates a metric thread with a 10 mm major diameter and a pitch of 1.5 mm between crests of the thread. The number of threads per mm is 1 divided by the pitch. Other letters and numbers may follow the thread specification to denote tolerances and deviations of the thread, but for many cases these are not necessary. In addition, for a blind hole, the depth of the thread can be specified in several ways. Following the thread designation, the notation X .50 DEEP, THD .50 DP, or a downward arrow with a horizontal bar at its tail followed by .50 all indicate that the thread should extend .50 inches below the surface of the piece, as shown in Figure 12.11. (THD indicates "thread," and DP indicates "deep.") The threaded depth is usually 1.5 to 2 times the nominal diameter of the screw thread.

The dimensions for a threaded hole are indicated on a drawing using a leader line with the arrow pointing at the major diameter, as shown in Figure 12.11. Threaded holes are usually dimensioned in the view where they appear as circles, rather than in a side view of the threaded hole. Multiple threaded holes of the same specification are typically denoted in the same way as other multiple features using the notation (2X) or 2 TIMES at the end of the thread designation.

Nuts and bolts are usually only shown in a parts list and not on any drawings. They are specified in the same way as threaded holes, plus a bolt length and the type of head. For instance .25-28 UNF X 1.50 HEXAGON CAP SCREW or .25-28 NF X 1.50 HEX CAP SCR indicates a bolt that is 1.5 inches long with hexagonal head. Nuts are specified in terms of their thread and shape, such as M8 X 1.25 HEX NUT.

12.7 ASSEMBLY DRAWINGS

An assembly drawing shows all of the components of a design either assembled or in an exploded view. Many times assembly drawings include sections. Most dimensions are omitted in assembly drawings. Individual parts are not dimensioned, but some dimensions of the assembled mechanism may be included. Hidden lines are seldom necessary in assembly drawings, although they can be used where they clarify the design. Leader lines attached to a ballooned letter or detail number, as shown in Figure 12.12, reference the parts of the assembly. The leader lines should not cross and nearby leader lines should be approximately parallel. Sometimes parts are labeled by name rather than number. The parts list may be on the assembly drawing (usually on the right side or at the bottom) or it may be a separate sheet. The assembly drawing may also include machining or assembly information in the form of notes on the drawing.

Often assembly drawings include assembly sections. These are typically orthographic or pictorial section views of parts as put together in an assembly. Adjacent parts in assembly drawings are cross-hatched at different angles to make the separate parts clear. The assembly cross-section on the left side of Figure 12.10 shows the interior structure of the parts of a pizza cutter and how they fit together. The detail view in the upper right of Figure 12.10 shows the cross-section through the rivet to indicate how the parts are assembled. Usually standard parts such as fasteners, washers, springs, bearings, and gears are not cross-hatched. But in the case of Figure 12.10, the rivet detail is integral to the assembly, and it is helpful to show its cross-section with cross-hatching to indicate how it fits with the other parts.

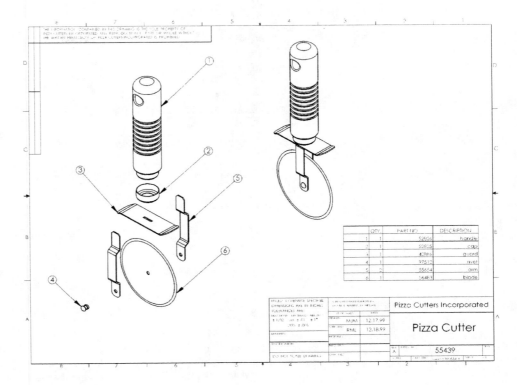

Figure 12.12

KEY TERMS

Centerlines	Dimension lines	scale
contour dimensioning	Extension lines	section views
cutting plane lines	Hidden lines	title block
detail view	Leader lines	Visible lines

Problems

1. Three orthographic views and an isometric view of an object that has overall dimensions of 4 × 4 × 4 inches are to be shown in a drawing. Determine the best ANSI sheet size for an object of this size at the scales indicated below:

   a. Half Size.

   b. 2:1.

   c. 1 = 1.

2. Three orthographic views and an isometric view of an object that has overall dimensions of 200 × 200 × 200 mm are to be shown in a drawing. Determine the optimal standard metric scale to be used for the ISO sheet sizes indicated below:

   a. A1.

   b. A3.

   c. A4.

3. The drawing shown in Figure 12.13 has many errors in the dimensioning. Sketch the ortho-
    graphic views and show proper placement of dimensions.

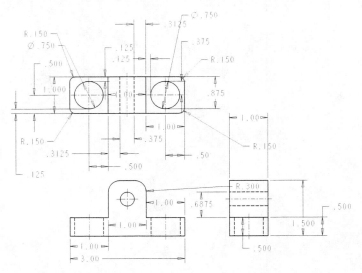

Figure 12.13

4. The drawing shown in Figure 12.14 has many errors in the dimensioning. Sketch the ortho-
    graphic views and show proper placement of dimensions. The M10 × 1.5 threaded hole
    requires a tap drill of 8.5 mm. Only two views are needed for this part.

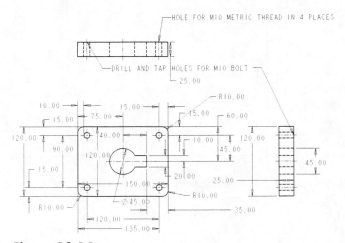

Figure 12.14

5. Sketch the following section views for the object shown in Figure 12.15. The threaded holes extend from the top surface approximately halfway through the thickness of the part. The other holes extend through the part.

    a. A-A.
    b. B-B.

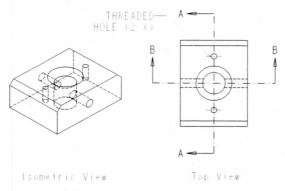

Figure 12.15

6. Sketch the following section views for the object shown in Figure 12.16. All holes extend through the part.

    a. B-B.
    b. D-D.

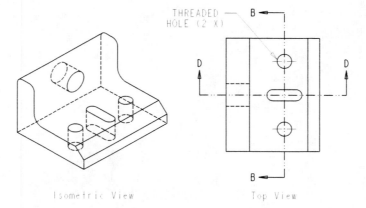

Figure 12.16

7. Look up the following machine screw threads in an engineering graphics book (such as *Engineering Graphics* by Giesecke, et al), a machinists or engineering handbook (such as *Marks' Standard Handbook for Mechanical Engineers*), an industrial supply catalog (such as McMaster-Carr), or on the World Wide Web (search on "tap drill size"). Specify the series (UNC or UNF), tap drill size or number, number of threads per inch, pitch, and nominal diameter.

    a. 4-40.
    b. 6-32.
    c. 8-32.
    d. 3/8-24.
    e. 6-40.
    f. 1/4-28.

8. Look up the following machine screw threads in an engineering graphics book (such as *Engineering Graphics* by Giesecke, et al), a machinists or engineering handbook (such as *Marks' Standard Handbook for Mechanical Engineers*), an industrial supply catalog (such as McMaster-Carr), or on the World Wide Web (search on "tap drill size metric"). Specify the series (course or fine), tap drill size, number of threads per mm, and nominal size.

    a. M2 × 0.4.
    b. M12 × 1.75.
    c. M30 × 3.5.
    d. M30 × 2.
    e. M10 × 1.25.

13

Tolerances

SECTIONS

OBJECTIVES

- Explain interchangeable parts
- Explain the necessity of tolerancing
- Read a general tolerance on a drawing
- Read limit dimensions and tolerances on individual dimensions
- Determine a tolerance stackup
- Determine the range of tolerances for manufacturing processes
- Read a surface finish specification
- Understand basic form tolerances
- Understand simple positional tolerances
- Read geometric dimensioning and tolerancing symbols

OVERVIEW

Tolerances on dimensions are necessary to specify the acceptable variability in the dimension of a part. Tolerances can be indicated for all dimensions using a general note or they can be specified for each individual dimension. Tolerances are based on the function of the part or are used to assure that mating parts fit together. However, in many cases the manufacturing process determines the tolerance. The surface finish may also be specified on a drawing to indicate the roughness of the surface. To further minimize ambiguity in engineering drawings, geometric dimensioning and tolerancing is used to specify the form of a feature, such as flatness or roundness, or to indicate the ideal position of a feature.

13.1 WHY TOLERANCES?

In 1815, it was hoped that muskets could be produced in a number of different U. S. Government and private armories so that the parts of the musket would be interchangeable. Before this time, muskets were individually handcrafted, so parts from one musket rarely fit another musket. Because engineering drawings were not commonly used, a number of "perfect" muskets were made according to master gages and jigs. *Gages* are devices used to check the individual dimensions of a part. For instance, the diameter of a shaft could be checked using a gage consisting of two holes: one of the maximum allowable diameter of the shaft and one of the minimum allowable diameter. If the shaft fit through the larger hole but not the smaller hole, then it was within the allowable dimensions for the shaft. *Jigs* are devices used to hold a workpiece and guide the tool to assure repeatable machining. The master gages and jigs were sent to the armories with the instruction that "no deviations from the pattern were to be allowed." In 1824, this concept of *interchangeable parts* was tested by disassembling a hundred rifles from several different armories, mixing the parts, and then reassembling at random. Most reassembled rifles worked as they should, proving the concept and value of interchangeable parts.

The interchangeability of parts is so common now that it is hard to imagine anything different. The concept allows parts made in various locations by different manufacturers to be successfully assembled and to function properly as an assembly. Although engineering drawings rather than "master parts" came into use in the mid-19th century, it was the two world wars in the 20th century that brought about the development of methods of showing the acceptable variation in a dimension on a drawing, or *tolerancing*

The need to control precisely the geometry of a part arises from the part's function. For instance, the cross-sectional geometry of an airfoil, such as the wing of a jet aircraft or a turbine blade, must be accurately controlled to assure aerodynamic efficiency. The more commonplace need for controlling geometry results from the requirement for parts to fit together. But it is quite difficult to make every part the exact size that is specified in a dimension because of slight differences in tool size, machine tool wear, human operator error, and other factors. As a consequence, tolerances are used in engineering drawings to specify the limit in the variation between mating parts and to provide guidelines to control the manufacturing process. The *tolerance* is the amount that a specific dimension is permitted to vary, or the difference between the maximum and minimum limits of a dimension.

Consider a dimension on a drawing specified as 3.750 ± .003. This dimension indicates that the part has a *nominal size*, or general size, of 3 3/4 inches (usually expressed as a common fraction). The *basic size*, or theoretical size for the application of the tolerance, is 3.750 inches (expressed as a decimal). The tolerance of the dimension is .006 inches. Thus, an acceptable machined part can have an *actual size* ranging from 3.747 to 3.753 inches, which are the minimum and maximum limits of the dimension. If the actual size is smaller than 3.747 or larger than 3.753, then the part is not acceptable.

Of course, it is desirable to make the part as close as possible to the basic size, sometimes called the *target size*. But the more accuracy needed in a machined part, the higher the manufacturing cost. Furthermore, the method of machining a part limits the tolerance that can be specified. For instance, the tolerance in drilling a .500 inch hole is between .002 and .005 depending on the quality of the drill press and drill bit. To require a tolerance smaller than .002 would require an additional machining process, such as reaming. Consequently, tolerances can play a large role in the cost of manufacturing a part. Therefore, the tolerances should not be specified tighter than necessary for the product to function properly.

An increased awareness of the importance of tolerances in manufacturing has led to an approach in which the deviation of the actual size of a part from the target size has a cost in terms of reworking of the part, scrap, customer dissatisfaction, and poor reliability. An approach to handle this is to design a product so that it is less sensitive to manufacturing tolerances. The idea is to design the part intelligently so that easy-to-manufacture tolerances, rather than exceptionally tight tolerances, are necessary. Consequently, proper fit between mating parts comes about because of good design, instead of depending on tight tolerances. This approach is known as *robust design*.

13.2 DISPLAYING TOLERANCES ON DRAWINGS

Every dimension on a drawing should have a tolerance. Tolerances can be displayed on engineering drawings in several ways depending on the situation.

General tolerances can be given in a note on the drawing or in the title block. An example would be the note ALL DIMSENIONS TO BE HELD TO ± .003'. Thus, a dimension of .375 would have a minimum limit of .372 and a maximum limit of .378. Often general tolerances are specified in terms of the number of digits following the decimal point in a dimension. In this case, a note would appear on the drawing such as:

UNLESS OTHERWISE SPECIFIED
TOL:.XX = ±.010
.XXX = ±.005
HOLES = ±.002
ANGLES = ±.5 DEG   ***Equation 13.1.***

Thus, a dimension of .50 on a drawing would indicate an actual size between .490 and .510. A dimension of .500 would indicate an actual size between .495 and .505. For metric dimension, a similar form for general tolerances would be X.X METRIC = ±.08.

Two other methods of displaying tolerances on a drawing are shown in Figure 13.1. The maximum and minimum sizes are specified directly when using *limit dimensions* to specify the tolerance. Usually the upper limit is placed above the lower limit. While this method clearly shows the limits of the dimension, many engineers, designers, and machinists think in terms of the nominal or basic size plus a tolerance, neither of which are immediately evident using limit dimensions. Thus, a more common approach is to use *plus and minus dimensions* where the basic size is shown followed by the tolerance values. If the plus and minus tolerance values are identical, then the basic dimension is followed by a plus/minus sign and half of the numerical value of the tolerance. Otherwise, the plus and minus tolerances are indicated separately with the plus above the minus. A *bilateral tolerance*, such as the tolerance for the 1.500 inch dimension in Figure 13.1, varies in both directions from the basic size. A *unilateral tolerance*, such as the tolerance on the shaft in Figure 13.1, varies in only one direction from the basic size. In both cases, the number of digits to the right of the decimal point for the dimension should be the same as the number of digits to the right of the decimal point for the tolerance.

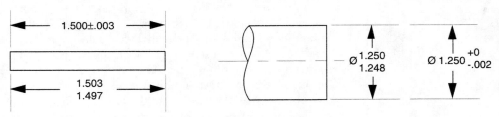

Figure 13.1

Sometimes it is not necessary to specify both limits of a tolerance and only one limit dimension is needed. MIN or MAX is placed after a numerical dimension to indicate that it is a *single limit dimension*. The depth of holes, length of threads, and radii of corner rounds are often specified using single limit dimensions.

Many times several methods of representing tolerances are used on a single drawing. For instance, general tolerances may be listed in the title block and plus and minus dimensions or limit dimensions may be used for a few dimensions to which the general tolerances do not apply.

An important consideration in applying tolerances is the effect of one tolerance on another, especially because tolerances are cumulative. This is known as *tolerance accumulation* or *tolerance stackup* for a chain of dimensions. In the example shown in Figure 13.2, two dimensioning schemes are shown. Above the part, *chain dimensioning* shows the distance from one feature to the next. This would be an appropriate dimensioning scheme if the distance from one hole to the next were critical, because the distance between holes must be between .995 and 1.005. But if the distance of the holes from left edge of the part were critical, a large tolerance would accumulate. The third hole would be 2.985 from the left edge if all of the dimensions happened to be at the minimum limit of the dimension, or 3.015 from the left edge if all dimensions were at the maximum limit. Thus, the actual dimension of the third hole from the left edge using chain dimensioning is 3.000 ± .015. This tolerance accumulation could be avoided using *datum dimensioning*, where the dimensions are given with respect to a datum, in this case the left edge of the part as shown below the part in Figure 13.2. Using this scheme the third hole is specified to be between 2.995 and 3.005 from the left edge. Of course, the distance between the second and third holes could be as small as .990, if the second hole is at 2.005 and the third hole is at 2.995. The distance between the second and third holes could be as large as 1.010 if the holes are at 1.995 and 3.005. Consequently, the decision about which way to dimension the holes depends on whether the distance between holes is critical, or whether the distance from each hole to the left edge is critical.

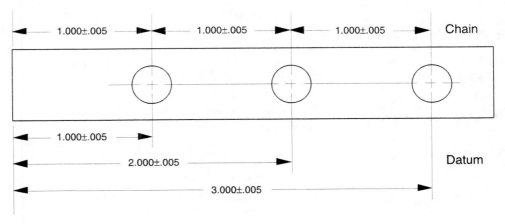

Figure 13.2

13.3 HOW TO DETERMINE TOLERANCES

One of the most difficult aspects of dimensioning and tolerancing for inexperienced engineers and designers is to determine what tolerance to specify on a drawing. In some cases a specific tolerance is quite clear based on the function of the design. For instance, if a 3/4-inch shaft must rotate at moderate speed in a hole, the tolerances on the shaft and the hole can be determined based on standard classes of fits that are available in many engineering and machinist handbooks. In this particular case the hole could be between .7500 and .7512, while the shaft could have a diameter of .7484 to .7492. A shaft any bigger or a hole any smaller would result in too tight of a clearance for the shaft to rotate freely, or could result in the shaft being too big for the hole. A smaller shaft or larger hole than the specified limits would result in a sloppy fit between the shaft and the hole. The point here is not the details of how the tolerances are determined. That is too specific to individual cases for this discussion and is presented in many handbooks and texts. Instead, the point is that the function of the system that is being designed drives the tolerances. In this case, *the tolerances drive the manufacturing process* used to machine the hole and the shaft.

But more a more common situation is the opposite: *the manufacturing process drives the tolerance.* If the only machine tool that is available to form a hole is a drill press, the 3/4-inch hole that will result will be between .748 and .754 in diameter based on expected tolerances for the drilling operation. But this means that the hole in the example above would have too much variability to assure that the shaft rotates in it properly. Of course, if only one shaft-hole assembly was being made, the hole could be drilled first and measured. Then the shaft could be turned on a lathe to a diameter just slightly smaller to achieve the fit described above. But this approach will clearly not work for mass-produced, interchangeable parts. Either a more accurate machining method is needed to create the hole or the design must be altered to avoid drilling a tightly dimensioned hole altogether. (In this example, a standard-size, off-the-shelf bearing could be inserted into a larger drilled hole to mate with the shaft.)

When the manufacturing processes that are available drive the tolerances, the tolerances on the drawing must reflect the manufacturing process that is used to make the part, and the design must be altered to ensure that the part can be made with the available machining processes. Guidelines are available for the tolerance range of various common machining processes. These processes include the following:

Lapping: A process to produce a very smooth and accurate surface by rubbing the surface of the workpiece against a mating form, often using a fine abrasive between the surfaces.

Honing: A process in which a honing stone made of fine abrasive is used to form a surface on a workpiece.

Grinding: A process to remove a small amount of material from a workpiece with a rapidly rotating grinding wheel.

Broaching: A process similar to filing in which a cutting tool is reciprocated along its axis to remove a small amount of material from a workpiece.

Reaming: Removal of a small amount of material from a drilled hole using a rotating cutting tool (reamer).

Turning: Axisymmetric removal of material from a rotating workpiece by feeding a cutting tool into the workpiece using a lathe.

Boring: Axisymmetric removal of material from a workpiece using a tool with a single cutting surface. Either the workpiece or the tool may be rotating.

Milling: Removal of material by feeding workpiece into a rotating cutting tool.

Drilling: Creating a hole by feeding the end of a sharpened cylindrical cutting tool (drill bit) into the material.

Stamping and *Punching*: Cutting material using a punch and a die to shear the material, much like a paper hole-punch.

The tolerance typically depends on the size of the feature, as well as the quality of the machine tool, sharpness of the cutting tool, and skill of the operator. Figure 13.3 indicates the range of tolerances to be expected for various machining operations. To use this table, first consider the size of the feature in the left column. Then go below the sizes in the left column to the type of machining operation used. The bar associated with that process indicates the range of tolerances in the row associated with the feature size. For instance, consider a feature that has a dimension of 2 inches. If broaching were used to create that feature, the chart indicates that the total tolerance would be .0004 to .0015, depending on the machining conditions. Thus, this dimension could be specified as 2.0000 ±.0002 up to 2.0000 ± .0008 (rounding up). If the same piece was created on a milling machine, the tolerances would be .0025 to .010, indicating a dimension of 2.0000 ± .0013 up to 2.000 ± .005. If broaching were not available, we would have to be satisfied with the tolerances of a milling machine and adjust the design accordingly, if the milling tolerances are too large. If both broaching and milling were available, the criticality of the tolerance and the cost of manufacturing would drive the tolerance that would be specified on the drawing. (Broaching, a mass-production process, is usually more expensive than milling, so milling would be preferred if the milling tolerances are acceptable.) Tolerances for metric dimensioning can be determined by converting the values in Figure 13.3 to millimeters and rounding off the result to one less place to the right of the decimal point.

Typical tolerances on drills depend on the drill size. Standard drill sizes are fractional in increments of 1/64-inch from 1/16-inch to 4-inch and according to an alphanumeric code. The coded drill sizes range from 80 (.0135 inch) to 1 (.2280 inch) and from A (.234 inch) to Z (.413 inch). The dimensions for the coded drill sizes are widely available in engineering and machinist handbooks. In addition, the proper drill sizes for

Size (in.)	Total Tolerance (in.)								
0.000-0.599	0.00015	0.0002	0.0003	0.0005	0.0008	0.0012	0.002	0.003	0.005
0.600-0.999	0.00015	0.00025	0.0004	0.0006	0.001	0.0015	0.0025	0.004	0.006
1.000-1.499	0.0002	0.0003	0.0005	0.0008	0.0012	0.002	0.003	0.005	0.008
1.500-2.799	0.00025	0.0004	0.0006	0.001	0.0015	0.0025	0.004	0.006	0.010
2.800-4.499	0.0003	0.0005	0.0008	0.0012	0.002	0.003	0.005	0.008	0.012
4.500-7.799	0.0004	0.0006	0.001	0.0015	0.0025	0.004	0.006	0.010	0.015
7.800-13.599	0.0005	0.0008	0.0012	0.002	0.003	0.005	0.008	0.012	0.025

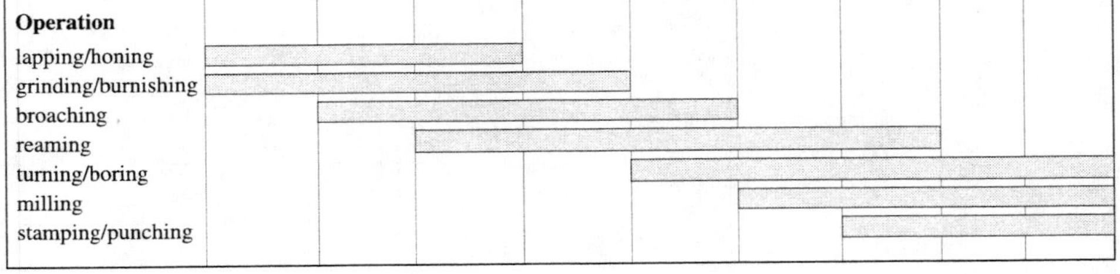

Operation

lapping/honing
grinding/burnishing
broaching
reaming
turning/boring
milling
stamping/punching

Figure 13.3

drilling holes that will be tapped are listed in these handbooks. The standard tolerance for drilled holes is given in Table 13-1.

TABLE 13-1   Standard Tolerance For Drilled Holes

Drill Size (in.)	Tolerance (in.)	
	Plus	Minus
0.0135 (80)-0.185 (13)	0.003	0.002
0.1875-0.246 (D)	0.004	0.002
0.250-0.750	0.005	0.002
0.7656-1.000	0.007	0.003
1.0156-2.000	0.010	0.004
2.0312-3.500	0.015	0.005

13.4   SURFACE FINISH

All surfaces are rough and irregular on a microscopic scale. The roughness can be described in terms of asperities (peaks or ridges) and valleys. The irregularities of a surface are classified into *roughness* and *waviness*. Roughness describes the small scale, somewhat random irregularity of a surface, while waviness describes a more regular variation in the surface that typically has a wavelength of 0.8 mm or more. The surface can be thought of as a roughness superimposed on waviness. The roughness and waviness can be measured in several ways, but the most common is a profilometer, which drags a fine-pointed stylus over the surface and records the height of the stylus. The roughness is measured in terms of the roughness average (R_a). The roughness average is defined as the average of the absolute values of the deviation of the local surface height from the average height of the surface. This is equivalent to half the average of the peak to valley height. In addition, the *lay*, or predominant direction of the marks left by the machine tools, may be important to describing the surface.

The surface finish resulting from several machining and forming processes are shown in Figure 13.4. This figure shows the range of possible surface roughness averages (R_a) in both micrometers ($1\mu m = 10^{-6}$ m) and microinches ($1\mu m$ in $= 10^{-6}$ in). For instance, surfaces formed by drilling are likely to have a roughness from 12.5 down to $0.8\mu m$ (500 down to $32\mu m$ in). Typically, the roughness is in the middle of the specified range, about 6.3 down to 1.6 m for the case of drilling. In addition to the machining processes described in Section 13.3, the following processes are also included in Figure 13.4:

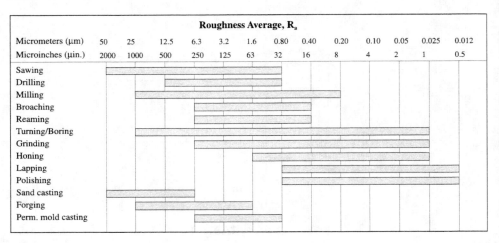

Figure 13.4

Sawing: Cutting material by moving a toothed blade through the material.

Polishing: Removal of scratches and tool marks on a surface using a belt or rotating wheel of soft material such as cloth or leather, often with a fine abrasive.

Sand Casting: Forming a part by pouring molten metal into a mold made of sand.

Forging: Shaping of metal to a desired form by pressing or hammering, usually with the metal hot.

Permanent Mold Casting: Forming a part by pouring molten metal into a permanent mold.

To put the roughness averages in perspective, consider that a $0.10\mu m$ roughness is a mirrorlike surface, free from visible marks of any kind. A $1.6\mu m$ roughness is a high-quality, smooth machined finish. A $6.3\mu m$ roughness is the ordinary finish from typical machining operations.

The surface finish may be specified on a drawing using the special symbols touching the surface or with a leader line to the surface as shown in Figure 13.5. For the top surface, the roughness is specified as $1.2\mu m$, corresponding to a high quality, smooth machine finish. The surface finish symbol on the right side of the object includes a horizontal bar that indicates that material removal by machining is required for this surface. The surface finish symbol on the left side of the object indicates that material removal from this side is prohibited. This surface must be that resulting from the original process used to produce the surface such as casting, forging, or injection molding.

Other notations can be added to the surface roughness symbol. A number to the left of the surface finish mark describes the material removal allowance indicating the amount of stock material to be removed by machining. A symbol to the right of the surface roughness mark indicates the lay, or predominant direction of machining marks: perpendicular, parallel, circular, or radial. Other notations can be used to specify the

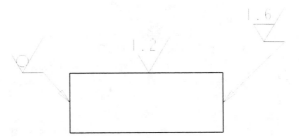

Figure 13.5

waviness. Details of surface finish notation are available in engineering and machinist handbooks.

13.5 GEOMETRIC DIMENSIONING AND TOLERANCING

Ideally, engineering drawings should be unambiguous in their interpretation. In many cases, stating dimensions and tolerances provides adequate information so that the part can be manufactured to ensure interchangeability of parts and optimal performance. But sometimes, the traditional dimensioning using the plus and minus scheme does not adequately describe the geometry of the part. For instance, consider the part shown in Figure 13.6. The dimension shown in the drawing could have several possible interpretations. For instance, the dimension at the top edge could be 14.9 mm while the dimension at the bottom edge could be 15.1 mm, resulting in a trapezoidal part instead of a rectangular part. Or the right edge of the part could be bowed so that the part is 15.1 mm wide at the top and bottom, but 14.9 mm wide at the middle. As a result, the part would not fit flush against another flat surface even though the part is 15 ±.1 mm wide at any particular location. In both of these cases, the geometry of the part is not described fully by the plus and minus tolerances on the dimension.

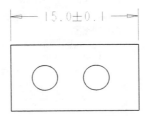

Figure 13.6

A system known as *geometric dimensioning and tolerancing* is used to prevent such ambiguities in the design to present the design intent more clearly. Geometric dimensioning and tolerancing supplements the traditional dimensioning system with specifications that describe the geometry of the part to enhance the interpretation of the drawing. It is used to indicate dimensions critical to a part's function and ensure part interchangeability. Items related to geometric dimensioning and tolerancing are indicated on a drawing by a feature symbol consisting of a frame or box around information describing the geometry. A complete discussion of geometric dimensioning and tolerancing is beyond the scope of this book—there are entire books on the subject. Nevertheless, several of the key aspects and applications of geometric dimensioning and tolerancing are presented here to familiarize the reader with the basic terminology and symbols that are used.

The various types of tolerances and the characteristics that they describe are indicated in Figure 13.7. Each has its own symbol that is used on a drawing. Perhaps the easiest type of geometric tolerances to understand are the *form tolerances*, which describe the shape of a single feature. For instance, straightness indicates the limits on how much a surface or axis can bow with respect to a straight line. Figure 13.8 shows the *straightness* specification for a surface. A feature control box with the straightness symbol (a horizontal bar) and a numerical dimension are connected by a leader line to the surface. The interpretation is that the upper surface must be straight enough so that all points on the surface are within the tolerance zone of 0.010 mm. An example of a *flatness* specification is shown in Figure 13.9. The parallelogram symbol with a numerical dimension in a feature control box indicates that the planar surface must lie between two parallel planes 0.20 mm apart. Other single feature specifications include *circularity* or *roundness* (for circular features to be within a tolerance zone defined by two concentric circles), and *cylindricity* (for cylindrical features to be within a tolerance zone defined by two concentric cylinders). Closely related to form tolerances are *profile tolerances*, which define the acceptable deviation of the outline of an object (profile) from that specified in the drawing. These tolerances define a zone on either side of the true profile shown on the drawing within which the line or surface should remain. Profile tolerances can be applied to either a line or a surface.

	TYPE OF TOLERANCE	CHARACTERISTIC	SYMBOL
FOR INDIVIDUAL FEATURES	FORM	STRAIGHTNESS	—
		FLATNESS	▱
		CIRCULARITY (ROUNDNESS)	○
		CYLINDRICITY	⌀
FOR INDIVIDUAL OR RELATED FEATURES	PROFILE	PROFILE OF A LINE	⌒
		PROFILE OF A SURFACE	⌓
FOR RELATED FEATURES	ORIENTATION	ANGULARITY	∠
		PERPENDICULARITY	⊥
		PARALLELISM	//
	LOCATION	POSITION	⊕
		CONCENTRICITY	◎
		SYMMETRY	=
	RUNOUT	CIRCULAR RUNOUT	↗
		TOTAL RUNOUT	↗↗

Figure 13.7

Orientation tolerances prescribe the relation between features. *Parallelism* controls the degree to which a surface is parallel to a reference plane, or datum plane. In Figure 13.10, the horizontal datum plane that coincides with the bottom edge of the part is identified with a box around B attached to the bottom edge. The parallelism fea-

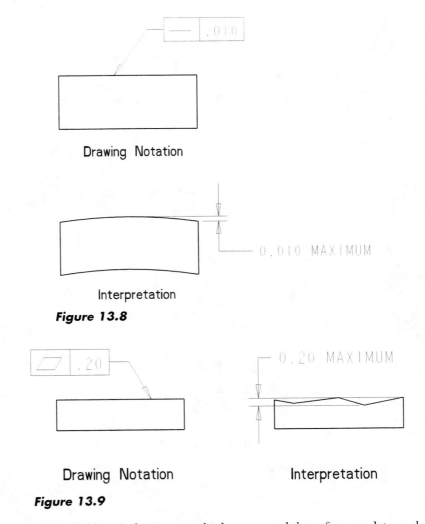

Drawing Notation

0.010 MAXIMUM

Interpretation

Figure 13.8

0.20 MAXIMUM

Drawing Notation

Interpretation

Figure 13.9

ture symbol (parallel lines), the numerical tolerance, and the reference datum plane are included in a feature control box with a leader line to the surface to which the tolerance applies. In this case, the upper surface must be within .10 mm of parallel to datum plane B. *Perpendicularity* with respect to a datum plane is indicated in a similar way, as shown in Figure 13.11. Here the vertical plane must be perpendicular to datum plane A to within .20 mm. In this example, an alternative notation for specifying datum plane A is used. The datum plane symbol used in Figure 13.11 is common, but the datum plane symbol used in Figure 13.10 and Figure 13.12 is preferred. The datum plane symbol can be applied in several different ways as shown in Figure 13.10 and Figure 13.12. Several other relations between features can be specified, including the tolerance zone for *angularity* from a datum plane or axis, the tolerance zone for *concentricity* of a surface of revolution with respect to an axis, the tolerance zone for *symmetry* with respect to a datum plane, and the tolerance zone for *runout*, which describes the circularity with respect to an axis of revolution.

The most difficult concept in geometric dimensioning and tolerancing is the concept of *positional tolerances*. It is demonstrated most easily in indicating the position of a hole, as shown in Figure 13.12. In this case, the ultimate goal is to have a circular open

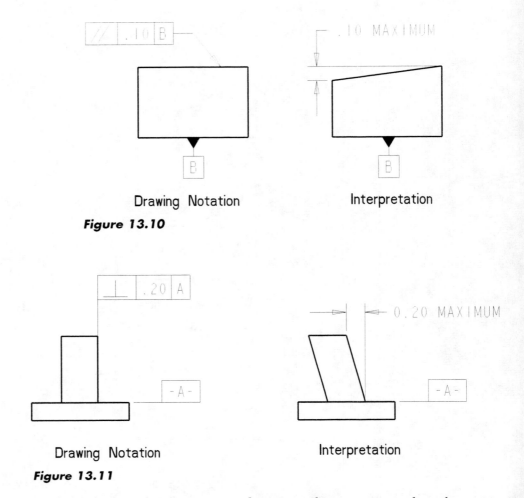

Figure 13.10

Figure 13.11

area (hole) that is at least 25.0 mm in diameter with its center exactly at the position indicated in the drawing. Note that even though we want a 25.0 mm hole, the hole is dimensioned as 25.3 mm in the drawing. The reason for this will shortly become evident.

Rather than describing the position of the hole with a plus-or-minus tolerance, the ideal position of the hole is prescribed. The boxed dimensions indicate that they are basic *true-position dimensions*, which describe the perfect position of the center of the hole. Then the feature control box below the dimension of the hole shows how close the center of the hole should be to the true position. In this case, the hole should be within a circular tolerance zone with a diameter of .1 mm of the true position (indicated by the plus in the circle within the feature control box followed by ø .1). The reference datum planes are also included in the feature control box. Datum plane A is the surface of the part in the plane of the page. Datum planes B and C are references for the true-position dimensions of 40 and 60 mm. These three mutually perpendicular datum planes provide a reference point for the positional tolerance of the hole.

The positional tolerance zone for the center of the hole is shown in Figure 13.12. The "true position of hole center" is based on the 40 and 60 mm dimensions. Around this center is a circle with a diameter of .1 mm (not drawn to scale in Figure 13.12) that defines the "positional tolerance zone." The center of the actual hole must be within this

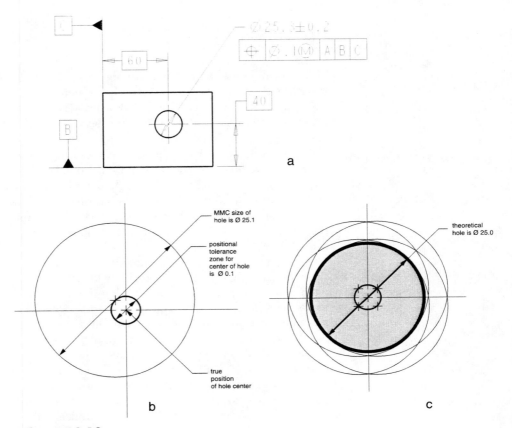

Figure 13.12

circle. For instance, an acceptable hole would be a 25.1 mm diameter hole with its center on the edge of this circular tolerance zone, as shown in the Figure 13.12.

The M in a circle in the feature control box in Figure 13.12 indicates that the .1 mm circular positional tolerance zone is applied at the *maximum material condition* (MMC). For a hole, the maximum material condition is the smallest acceptable dimension of the hole, because this is the situation in which the most material would be present. For the part in Figure 13.12, the diameter of the hole for the maximum material condition is 25.1 mm, given a dimension of 25.3 ± .2 for the diameter of the hole. Thus, the circle representing a hole with its center on the edge of the positional tolerance zone has a diameter of 25.1 mm, as shown in Figure 13.12. Of course, the 25.1 mm diameter hole could be anywhere within the positional tolerance zone or on its edge. Three more 25.1 mm diameter circles are drawn in Figure 13.12 in addition to the original 25.1 mm circle. The centers of all four circles are on the edge of the positional tolerance zone. Note that there is a circle that lies inside all of the 25.1 mm diameter circles, which we call the "theoretical hole." It is relatively straightforward to find the diameter of the theoretical hole, based on the positional tolerance zone for the center of the hole and the MMC size of the hole. The radius of the theoretical hole is the distance from the true position of the hole center to the nearest portion of any one of the MMC circles. Here the theoretical hole has a diameter of 25.0 mm. In fact the theoretical hole always has a diameter equal to the diameter for the maximum material condition minus the diameter of the positional tolerance (in this case, 25.1 mm − .1 mm = 25.0 mm).

The key result is that if the hole diameter is within the specified tolerance (25.3 ± .2 mm) and the center of the hole is within the positional tolerance zone (.1 mm), there will always be a circular opening in the part with a diameter of at least 25.0 mm. Now assume that the hole must mate with a circular pin that is positioned at the true center of the hole and is exactly 25.0 mm in diameter. Given the dimensioning scheme in Figure 13.12, the pin will always align with the theoretical hole and fit through the theoretical hole, even if the actual hole is not positioned so its center is exactly at the true position of the hole center. Of course, the theoretical hole is based on the maximum material condition (smallest hole allowed). If the hole is at the large end of the acceptable tolerance, 25.5 mm in diameter, circles drawn in Figure 13.12 will be larger. But the theoretical hole will still be open for the pin. Likewise, if the circles drawn in Figure 13.12 are not on the edge of the positional tolerance zone, but inside of the zone, the entire theoretical hole will still be open for the pin. Thus, defining the position and diameter of the hole as in Figure 13.12 forces the existence of an open area (theoretical hole) that is at least 25.0 mm in diameter and centered at the true position of the hole center.

The maximum material condition reflects the practical aspect of assembly. Consider two parts that are bolted together with several bolts. If the bolt holes are not accurately positioned, not all of the bolts can be inserted. Either drilling out the holes to make them larger or using smaller diameter bolts fixes the problem. The idea of the maximum material condition is to capture these trade-offs. The maximum material condition indicates the inner boundary (the theoretical hole) for the actual hole. The boundary of the actual hole must always be outside of this inner boundary. In this way, a bolt or pin that is positioned at the true position of the hole will always fit through the actual hole. Likewise, the least material condition (LMC) , or largest hole size, can be used to define a theoretical circle within which the actual hole will be. The boundary for the actual hole must lie inside of the theoretical circle defined by the LMC. Further information regarding geometric dimensioning and tolerancing is provided in handbooks and graphics textbooks.

KEY TERMS

actual size
basic size
form tolerances
General tolerances
geometric dimensioning and tolerancing

limit dimensions
maximum material condition
nominal size
Orientation tolerances
plus and minus dimensions

positional tolerances
roughness
target size
tolerance stackup
true-position dimensions

Problems

1. The part shown in Figure 13.13 is made using a very accurate milling machine by a skilled machinist. The hole is reamed. Specify plus and minus tolerances for each dimension assuming that it is critical to hold all dimensions as close as possible to those specified. Use four digits past the decimal point to specify the tolerances, even though typical practice would be to specify only three digits past the decimal point. Dimensions are in inches.

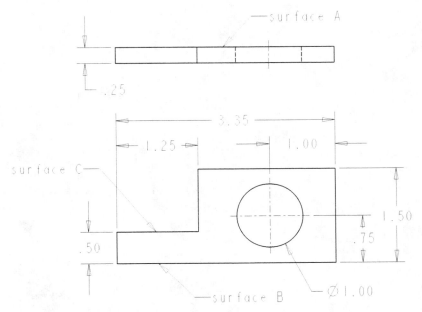

Figure 13.13

2. The part shown in Figure 13.13 is made by an unskilled student using an old milling machine in a university student shop. The hole is drilled. Specify plus and minus tolerances for each dimension that are reasonable for these conditions. Use four digits past the decimal point to specify the tolerances, even though typical practice would be to specify only three digits past the decimal point. Assume dimensions are in inches.

3. Sketch a view of the object shown in Figure 13.14. Specify the horizontal dimension of the steps using chain dimensioning from the left end. The length of each horizontal section from left to right is .50, .75, 1.25, and .25 inches. Base the plus and minus dimensions on the worst expected tolerances for milling. What are the maximum and minimum dimensions for the overall horizontal length of the object? Use four digits past the decimal point to specify the tolerances, even though typical practice would be to specify only three digits past the decimal point.

4. Sketch a view of the object shown in Figure 13.14. Specify the horizontal dimension of the steps using datum dimensioning from the left end. The length of each horizontal section from left to right is .50, .75, 1.25, and .25 inches. Base the plus and minus dimensions on the best expected tolerances for milling. What are the maximum and minimum dimensions for the overall horizontal length of the object? Use four digits past the decimal point to specify the tolerances, even though typical practice would be to specify only three digits past the decimal point.

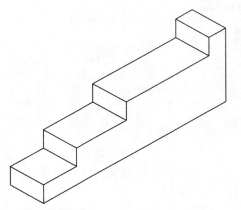

Figure 13.14

5. Sketch a side view of the shaft shown in Figure 13.15. Specify the horizontal dimension of each section of the shaft using chain dimensioning from the left end. The length of each horizontal section from left to right is .75, 2.00, .50, 1.25, and 3.00 inches. Base the plus and minus dimensions on the best expected tolerances for turning. What are the maximum and minimum dimensions for the overall horizontal length of the object? Use four digits past the decimal point to specify the tolerances, even though typical practice would be to specify only three digits past the decimal point.

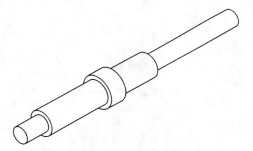

Figure 13.15

6. Sketch a side view of the shaft shown in Figure 13.15. Specify the horizontal dimension of each section of the shaft using datum dimensioning from the left end. The length of each horizontal section from left to right is .75, 2.00, .50, 1.25, and 3.00 inches. Base the plus and minus dimensions on the worst expected tolerances for turning. What are the maximum and minimum dimensions for the length from the left end to the left edge of the largest diameter section? Use four digits past the decimal point to specify the tolerances, even though typical practice would be to specify only three digits past the decimal point.

7. Draw the appropriate surface finish symbol for:

   a. surface roughness typical for drilling.

   b. surface roughness typical for grinding.

   c. the best possible surface roughness for milling with material removal required.

   d. surface finish of 12.5 microns with material removal prohibited.

8. Sketch the appropriate Geometric Dimensioning and Tolerance form tolerance for:

    a. an edge straight so that all points on the surface are within a tolerance zone of 0.020 mm.
    b. a surface that is flat to within 0.015 mm.
    c. a surface that is parallel to datum plane C to within 0.20 mm.
    d. a surface that is perpendicular to datum plane B to within 0.10 mm.
    e. a hole that is perpendicular to datum plane B to within 0.12 mm.

9. The part shown in Figure 13.16 is dimensioned in millimeters using the traditional coordinate method. Sketch the same views of the part and dimension using Geometric Dimensioning and Tolerancing procedures so the following functional requirements are met:

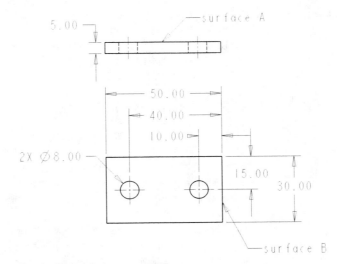

Figure 13.16

Set surfaces A and B as datum planes.

Surface A is flat to within 0.15 mm.

The upper edge in the front view from which the holes are located vertically is perpendicular to surface B to within 0.20 mm. Set this edge as datum plane C.M

The edge-forming surface A in the top view is straight to within 0.05 mm.

The 10, 15, and 40 mm dimensions are true-position dimensions.

The 5, 30, and 50 mm dimensions must be held to the tightest possible tolerance that can be achieved using milling. (Convert the dimensions to inches to determine the tolerances to two places after the decimal (round as necessary). Specify the tolerances as plus and minus dimensions in millimeters.)

The holes have a tolerance of ±0.05mm. The theoretical hole size is 8.00mm.

The holes are located within 0.15 mm of the true position at the Maximum Material Condition.

10. The part shown in Figure 13.13 is dimensioned in inches using the traditional coordinate method. Sketch the same views of the part and dimension using Geometric Dimensioning and Tolerancing procedures so the following functional requirements are met:
    Set surfaces A and B as datum planes. Set the right edge as datum plane D.

    Surface A is flat to within .005 inches.

The hole is perpendicular to surface A to within .010 inches. (Place this tolerance just below the dimension.)

Surface C is parallel to surface B to within .012 inches.

The .75 and 1.00 dimensions for the location of the hole are true-position dimensions.

The 1.50 and 3.35 dimensions must be held to the tightest possible tolerance that can be achieved using milling (use three digits past the decimal point for the tolerances).

The hole has a tolerance of ±.002. The theoretical hole size is 1.000.

The hole is located within .004 inches of the true position at the Maximum Material Condition.

REFERENCES

ASME Y14.5M-1994, Dimensioning and Tolerancing. New York, NY: American Society of Mechanical Engineers, 1995.

G. R. Bertoline, *Introduction to Graphics Communications for Engineers.* New York, NY: McGraw-Hill, 1999.

P. J. Booker, *A History of Engineering Drawing.* London, England: Northgate Publishing Co. Ltd., 1979.

S. H. Chasen, Historical highlights of interactive computer graphics. *Mechanical Engineering,* November 1981, 32-41.

G. E. Dieter, *Engineering Design: A Materials and Processing Approach.* New York, NY: McGraw-Hill, 1991.

A. R. Eide, R. D. Jenison, L. H. Mashaw, L. L. Northup, and C. G. Sanders, *Engineering Graphics Fundamentals.* New York, NY: McGraw-Hill, 1985.

J. Encarnacao and E. G. Schlechtendahl, *Computer Aided Design.* Berlin, Germany: Springer-Verlag, 1983.

E. S. Ferguson, *Engineering and the Mind's Eye.* Cambridge MA: The MIT Press, 1992.

E. S. Ferguson, The mind's eye: Nonverbal thought in technology. *Science* 197:827-836, 1977.

F. E. Giesecke, A. Mitchell, H. C. Spencer, I. L. Hill, R. O. Loving, J. T. Dygdon, J. E. Novak, and S. Lockhart, *Engineering Graphics.* Upper Saddle River, NJ: Prentice Hall, 1998.

K. Hanks, *Rapid Viz: A New Method for the Rapid Visualization of Ideas,* Menlo Park, CA: Crisp Publications, 1990.

C. M. Hoffman, *Geometric and Solid Modeling,* San Mateo, CA: Morgan Kaufmann Publishers, Inc., 1989.

S. Pugh, *Total Design,* Reading, MA: Addison Wesley, 1990.

D. G. Ullman, *The Mechanical Design Process,* 2nd Edition. New York, NY: McGraw-Hill, 1997.

D. G. Ullman, S. Wood, and D. Craig, The importance of drawing in the mechanical design process. *Computers and graphics,* 14:263-274, 1990.

W. R. D. Wilson, Course Notes for ME B40: Introduction to Mechanical Design and Manufacturing. Northwestern University, March 1998.